POLICING THE INNER CITY

POLICING THE INNER CITY

A Study of Amsterdam's Warmoesstraat

Maurice Punch
Reader in Sociology
The Netherlands School of Business
Nijenrode

Archon Books
Hamden   Connecticut

363.209
P96

© Maurice Punch 1979

First published 1979 in England by
THE MACMILLAN PRESS LTD
*and in the USA as an Archon Book
an imprint of*
THE SHOE STRING PRESS, INC.
*995 Sherman Avenue,
Hamden, Connecticut 06514*

Library of Congress Cataloging in Publication Data

Punch, Maurice.
  Policing the inner city.

  Bibliography: p.
  Includes index.
  1. Amsterdam–Police. 2. Law enforcement – Netherlands –
Amsterdam. I. Title.
  HV8225.A5P85   1979   363.2'09492'3   79–4553

  ISBN 0–208–01819–0

Manufactured in Great Britain

For Corry, Julio and Maria

Contents

Preface

I am indebted to the Amsterdam Police for the excellent co-operation and hospitality which marked the research. In particular, I should like to express my sincere thanks to the Chief Constable of Amsterdam, Mr Th. Sanders, for opening the doors of his force to scrutiny from outside, and also Chief Inspector J. H. Nicaise, Head of the Warmoesstraat Police District, who allowed me the freedom of his station and supported the research at every stage. I also received inestimable help within the force, and in some cases comments on drafts of papers and the typescript of this book, from Jella Kuiper, Bob Visser, Henny Elout, Aaldert van de Vlies, Hans van de Horst, Evert Jagerman, Harry van der Woude, Willem van Lieshout, Iebe de Wolf and Jaap de Vries. In the Warmoesstraat itself I was identified with one group, who put up with me uncomplainingly, and the research was greatly dependent upon their co-operation. I am grateful to them all, but especially the 'brigadiers' – Gouke Nijholt, Ernst Wetjens and Helmut Olivier – and the 'agenten' – particularly Ruud Valentijn, Hans Achterberg, Willem van Hattum, Tinus Noorlander, John Voorn, Jan van Looijen, Paul Walgering, Joop Meijer, Jan Steiner, Rob van de Kwast, Rob Drenthe, Rob Raat and Gerrit Bouwhuis. Initially I was put on the police trail by my involvement with policemen studying at the University of Essex and I learnt a great deal from Terry Watson, Geoffrey Markham, Trevor Naylor, Barry Devlin, Robin Blackmore, Ralph Crawshaw, John Watson and John Sutton.

A number of people commented on a sprawling manuscript and their criticisms helped me to shape and prune the material into acceptable form; my thanks are due to Wim Broer, Kees Schuyt, Lo Brunt, Frank Bovenkerk, Joep Toebosch, Jim Olila, Simon Holdaway, John Brown, Peter Manning, Mike Chatterton, Garry Brana-Shute, Michael Banton, Bram de Swaan, Ton Peters, and the anonymous reader of the publisher. Dennis Marsden wasted two sunny days of a sabbatical struggling with the meandering script and my guilt is mixed with respect for his shrewd and useful comments. A special mention must go to Derek Phillips, who not only helped to preserve my sanity during periods of acute culture-conflict by permitting me to beat him weekly at squash, but who acted as an informal supervisor to the project. He brought my attention to books and articles, helped to develop a theme for the work, and closely read various drafts. His help and encouragement were invaluable. I also appreciate the speed and efficiency of Mevrouw G. de Wit-Smit, Mary Girling, Linda Peachey, Eleanor Hunter, Hanneke Beyer and Nely van Westerop, who worked on the typescript. Henk Jarring kindly helped with the index.

I should also perhaps mention here four important pieces of work which I read only after the field-work was completed. I only obtained a copy of Rubinstein's *City Police* in 1976; was provided with two draft articles by Simon Holdaway this year; was kindly sent a typescript of *Police Work* by Peter Manning in the early summer (it has since been published); and could only get my hands on Mike Chatterton's excellent thesis when it was too late to incorporate his material into my book.

Finally, virtually moving house five times in five years, for various periods associated with research and study-leave, with two small children and enduring the strains of shift-work placed no small burden on my family. That is why this book is dedicated to the three people who suffered the absences and the restlessness while I was playing at policeman and who survived the gloomy, quasi-masochistic preoccupation with 'the book'.

MAURICE PUNCH
Amstelveen, December 1977

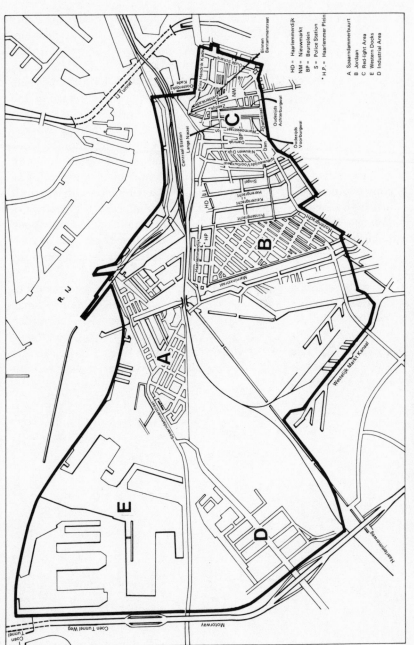

MAP SHOWING BOUNDARIES OF THE WARMOESSTRAAT POLICE
DISTRICT, INCLUDING CENTRAL AMSTERDAM

HD = Haarlemmerdijk
NM = Nieuwmarkt
BP = Beursplein
S = Police Station
* H.P. = Haarlemmer Plein

A Spaarndammerbuurt
B Jordaan
C Red-light Area
E Western Docks
D Industrial Area

1 Observation and the Police: the Research Experience

(i) INTRODUCTION

My first murder – this is not, I hasten to add, a confession – was that of a young woman whose suspected infidelity had caused her husband to stab her to death. That evening I had arrived at Police Headquarters in Amsterdam for a night duty with a young inspector who was responsible for supervising major incidents in the town. Almost immediately we were called to a suspected murder which involved a long interrogation of an English suspect (which I helped to translate) and the dragging and searching of a canal by divers for the body. It was a bitterly cold night and the eye-witness account of the alleged murder became increasingly discredited as old bicycles, but no body, were brought to the surface. After several hours of interrogations and a long period of standing by the canal the suspect was sent home and we sat down for a welcome cup of coffee at about four o'clock. Immediately the telephone rang and the inspector said, 'It looks like a murder in Amsterdam-South'.

We drove through the slumbering city to a quiet and respectable street where the only indicator of trouble was the patrol-car parked outside a neat row of low-rise flats. We climbed the stairs, met the two policemen who had been first on the scene, and entered a small flat, conspicuously clean like most Dutch homes. The gas-fire was still burning, a woman's clothes were tidily folded over the back of the chair, and there were mementoes from Sicily on the shelves and wedding and family photos on the walls. The bedroom door was slightly ajar and a bare foot was visible on top of the bed. The inspector

---

This chapter appeared as 'Backstage: Observing Police Work in Amsterdam' in *Urban Life*, vol. 7, no. 3 (October 1978) and is reprinted by permission of the publisher, Sage Publications, Inc.

entered the room and returned to talk in a hushed voice to the
policemen. Steeling myself against an innate fear of death I entered the
bedroom. A young, attractive woman in pyjamas lay on her back on
top of the bed with her legs slightly drawn up and her arms spread wide.
Her open eyes stared glassily like those of a stuffed animal. There were
stab wounds in her stomach, neck and face and the sheets and walls
were spattered with blood. The holes in her neck were a brown-purple
colour with surprisingly little blood around them while a slit on her
upper lip made it appear as if she was grinning. With only the hiss of the
gas-fire breaking the silence we waited for the other services to arrive.

The husband had discovered some evidence of his wife's unfaithful-
ness and had stabbed her about thirty times with a stiletto. He then
phoned the police and brought his two children downstairs to a
neighbour and began walking to the station, but was intercepted by a
patrol-car on his way. Below there was an attractive little girl of three
and a boy of about nine. The little girl cried when she saw the uniforms
and the inspector went down on his haunches and started talking
kindly to her. 'Mummy is dead', she said. Upstairs, the reverential
silence in the flat was soon broken. A procession of people arrived –
two detectives, two ambulancemen, a doctor, a photographer, and an
officer from the detective branch – and joined the four people already
there (the two patrolmen, the inspector and myself). Each new arrival
introduced himself and shook hands and the conversation became less
stilted and more jovial as old acquaintances met up and began to chat
amicably. Each newcomer went casually to inspect the body and then
the routine surrounding a murder – the removal of the body to the
morgue for an autopsy and the bringing of the children to relatives –
took over from the particular circumstances of the case. We went to the
station and opened the spy-hole in the cell door; the husband raised a
weary head from beneath the blankets. He looked quite ordinary. I
went home and slept until mid-afternoon. When I woke up I felt ill and
went to the toilet where I was sick.

This incident was part of a study carried out with the Amsterdam
Police in several periods between 1974 and 1976. The original orientation of the research was to use the approach of Reiss (1971), in his
observational study of police–citizen contacts in three high-crime-rate
areas of American cities, as an entrée to police work in the city-centre
of Amsterdam. But, in a sense, that initial goal was merely a peg on
which to hang a diffuse, long-standing interest of mine in the police.
This interest had been stimulated by contact with policemen who came
to study at my university in England. I found them practical, realistic,
humorous and refreshing and developed a certain affinity with them.

Increasingly I turned towards an academic interest in the police and, initially, that was focused on the 'social' role of the police (Punch and Naylor, 1973). Twice I attempted to carry out projects with the local police, but on both occasions I encountered a negative response from the academic watchdogs of the Home Office who control all research proposals on the police. I was disappointed by the lack of response and decided that The Netherlands might prove a more suitable climate for research, partly because each force makes its own decisions regarding research. In 1973 I had spent a half-year in The Netherlands on a Nuffield Fellowship and had begun to learn Dutch (assisted by my wife who is Dutch).

Through informal contacts, namely mutual acquaintances in the International Police Association, I was able to spend a couple of weeks with two experienced beat officers who operated in the experimental role of 'community relations officers' in a working-class area of Rotterdam (Punch, 1974b, c). This got the ball rolling and one influential contact which was made in this period was with the psychologist, Dr Tom Fris, who worked for the Amsterdam Police. I planned to return to The Netherlands in the summer of 1974 with the help of a Leverhulme Fellowship, and asked Fris if he could arrange for me to spend one month on patrol with the uniformed branch in the city-centre of Amsterdam. I emphasised the city-centre because I knew the stations there were busy. Given my limited time, I wanted to observe as much as possible and had little inclination to spend my time in a sleepy suburb with traffic accidents and violations as the major diversions from tedium and drinking coffee. Like many foreigners in The Netherlands I tend to see it as a one-city society, with Amsterdam standing out as worldly and cosmopolitan compared to the stiffness of The Hague, the vulgarity of Rotterdam, and the suffocating provincialism of the smaller cities. And there is one police station in Amsterdam which everyone has heard of and which is strategically placed in the heart of the thriving inner city. Instinctively that was where I wanted to be.

Clearly, the influential middle-man role of a social scientist within the police apparatus greatly facilitated my access (cf. Fox and Lundman, 1974). The fact that I was a foreigner was also doubtless an advantage in gaining entry. I was a visiting academic, seemingly a bird of passage, whose intention was to publish in English. In any event, it was not necessary, given my previous police contacts, to establish my bona fides and my request was handled through the police hierarchy by Fris. When I arrived in The Netherlands he had arranged a station, a group which I would be attached to, and a policeman 'mentor' who

would take me in tow so that I would not have to work with too many
different people. My involvement in a cross-cultural study of a police
force was something of a moral apprenticeship in the virtues and value
of field-work. Here I should like to employ that experience to clarify
some salient issues in the observational study of the police and in the
use of qualitative methods.

(ii) OBSERVATION AND THE POLICE

The police is often held to be the most secluded part of the criminal
justice system (Skolnick, 1975, p. 14). Like other agencies of social
control and like some client-serving bureaucracies, the police organisation erects barriers against prying outsiders and endeavours to
present a favourable image of itself to the extent of mystifying and
even falsifying accounts for public consumption (Manning, 1974a).
These structural features of isolation and secrecy, coupled with the
intrinsic dangers of police work, help to form an occupational culture
which is solidaristic, and wary of non-initiates (Westley, 1970). The
researcher's task becomes, then, how to outwit the institutional
obstacle-course to gain entry and how to penetrate the mine-field of
social defences to reach the inner reality of police work. Prolonged
participant observation seems to me to be the most appropriate, if not
the sole, method for achieving these ends. This becomes even more
likely when we examine the nature of police work.

The essence of uniformed police work is relatively solitary patrolling, free of direct supervision, with a high degree of discretion, in
face-to-face interaction with the public, and with decision-making
behaviour that is frequently not reviewable. Quinney (1970, p. 114)
states, 'Most of the operating policies of the police are beyond public
scrutiny; that is, they are secretive and known only to the police
themselves'. Only observation can tap that initial encounter on the
streets, or in a private dwelling, with all its implications for the
individual citizen concerned and for his potential passage through the
criminal justice system. Indeed, the theoretical developments in this
area over the past decade have accentuated the need for carefully
sketched ethnographies of police–citizen encounters. The insights of
deviancy and labelling theory have helped us to focus on the transac-
tional and socially created nature of law-enforcement – so that even
when the actors are unlikely to be nominated for Oscars and when
their scripts are hackneyed and stereotyped, the spotlight has been

turned on the *drama* of police work (Manning, 1974b).

This perspective of mine is strengthened as I am a foreigner working in a Dutch environment. One almost senses a latent hostility among Dutch sociologists against field-work as if they are frightened of involvement in society or feel incapable of taking the role of the other, so that they use their research instruments as a protective barrier to preserve unsullied their self and their ideology (this does not apply to anthropologists; cf. Brunt, 1977). Dutch criminology in particular seems to be dominated by a dehydrated fifties positivism. In contrast, Anglo-American sociology and criminology have to a degree been influenced by the rediscovery of the Chicago School, by the work of ethnographers of deviancy, and by the frontal attack on positivistic methods (Becker, 1970; Faris, 1970; Phillips, 1973). These intellectual forces have helped to re-accentuate interactionism and to reaffirm the value of participant observation. Although observation has been a key technique in most of the standard police studies, there has not been a great deal written about the problems of observing police work except for Manning (1972) and van Maanen (1975).

There were a number of reasons why I used observational techniques. Firstly, when I began this study there was little or no previous Dutch research on the police to guide me; my models then were Anglo-American studies based largely on observation. Secondly, I was conscious of the ecological nature of police work, with Bittner's (1967a) analysis of 'peace-keeping on skid-row' fresh in mind, and felt that the inner city had to be experienced at first hand. The members of the Chicago School were great pounders of the streets, and police patrols on foot took me slowly around the narrow streets of the Amsterdam red-light district and into bars, cafés, opium dens, gambling saloons, communes, houseboats, brothels, sex-cinemas, porn shops and private clubs. Thirdly I was interested in police–citizen encounters on the streets and these could only be witnessed *in situ*. Fourthly, my desire to penetrate the social world of the policemen meant that I wanted to see their 'backstage' performances (Goffman, 1959) – inside the station, away from the public, relaxing in the canteen, taking time off when on duty, socialising with them outside of duty and out of uniform. Fifthly, and finally, I rejected more structured techniques as unable to penetrate to where the 'action' is (Goffman, 1972), and mistrusted them as likely to provide unreliable guidelines to actual behaviour.

The essence of participant observation is the prolonged participation of the researcher in the daily life of a group (though not necessarily *as a member* of the group) and his or her attempt to empathise with the norms, values and behaviour of that group (Becker, 1970). As such the researcher becomes his own research instrument and is necessarily involved in a social relationship with the subjects of his research. It is perhaps not surprising, then, that people who research the police generally end up with more positive attitudes to the police as they come to perceive policemen as workers coping with client emergency, an imperfect legal system, pressures to accept gratuities, and the necessity of conforming to the informal colleague code (Punch, 1976a, p. 22). A number of academics have actually worked in uniform as policemen – I know of Kirkham (1976) and Buckner (1967) in America, Toebosch (1975) in The Netherlands, and Kurzinger (Punch, 1976a, p. 16) in West Germany. For example, in the much-publicised case of Kirkham in Florida, he became a police officer for six months and reports a personality change that fundamentally al-tered him (1974, p. 129). Kirkham seems to have 'gone native' and to have over-identified with the policeman's role, although it may be that he is just more honest and open about the unexplicated strains of field-work (Clarke, 1975).

Rubinstein (1973), on the other hand, went almost to the point of becoming a policeman – he worked as a crime reporter, completed the police training, and rode as an 'armed observer' in patrol cars in Philadelphia – and perhaps that degree of involvement has helped to produce what will surely become a classic. His *City Police* is an insider's view of backstage police behaviour which affirms the essential role of observation. For in microscopic detail, Rubinstein takes us into the policeman's world of body cues, symbolic assailants, selective inatten-tion, implicit meanings, perceptions of space and situated 'normality'. Although he never directly spells out his own involvement in encoun-ters – did he ever draw or use his gun? did he ever have to fight? did he assist in arrests? – he clearly got inside the skins of the patrolmen. The information he collected on violence and corruption could only have been gained by a trained observer who was accepted by the policemen. The complete observer role is a fiction because he or she is always part of the situation and because distancing oneself from the police role – say by explaining at each encounter to the citizen the reason for an academic's presence – may destroy precisely what one wishes to observe. Ineluctably, the researcher is drawn into some participation and must decide for himself where the border of legitimacy lies. Cain (1973, p. 199) reports being tested out by the policemen before she was initiated into 'easing' behaviour, which included drinking beer in a cupboard. She considers that the rapport built up during the observation period was essential to the success of her interviews with policemen and she admits that her qualitative material has possibly more validity than the quantitative data.

But, in general, the dilemmas of observational research with the police are likely to display considerable correspondence with qualitative studies employing immersion in field-work in other areas (Johnson, 1975; McCall and Simmons, 1969). To a certain extent there is an advantage in single-person research with the police because, as Manning argued at Leuven, this often entails easy access, a less threatening profile, low intrusiveness in the organisation, and a high capacity for personalised relationships (Punch, 1976a, p. 25). This 'lone maverick' approach, however, does depend on the nature of the research problem, funding, and the sorts of data to be collected

(iii) FIELD-WORK: ON PATROL IN THE WARMOESSTRAAT

The station selected for my research was Bureau Warmoesstraat (Punch, 1976b), in the heart of the red-light district, which had been receiving adverse publicity about alleged mistreatment of Surinamers from the former Dutch colony in the West Indies (Bagley, 1973b). Fris had chosen a group (of about fifteen men) who were not too 'fanatical' or idle, thus he hoped middle-of-the-roaders in terms of their attitude to police work, and a young, self-confident policeman, whom I shall call 'Willem', to take me under his wing. I had asked to be assigned to one shift in order to avoid meeting a large number of people on different shifts with whom it would be difficult to build up a relationship (Veendrick and Jongman, 1976, p. 13, worked with 84 policemen in a period of two months). There was a brief meeting with the station chief, where acquaintance was made with key personnel, and I was ready to begin my field-work.

I could speak and understand Dutch. My command of the language was fairly elementary but I could pick up the meaning of most conversations (incidentally the immersion in field-work dramatically improved my Dutch). This proved vital on a number of levels. Communication with the policemen was much easier than if they had been forced to speak in English. More importantly, interaction with the public was comprehensible and, while it was often necessary to clarify situations afterwards (with the danger of getting a one-sided account),

I could follow radio messages, conversations between policemen, and verbal exchanges during incidents. Additionally I could read the extensive documentary material in the station – telegrams, the station diary, reports, charge-sheets, complaints, 'wanted' notices, telex messages, etc.

The first few patrols took place in day-time and much of the activity was routine – stopping and checking the papers of cars, dealing with harmless drunks, and giving information to the public. In the day-time it was pleasant to stroll – although adjusting to the patrolmen's measured tread took some time – around Amsterdam in the sunshine, yet I still felt strange on the streets. Policemen always attract interest and I began to feel that everyone was looking at me too. Gradually, instead of avoiding eye-contact, I began to return stares, forcing people to look away. It was noticeable that, when the policemen interacted with the public, the people concerned seemed naturally to accept my presence as if assuming that I was a policeman in plain clothes. In fact my presence with the police scarcely ever raised comment in six months of field-work. Occasionally the men referred to me as a detective for the public's benefit:

Riding in a patrol-car along the Zeedijk, Tom noticed a battered Simca parked near a club for Surinamers with a scruffy youth sitting in the passenger's seat. 'Heroin birds', he said and parked further down the street. The driver returned and the car passed us, moving out into the Prins Hendrikkade. We overtook them outside Central Station and forced them to stop. The two policemen each took a door and hauled out the two youths. Tom pushed his suspect up against a bus-shelter and began to search him. In a detached and almost bemused way the young man said immediately, 'I bought a shot in —— but otherwise I don't have any stuff on me and I'm not armed, honest, I'll take it easy, don't worry'. Tom wanted to move the cars which were blocking the narrow and busy street in front of the station, and said sternly to the suspect, but with a smile at me behind his back, 'You stay here with your hands up and don't try anything because this detective here [pointing at me] is keeping an eye on you'. I frowned authoritatively.

(Field notes)

In deciding to work with one group, I also decided to do exactly the same duties as they did. There are shifts, such as the late evening shift (6 p.m. to 2 a.m.) at weekends, where action is practically guaranteed and it would have been easy to select attractive shifts and avoid dreary shifts (like 7 a.m. until 3 p.m. on Sundays). But my introductory story was that I wanted to observe general police work, without the frills and without selection of particular problems or offences. To share their experience I went on night duty, weekend duty, day duty, and so on. I went on foot patrol, in weather from drenching rain to humid heat, and in cars. During my second period of research (January to March 1975) there were some bitterly cold nights and I went out on patrol wearing two pairs of socks, wool pyjamas inside my trousers, two pullovers, scarf, gloves, and a woollen cap pulled over my ears. I prayed that we would not have to rescue someone from a canal! When the chance arose I showed willingness to help. Sometimes this meant clearing up in the canteen, making coffee, helping with English-speaking suspects or 'customers' asking about something at the counter, giving a hand to load a damaged motor-bike into a van, sweeping glass off the road after an accident, searching a house, helping to lift a drunk off the street and fetching take-away meals. I began with the notion that my role should be passive but, for a number of reasons, this became more and more difficult.

However, my willingness to adopt precisely the same work hours as the policemen paid dividends in terms of acceptance. In the first place, almost all officers and specialised police services, including most of the detectives, work office hours and the patrolmen are left to themselves in the evenings and at night. This accentuates their ideology that they bear the brunt of the work, on a twenty-four-hour basis, while the bosses are at home watching television or relaxing. The appearance of someone who was prepared to share their life of constantly changing shifts, which causes a number of domestic problems, and of sometimes dreary routine, in all sorts of weather, elicited a positive response. I was seen as willing to experience police life 'where it's at', on the streets, at times when the patrolman was abandoned by his own superiors. I also learnt to distance myself with disparaging remarks from the effete, bohemian image of radical intellectuals. It was not difficult to give vent to my love–hate relationship with academia, but, perceiving the warm response of policemen to a tirade about the idle, shiftless, ideologically blinkered, sexually promiscuous world of sociologists, I began to use this litany to puncture the initial defences of new acquaintances within the police. It always worked.

After my initial month in August 1974 I returned to England, wrote a report analysing the contacts which I had observed on the street between the police and the public (and sent copies to strategically placed people within the Amsterdam Police) and requested a further three months in the following year, which was promptly granted. During that month I had always been accompanied by Willem. Willem was twenty-six, had been a sailor, was unmarried, and was active in sports – namely parachute jumping, boxing, judo and karate (in which he was an instructor, having received advanced training in Japan). The son of a policeman, he was a 'hardliner' interested chiefly in catching criminals and was highly disparaging about other duties. He believed in tough enforcement and hard work. The appearance of a large American-style car in the red-light district would invariably arouse his attention and he would step in its path, hold up an authoritative hand, and politely but firmly ask for the driver's papers. His major interests were finding weapons or drugs.

When I returned to Amsterdam in January 1975, Willem had left for detective training. But the fact that I was prepared to return to the same group for a further three months greatly accelerated my general acceptance. Most of the men soon began to use my Christian name. Also they began to tell me that Willem was a 'fanatic', that he went out of his way to look for work, and that most of them were more easy-going. Indeed, I became worried about the low number of police–public contacts which I was recording until I realised that those of the previous period had been inflated by Willem's 'control everything' philosophy. My analysis of these contacts was really an analysis of the work of a 'rate-buster' rather than an indicator of a general picture of police–public relations. It is also fair to add, however, that police work in Amsterdam has a seasonal element responding to the ebb and flow of tourism, and the winter months are the off-season whereas in the full season the days are long and the streets crowded. However, my acceptance seemed to be complete when 'Jan' ostentatiously lifted his buttocks from the seat of the patrol car and broke wind with aplomb. It was the turning-point of the research and I felt like Whyte (1955, p. 318) stumbling on the informal social structure of Cornerville.

I soon found that some policemen were more sympathetic to me than others, some were more fun to be with, and some always seemed to be getting interesting cases. I now had a floating role free from a mentor, where I could more or less choose with whom I patrolled. I could go to the roster and select a car or a foot patrol and ask the sergeant if it was all right. More and more I went out in cars, not simply because I was lazy or to get out of the cold, but because they were linked by radio with headquarters and tended to get the most interesting calls. The foot patrols were in radio contact with the station but were limited by their beat area and their restricted mobility. More and more I went out with a select half of the group and tried to avoid the dull or uncommunicative other half. I got to know these men well and one of them, 'Hans', almost filled a 'Doc' role (Whyte, 1955, p. 291, was adopted by Doc in Cornerville) because he was so perceptive and articulate.

By now we had shared many incidents together and my regular appearance had led to me being as familiar as a piece of furniture. Hans, for example, would come and get me if something interesting was happening such as plain-clothes duties. Working on tips or with a specific goal, these occasions usually produced results and were much sought after by the men who welcomed the break from uniform and the chance to do some 'real' police work. Once Hans rushed into the canteen and beckoned to me. Three men in plain clothes were to move in on a suspected drugs deal in a hotel. On arrival at the hotel the suspects had just left for the train to Switzerland. We rushed off and arrived at the station with minutes to spare and delayed the train. I noticed a young man and woman in a compartment but Tom said we were looking for three people, not two. I insisted on asking for their passports because I felt intuitively that they might be the suspects. They were, and we started to search the compartment. The train could not wait for more than a few minutes. Suddenly Hans pulled out a small packet of white powder from behind the central heating and shouted 'Bingo!' 'What's that?' asked the youth. 'Sugar?' said Hans, contemptuously slapping the man's face with the packet. Handcuffed, they were hauled off to the station. The pleasure at being right was an indicator that by now I had a strong identification with the work of the patrolmen. I considered them my colleagues, felt a unity with the group, and was prepared to defend them in case of physical (or intellectual) attack (Punch, 1977a).

At the same time some of the men began to treat me almost as a colleague (I say 'almost' because collegiality is highly prized among policemen), and would give me the portable radio to carry or ask me to hold a suspect's arm. Once I was handcuffed to a suspect to prevent him running away and on another occasion a policeman asked me to hold his pistol while he handcuffed a suspect. I felt somewhat foolish as I stood gingerly holding a pistol in the middle of the street while onlookers stared dumbly at the arrest. But more and more I became involved in a participant role. I chased people, searched people, searched cars, searched houses, held people, and even shouted at people who abused my 'colleagues'. Fortunately I was never placed in a situation where I had to decide whether or not to fight on behalf of the policemen. In the few violent occasions that occurred I found that my reactions were so slow and my inability to decide what to do so chronic that the incident was over before I could weigh in. As if I believed in the cool voice of academic reason, I used to rush around the combatants futilely imploring them to calm down.

In fact, during the research, nobody aimed a fist or a gun at me. Sometimes I would stand between two squabbling drunks to show the patrolmen that I was not frightened. But, in fact, I always felt fortified by the presence of two policemen (normally I am a physical and moral coward). There was frequently an element of danger and yet it never seemed very real. On numerous occasions we went into buildings with drawn pistols or arrested people who were thought to be armed. But I never had to lead the charge and could simply stay to one side or stand behind a pillar. Probably there was more danger in a high-speed chase through the narrow, cobbled streets, but some element of danger attends all observation with the police. There were frequent raids, for example, on clubs frequented by Surinamers, and their hostility to the police, based on claims of racial prejudice and mistreatment, made these potentially explosive occasions. Normally, raids would consist of at least six or eight men and yet if a real fight had developed then we would have been in trouble and hopelessly outnumbered. Normally I stayed by the door because I was told that to walk unarmed in plain clothes through a densely crowded club was asking for a knife in your back. Such situations were probably the most stressful that I encountered – as opposed to confronting victims injured in assaults or accidents – because of the intense hostility directed at me on the assumption that I was a policeman.

As with observation on some deviant and criminal groups, there arose the ethical question as to the observer's reaction to witnessing misbehaviour on the part of the policemen. The literature on the police alerts one to widespread and deeply engrained malpractices such as corruption, mistreatment of suspects, racial prejudice, and denial of legal rights to suspects (Humphry, 1972; Walker Report, 1968; Sherman, 1974). Initially I came to the conclusion that these abuses, amply documented in English and American material, were largely absent in Amsterdam policing. In six months graft and corruption were scarcely mentioned, not even jokingly or on informal occasions out of duty, and revelations of such practices in the papers were almost nonexistent.

In the summer of 1976 my contacts with the Warmoesstraat had tailed off as I had become more and more involved in writing. Around that time there were rumours internally of dubious police practices related to the Chinese gambling and drugs world. One evening I went to Hans's flat for a celebration and several policemen began talking excitedly about corruption. I learnt more in that evening, thanks to the liberating effects of alcohol, than in all my field-work. It was not so much a series of shocking personal revelations – indeed, the whole tenor of the discussion emphasised the honesty of the men present (one could hardly expect it to be otherwise) – but more that a subterranean police culture which had largely escaped me suddenly emerged. There was talk of policemen sleeping with prostitutes, accepting bribes, keeping an extra round from the range to use in case of a hasty shot which the constable did not want to report, covering up for colleagues in delicate situations, and running messages for members of the Chinese underworld. Hans and Tom explained, 'How much do you think you found out when you were with us? You wrote somewhere that you thought we were open-hearted. Well, we only let you see what we wanted you to see. You only saw about fifty per cent. We showed you only a half of the story.' Bert then said that as far as he was concerned I had seen ninety per cent. Tom had had a young constable in tow for three weeks and he turned to him and said, 'How long have we been working together? Three weeks? Well, I haven't let you see a thing. Not a thing.'

It would almost require another book to go into the intricacies of that corruption scandal, which did not really touch the uniformed patrolmen but was focused on plain-clothes men in vice and drugs, and Hans almost deserves a book to himself. He would have made a good sociologist. But I cannot go into detail because I identify the station where I worked and individuals would be easily recognisable. To capture the stories behind the stories it would probably be necessary to write a novel, as Wambaugh (1970, 1972, 1975) has successfully done for police work in Los Angeles. However, it is worth noting that my favourable field impressions were based on a partial picture and that keeping in contact with my informants proved invaluable during the writing-up phase. The field-work may have been essential in gaining the trust of these men, but it is probably true that I have learned far more about the police since I stopped observation, and am still learning.

After the research period in early 1975, there followed two more months in July and August when I also carried out a number of interviews (Punch, 1976d). I interviewed policemen of all ranks from commissioner to constable as well as a number of people outside the force. The interviews were carried out after I had developed rapport with the policemen and were informed by my practical experiences on the street. There was no attempt at a random sample and I simply selected people I knew or who occupied important organisational positions. In the closed social world of a police force, interviewing strangers can be a futile and frustrating business, and interviews with constables not in my group were not very successful. For police–citizen encounters on the street I had a check-list, based on Reiss's (1971) research, which enabled me to generalise about the sorts of people with whom the police interact. Thus, I could call on documentary and internal statistical evidence, interviews and accounts, and statistical data on suspects and other groups (e.g. using age, sex, nationality, attitudes to the police, and police attitudes to the public) based on observations from police work on the street.

In the meantime I had taken up a teaching appointment in The Netherlands. Initially I suffered withdrawal symptoms and hankered after the atmosphere of the station and the friends I had made among the policemen. The university seemed a pedantic and unreal world and I had considerable difficulty in readjusting. Fortunately, I more or less had 'carte blanche' to return to the station. This proved less and less satisfying, as the group gradually split up when people applied to forces in other towns or were selected for the detectives. But the good old days had gone, and my appearances gradually tailed off, although I remained in informal contact with some officers and some men. But as Polsky (1971, p. 145) says, field-work is fun. To a certain extent it is a 'holiday' from academic rituals and it provides an opportunity to get away from books, papers, essays, seminars, and sedentary pontificating on the ills of the world. Working with the police takes you out of the university and into the entrails of society, where you witness incidents from sudden birth to sudden death. And basically all you have to do is watch and listen. The patrolmen, for instance, cannot escape the paperwork surrounding modern policing, but all such onerous tasks I could avoid. I could enter extreme situations yet without being responsible for settling them. In the car, I could lean back and watch pretty girls on the streets while the men kept their eyes open for incidents (as well as the girls). In the car you feel connected with the rising and falling rhythm of the city. Amsterdam is a beautiful city, marred in day-time by teeming streets, clogged with traffic. We, however, could drive through empty streets at night and cruise effortlessly alongside the canals watching the first rays of sunrise break over the artistic gables of the house tops. In effect, we saw Amsterdam at its best, and also at its worst.

(iv) COMMENT

In this final section I shall endeavour to generalise about my field experiences with the Amsterdam Police. Basically the problems encountered in researching the police overlap to a considerable extent with the dilemmas found in most observational studies (McCall and Simmons, 1969). There are some specific aspects peculiar to the police – such as danger, shift-work, the visibility of uniforms (and hence the visibility of the accompanying researcher), the ethical ambivalences of police work, etc. – and there now exist enough studies for someone to think of collecting reports of field-work with the police in order to draw up an analytical balance-sheet as to the parallels with, and divergences from, the standard accounts of qualitative and observational research. My research was given an added dimension by the fact that I was working in another culture and in a foreign language, unlike the majority of police studies to date. Of course the Amsterdam Police does not, to my knowledge, practise cannibalism, and popping over the North Sea is not like Evans-Pritchard setting off stoically into the bush. But, at times, the backwardness of Dutch sociology and its reluctance to enter the field made me feel like a lone anthropologist, addicted to his 'tribe' and resentful of the lack of understanding about it in the wider society (Clarke, 1975).

A favourable aspect of working with the police is that it is a routinised, bureaucratic organisation. With exceptions, you know when a shift begins and ends. And if you want to interview 'Constable Van der Linden' for two hours beginning at six o'clock, then the sergeant arranges for him to be free. The bureaucracy will work for you and organise things for you and that can greatly facilitate field-work. It avoids some of the aimless, diffuse aspects of field-work with deviant groups where the researcher is dependent on the mood and behaviour of the group and where prior planning of research activities proves almost impossible. There was at my disposal a room for interviewing, a photocopying machine for documentary material, a telephone for making appointments, and transport to bring me to incidents or to bring me home (once I was brought home in a patrol-car when I was ill and once to collect a cheque-book in order to get some money out of the bank). I even had a police bicycle lent to me because I had no car for getting home when the public transport stopped running. For much of the research I had no effective institutional base in The Netherlands so that these facilities greatly assisted the research.

Otherwise, the dilemmas and pitfalls of participant observation with the police are little different from those of studying other groups. There is an element of danger, but that is also true of research with certain deviant groups – Yablonsky (1973, p. 194) was threatened during his communes research, and Hunter Thompson (1967, p. 283) was beaten up by Hell's Angels. It may be necessary to absolve the police from responsibility in case of accident and sign a document stating that the researcher patrols at his own risk. This was not necessary in my case, but I did take out special insurance coverage.

There is, too, always the question-mark surrounding the extent to which individuals modify their behaviour in the presence of the observer. My feeling echoes that of Becker (1970, p. 46) in believing that people do not keep up such an act for long and that what they are engaged in is often more important to them than the fact that an outsider is present. A policeman may speak more politely to a citizen because a researcher is at his elbow, but in many situations he does not have time to think but must react instantly. In any event, my appearances were so commonplace that after a while I do not believe people noticed me during routine cases. However, the more I was accepted the more they expected me to act *as a colleague*. In my willingness to be accepted by the policemen I over-identified perhaps too readily and this doubtless endangered my research role. For the patrol group is a cohesive social unit and the policeman's world is full of seductive interest so that is is all too easy to 'go native'.

There also exists a potential dilemma of witnessing crimes either on the part of suspects, or, indeed, on the part of the policemen. Would it infringe the research role to appear as a witness against a suspect? Would one feel obliged to testify against a policeman who had been observed in violation of the law? The sociologist has no right to privileged information and may have to be prepared to suffer for protecting his respondents. Fortunately, this problem did not arise in my study. There is, however, a more general ethical issue as raised by Becker's (1967) query, 'Whose side are we on?' Frequently, research studies have emphasised the exposure of pernicious practices within control institutions and have tended to identify with those groups who suffer from such practices (Bianchi et al., 1975). In researching the police I was conscious that many academic colleagues have a critical, if not hostile, perspective on the police and this made me somewhat defensive about my research. Some radical criminologists, for example, had advised me to infiltrate the police organisation (they emphasised the advantage I enjoyed in being trusted by the police), to collect damaging material and to photocopy documents, and then to expose the police in the most embarrassing light possible. I rejected this espionage model of research, but there remained one's personal feelings about people who come into contact with the police.

During my study I have often shared the back seat of the patrol-car with a handcuffed suspect who had just been deprived of his freedom. Naturally this first-hand observation of suspects raises a number of moral questions about the nature and effects of law and crime and about the law-enforcement process. My own feelings were to have little sympathy for individuals concerned in crimes of violence and in dealing in hard drugs. It was difficult to get worked up about many of the minor offences, such as shoplifting, and the suspects were often either stupid, in drawing attention to themselves, or else just unlucky at being caught. But to a large extent I accepted police work as an enterprise and 'morally' approved of most of its activities. This feeling was accentuated by the fact that the predatory underworld of Amsterdam holds little romantic appeal for me. Quite frankly, the procession of pickpockets, ponces, prostitutes, dealers, muggers, car thieves, drunken drivers, burglars, bouncers, army deserters, shoplifters, delinquents and suspects accused of violence with knife or gun, were simply not the sort of people that, face to face, have a Damon Runyon appeal. And if the eye and ear are important for collecting data, then why not the nose? Some of these people literally stink. Perhaps that tells the reader more about me than about criminals, but I have seen, and smelt, enough suspects to raise severe doubts as to my ability of identifying with them. The role of drugs in criminality in Amsterdam can mean that suspects are in a very poor physical and hygienic state, while the city-centre world of bars and vice attracts a species of over-weight, over-dressed, loud-mouthed café-dwellers who seem willing to beat someone up at the slightest excuse. For a number of reasons, then, I reservedly accepted the side I was on.

There is often no definite end-point to a field study. I was restricted by teaching obligations and half of the research was carried out in time that was technically vacation. In total I spent about six months on patrol. This seems to be the acceptable *minimum* and compares unfavourably with classical anthropological studies, with Whyte's (1955) four years in Cornerville, and Suttles' (1968) three years in the Near West Side of Chicago. But, finally, I should like to re-endorse my earlier remarks that observation is essential to penetrating the police culture. Immersion in the field also provides a degree of life experience that is lacking in most academic environments. The police is an institution concerned minutely with regulating everyday behaviour and with applying societal norms. Its work is intrinsically interesting on a human level and its performance socially important in terms of providing data about a largely closed social world. Policemen work at the nerve-edge of society, where control is exercised, where sanctions are applied, and where crises are resolved. They inhabit profane areas of society, where good citizens fear to tread, and face situations where the buck can no longer be passed on. Encounters become instant morality plays with the abstract values of our civilisation – justice, liberty, equality before the law, etc. – being daily redefined in unedifying and irresolute conflicts accompanied by blood, blasphemy and violence. The magic and the mundane, the routine and the ritual, the sacred and the profane mingle in police work into a blend irresistible to the hackneyed plots of television serials and, less conspicuously, into rich and fruitful material for the study of social interaction. Participant observation enables one to go behind the public front of a conspicuous service bureaucracy to witness 'backstage' behaviour when the actors are off-stage, not performing to a public, and not peddling stereotyped scripts for the benefit of bystanders. In essence, the appeal of field-work is that it is concerned with real people and that confrontation with people, in all their baffling complexity, is a fruitful antidote to a positivist methodology and a natural science model for the social sciences.

2 Introduction: Crime and the Police in Amsterdam

(i) THE RESEARCH PERSPECTIVE

This book reports an observational study of the occupational culture and identity of uniformed policemen in a cosmopolitan city-centre. It sets out to build upon the existing Anglo-American literature on police work and to amplify it by adding a cross-cultural component, by emphasising the increasingly cosmopolitan element in the criminal world of metropolitan life, and by accentuating some novel elements in the occupational world of the contemporary policeman. In particular, this case study of police work in one inner-city station in a world city will focus on the complex factors which generate a vicious circle that dilutes the police culture, that creates an almost normless quality about police work and the decline of the police craft, and that leads to increasingly ineffective law-enforcement and 'repressive' norms of policing. A major purpose of this book, then, is to illuminate the reality of police work by going behind the often negative stereotype to observe and to listen to a group of policemen whose values and behaviour are intimately shaped by the unique area they police, namely the red-light district of Amsterdam.

A central concern is to demystify police practice by simply viewing it as work. As such, attention is drawn to the occupational culture, to values and norms surrounding work, to organisational directives and pressures, to informal practices and codes, and to the fact that 'a man's work is one of the more important parts of his social identity – his self' (Hughes, 1953). The fruitfulness of this approach is argued by Manning (1977, pp. 16ff) who emphasises the contradiction between the public symbolism of the police role as crime-fighter and the actual occupational activities of patrol work, while Chatterton (1976b, p. 114) maintains that 'unless we are prepared to invest time in looking into the policeman's world view, his occupational culture, we cannot hope to achieve an understanding of the way he approaches and does his job'. Rubinstein (1973, p. xi), moreover, argues, 'The lack of any systematic description of police work has enhanced the mystery and speculation which shroud the police'.

Skolnick (1975), in his study of Oakland detectives, makes the 'action perspective', whereby the investigator perceives the meaning of events through the eyes of the participants, a crucial element in his research and maintains that:

> A study of law in action, whether of judges, lawyers, or policemen, is a study of men interpreting and thereby transforming principles and associated rules within legal institutions. Above all, it is a study of men at work. The action perspective is intended to reveal the meaning of the work to the men performing it. (p. 25)

In elaborating his theoretical perspective, Skolnick argues that his prime focus is not with the police as an occupational group, and therefore not with a contribution to the sociology of work, but rather that an analysis of the policeman's working personality is the distinctive concern of the legal sociologist. In tackling this particular research I was not especially conscious of the overtly legal approach but considered it more as a contribution to a developing sociology of the police which falls somewhere within the overlapping perspectives of the sociology of law, the sociology of work, and the traditional concern of criminology with law-enforcement. Apart from the 'new wave' of police studies mentioned below, such as Rubinstein (1973), Chatterton (1975a) and Manning (1977), two works in particular helped to shape my approach to this research. One was Bittner (1967a), because he seemed to have captured the subtle relationship between police work and the norms and values of a specific area in his analysis of peace-keeping on 'skid-row', and the other was Whyte's (1955) study, *Street Corner Society*. While mentioning Whyte's classic may merely invite unfavourable comparisons with my work, it helped to stimulate and guide my research and gave me a model for participant observation.

A cross-cultural study of police work in Amsterdam may be useful in highlighting and contrasting the dilemmas of policing large, international cities such as London, New York and Paris. I mean by this that there is a specific style of predatory criminality associated with the anonymity of an inner-city area (Banfield, 1974, p. 10), with its mixture of urban decay and impersonal spaces, and that in some cities this is interrelated with mass tourism, open borders, and mobile foreign criminals. This international element is totally missing from previously published work on the police. One consequence is that Bittner's material on 'skid-row', where officers of long experience and deep local knowledge kept the peace, seems dated and not wholly applicable to less stable deviant communities. Bittner wrote (1967a, p. 707):

> As a general rule, the skid-row patrolman possesses an immensely detailed factual knowledge of his beat. He knows, and knows a great deal about, a large number of residents. He is likely to know every person who manages or works in the local bars, hotels, shops, stores, and missions. Moreover, he probably knows every public and private place inside out. Finally, he ordinarily remembers countless events of the past which he can recount by citing names, dates and places with remarkable precision.

In Amsterdam, certain such norms based on intimate local knowledge and particularistic acquaintances remain, but the rapid changes of the last decade have led to an increasingly criminalesque subculture and to the social estrangement and isolation of the policemen who operate there.

Amsterdam is considered to be the most difficult city in The Netherlands to police (Punch, 1947a) and Bureau Warmoesstraat, in the heart of the city-centre, enjoys a notorious reputation. As a case study of a unique station in a unique part of Amsterdam, the evidence presented here cannot be taken as representative of the Dutch Police as a whole. The Warmoesstraat has its own specific atmosphere and style, unlike stations not simply in other Dutch cities but even of suburban stations in Amsterdam. Perhaps one would have to compare the Warmoesstraat with, say, Soho in London or with parts of San Francisco. The city of San Francisco seems to share a number of features with Amsterdam, such as the hippy invasion of Haight-Ashbury (Smith, 1970), a wide range of ethnic groups (Davis, 1971) and fragmented political decision-making, and perhaps the most important is a degree of tolerance for deviance. Becker and Horowitz (1971, p. 6) describe this quality as 'civility', which involves accommodating to differing morals and life-styles in order to promote peace and stability. For example, they mention that the police do not harass homosexuals as is common in some other American cities (Wittman, 1970). But the culture of civility concept seems of value in describing the traditional libertarianism associated with a world city like Amsterdam.

In particular, the city-centre of Amsterdam can be viewed as a testing-ground for that tolerance because norms are pushed to their limits. On the one hand there is a traditional deviant community of prostitution, bars and underworld characters, and on the other hand there is a conglomeration of predatory criminals, migrant groups, rootless foreigners and transitory people. Deviance can be seen as patrolling the fringes of social change and as experimenting with potential directions for future social growth (Shoham, 1976), so that the 'enlightened' views of inner-city life afford a glimpse of potential future developments. Part of the dilemmas and predicaments facing the police and inhabitants of the city-centre arise from specific ecological problems such as urban decay, redevelopment, unbalanced age distributions, concentrations of migrants, high turnover of people, anonymity and so on (Heinemeyer et al., 1968; Newman, 1973). In such environments the police become estranged from the mixed population, are forced into repressive enforcement, and are perceived as critical gatekeepers maintaining the existing social system of rich and powerful citizens cloistered in their suburban enclaves against the poor, the weak and the newcomer in the urban ghetto. Westley (1974, p. 310) summed up this predicament:

> To combat crime the police have shaped themselves into a kind of army of occupation. Of course, they are ineffective, for what occupied territory co-operates with occupying patrols; and without co-operation the police find themselves separated from the sources of order. There is in fact little order to build upon, for the ineffectiveness of the police, through no fault of their own, has deprived these inner-city communities of vital public support in creating order.

It may, however, be too easy to conceive the inner city as an atomistic, predatory world of 'disorganisation'. Suttles (1968), on the other hand, has painstakingly documented the elements of organisation in a slum. For the Near West Side of Chicago he shows that there are patterns of 'ordered segmentation' regulating and defining social life. 'The city is seen as something like an irregular lattice work from which a person's behaviour and appearance can be gauged, interpreted, and reacted to depending upon the section to which he belongs' (p. 15). The tension between tolerance and repression, and the testing of moral boundaries, is played out visibly in the inner city of Amsterdam, and as such it may serve as a microcosm of value conflicts in the wider society and as an example of the limitations placed on deviance with its ambivalent origins in both creative innovation and potential disruption (Shoham, 1976, p. xv).

This book, then, is a sociological study of contemporary police work in a cosmopolitan city-centre. The occupational world and social identity of the uniformed policeman is taken as central to exploring the ambivalences and dilemmas of policing a deviant community. This also helps to get behind the stereotype to the nature of the social order which policemen help to create or to which they respond because there is a sense in which the police operate at the nerve-end of society, having to resolve on the streets legal ambiguities, cultural conflicts and normative confusion. As social regulators policemen make practical decisions in concrete situations which can tell us a good deal about the fluctuating and sometimes conflicting norms and values in a given society concerning control, respectability, tolerance of nonconformity, acceptance of ambiguity, the dividing line between legal and non-legal deviance, the reconciliation of social disputes and so on. The policeman is in the 'front-line' (Smith, 1965) and daily encounters the consequences of these pressures. In large cities police work is for much of the time a boring, monotonous, messy routine and I encountered an almost normless quality in contemporary policing.

Whitaker (1964, p. 30) argues that police work is becoming increasingly more difficult, and Cain (1973, p. 62) speaks of the 'low morale and disillusion, the sense of having a tough job to do with inadequate equipment and recognition' in urban policing. The almost jaundiced role obsession of the policeman emerges in many studies. Preiss and Ehrlich (1966, p. 22) talk of 'impotence and cynicism', while Westley (1970, p. 149) observed in 1953 that: 'Condemnation and his uniform stereotype him. Condemnation and his work make of him a pariah . . . his morality is one of expediency and his self-conception one of a martyr.' Seventeen years later Westley believed that the situation had merely been reinforced by the intervening period – which had seen riots, racial violence, protests and murders of policemen come to the fore – and Skolnick confirms this when reviewing the police response to the violent and critical sixties in the second edition of *Justice Without Trial*. The policeman in America has become a member of a low-status out-group who has turned to 'blue power' and to the police unions as right-wing, political interest groups (Juris and Feuille, 1973). Furthermore, the much-buffeted New York policemen are now perceived as a 'beleagured minority' who are reacting bitterly to exposure, criticism, and the promotion of minority groups (Alex, 1976). There was something of that sourness among the Amsterdam policemen with whom I worked, along with a variety of accommodations from indifference to alienation.

(ii) THE SOCIOLOGY OF THE POLICE

In this brief review of the literature on the sociology of the police it will become obvious that we are highly reliant on American studies. In explaining the impetus given to this area in America, Furstenberg (*Police Journal,* No. 4, 1973) maintained that initially the American academic community was uninterested in the police partly because it was considered a low-status area and partly because there were few funds available. Research grants and academic involvement were only generated following widespread criticism of police behaviour in the sixties when the cities threatened to explode and the police were stetched to their limits. Racial violence, urban unrest, massive demonstrations and spiralling crime led to intense public debate on 'law and order' and suddenly huge sums of money became available to study a range of pressing social problems including the behaviour of the police. The emphasis, however, tended to be on investigation of abuses and on deviations from the legally prescribed norms of law-enforcement. In other words, the spotlight on the police was generally critical and it highlighted the areas of violence, prejudice, corruption and abuse of legal powers (Chevigny, 1968). Or, as Maureen Cain (1977, p. 3) remarked when discussing press coverage of the police in Britain, they were only directly the focus of interest when 'dead, brutal or corrupt'.

Three standard works emerged from the extensive output of this period – Skolnick (1975), J. Wilson (1968) and Reiss (1971). In general, they were concerned with the gap between the universal prescriptions of the law book and the law in action. Their approach was not specifically theoretical but was more concerned with empirically documenting and amplifying the 'gap'. Manning (1977, p. 163) has criticised these works for being too 'legalistic' and for collapsing a series of processes into one, such as the arrest rate. The perspective of the studies was, however, dictated to a certain extent by the questions being raised about the police in the wider society at the time and by the backgrounds, training and research orientations of the academics concerned.

In Britain, Banton (1964) and Cain (1973) have written books which are often regarded as the authoritative texts. Banton, an anthropologist by training, was interested in the place of the policeman in the community and his responsibility for maintaining order as a 'peace officer' as well as a law officer. The fact that his work was a cross-cultural study gives it a valuable dimension in highlighting a number of contrasts between American and British (as represented by police work in Edinburgh) policing. Maureen Cain carried out a project which compared policing in rural Suffolk and in Birmingham; the research was concerned with 'the relevance of different role-definers for police-action and their role conception'. Because so much material on the police has been collected predominantly in urban areas, it is useful to have data on rural policing where the community appears to play an important role in defining the policeman's identity and where 'peace-keeping' is the first priority. Both these books were concerned with the policeman's role in the community and did not focus specifically on unravelling the nature of encounters with the public.

Although the books mentioned remain important studies of the police which have been valuable in promoting sociological insights on the police, they are now all somewhat dated. Skolnick, Reiss, Wilson, Banton and Cain carried out their field-work in the early or mid-sixties before the numerous technical innovations which radically altered patrol work. For example, since Cain's research commenced in 1962, Britain has seen the introduction of 'Unit Beat Policing', personal radios, mobile patrols, rapid promotions and the Police College disseminating a professional ideology (Holdaway, 1977a). I would argue that police work in the seventies contains many elements not previously discussed and that the ethnographic approach, employed so successfully in research on subcultures and in deviancy studies, can usefully highlight the social world of the contemporary policeman.

A second generation of police studies has recently emerged which are often more in tune with wider theoretical developments in sociology, particularly in interactionism and phenomenology. Among these I include as influential the work of Westley (1970), Bittner (1967a), Rubinstein (1973), Chatterton (1975a) and Manning (1977). These writers share in common a focus on the occupational culture of the policeman as an analytical framework for explaining his behaviour under different circumstances. Their approach is more intrepretative in that they take into account the meaning which the policeman gives to acting, and *not* acting, as alternative ways of handling situated events. Westley preceded this 'new wave' with his thesis of 1953, but his work was published as a book seventeen years later and holds its own as a study of an occupational morality of secrecy which shaped the use of illegal force against suspects and which protected the perpetrators of violence. In describing the isolation and alienation of the police from conventional society he foreshadows the predicament of the policeman in contemporary urban society where he is seen almost as a member of an army of occupation (this analogy is used by James Baldwin, 1962, pp. 65–7, and also by Colin MacInnes, 1969b, p. 467).

Bittner's essay on 'peace-keeping in skid-row' has played an important role in analysing the diffuse and largely unexamined work of literally keeping the peace. By concentrating on the particularistic norms of 'skid-row' he draws attention to the situated notions of appropriate behaviour, culpability and privacy. The right to search bodies and to search rooms without prior agreement is a taken-for-granted fact of life for the residents and patrolmen of skid-row, although this conflicts patently with civil liberties. But we should bear in mind that Bittner's skid-row policemen are unusual because of the area, the people, the policies of the station, and the experience of the patrolmen (Manning, 1977, p. 267).

Rubinstein has produced a study of police work in Philadelphia which Westley (1974, p. 311) predicts will become 'an enduring ethnography of urban life in America'. Written in a journalistic style and with little attempt to systematise his material, Rubinstein gives us an insider's view of backstage police behaviour and, in microscopic detail, takes us into the policeman's social world. Manning (1977) spent a relatively short time in the field with the Metropolitan Police but elicited a good deal of rich material which he analyses in terms drawn from the dramaturgical perspective, from formal ethnography and anthropology, and from information theory. Chatterton (1975a) has been influenced by interactionism and labelling theory and has sought to itemise the social and organisational constraints which influence decisions to arrest or not to arrest. His data were collected with uniformed men and detectives in a large northern city and promise to be the most comprehensive study of British policing at the operational, decision-making level. Holdaway (1977a) carried out a rare disguised participant observation study of an urban police force while working as a policeman, and this too looks likely to produce badly needed first-hand data on the dilemmas and routine practices of contemporary policing.

In the new wave there tend to be two common factors. This is, first, a focus on police work as *work*. Manning's book is actually entitled *Police Work* and he writes (1977, p. 373): 'We are only now beginning to make visible the implicit assumptions that the police make about their own work: why, how, where and when they do it.' Chatterton (1976b, p. 120) also observes that: 'It is surprising that when so much interest is shown in the products and consequences of police work so little is known about how that work gets done . . . unsupported inferences about the policing process have passed imperceptibly into our conceptions of police work.' And, second, they prise open the informal social world of the policeman which contrasts frequently with the police image as presented by administrators, policy-makers and senior officers. What from outside appears to be a highly articulated, authoritarian organisation, with a high level of control over its lower participants, is, in practice, an institution forced to grant considerable autonomy to its lower ranks, who manipulate their low visibility from control to take part in 'easing' (Cain, 1973, p. 74), 'perks' (Manning, 1977, pp. 151–3), 'cooping' (Maas, 1973, pp. 54–5) and corruption (Rubinstein, 1973, pp. 373–434).

Finally, before moving on to the perspectives used in this particular study, I should like to mention two important features of the literature on the police. One is that Dutch social science has displayed a conspicuous lack of interest in the police. The 'Coornhert Liga' (which performs a similar role to that of the Howard League for Penal Reform in Britain) lamented: 'The picture regarding research on the police is particularly sombre. It is unfortunate to have to conclude that, apart from incidental publications from university institutes and an occasional project by police officers, there can be no talk of regular research, let alone a policy for research' (1973 p. 43). The other is simply that the sociology of the police in general does not display the signs of a well-developed sub-discipline. The field is not theoretically homogeneous, does not appear to be particularly cumulative, but remains something of a disparate patchwork quilt of one-man studies. We do not possess an impressive array of data about the many facets of the police in society. In particular, not much attention has been paid to the police at the societal level, to the internal political culture of police organisations, to informal negotiations with other organisations, to comparative research, and to the non-occupational social world of the policeman (exceptions are Silver, 1967; Bent, 1974; Mitchell, 1975; Bayley, 1976). It is worth adding here that the 'new' criminologists have largely chosen to ignore the police as an object of study, perhaps because they feel it is sufficient simply to condemn the police rather than investigate them. Taylor et al. (1973), a leading text in the field, barely mentions the police. Indeed, they seem to insulate themselves from actually having to study control structures, as opposed to making declamatory statements about their commitment to change them, because such research can be denounced as offering 'advice and prescriptions to authority-holders' (ibid., p. 245).

(iii) DUTCH SOCIETY AND THE CRIMINAL JUSTICE SYSTEM

Here I should like to sketch briefly a few essential themes related to criminality and the police in Dutch society as a backcloth to the presentation of the research data. In general there have been very few attempts by social scientists to analyse The Netherlands at the macro level; Goudsblom's (1967) *Dutch Society* is indispensable but dated, while Lijphart's (1968) interesting study of pluralism and democracy is particularly concerned with the political process. It is tempting for a foreigner to compress the complex historical, economic and political features which help to shape social structure by generalising about national character. This is frequently not only painful for the host country but also misleading in posing a specious explanation of behaviour in terms of a national stereotype which may serve to conceal class and regional differences. Here I shall simply confine myself to a number of observations that have been made about the Dutch and Dutch society while appreciating that the social reality is infinitely more complex.

Foreign commentators tend to remark on the relative stability and orderliness of Dutch society. Bagley (1973a), for example, was obviously struck, during his research on race relations in The Netherlands, with the emphasis on deference and regulation; he quoted de Boer Laschuyt (1959),

> Dutch life is so regulated, so organised and ruled even in the smallest details, that it would become unbearable if not everybody stuck to the instructions and regulations. The fact that everybody lives according to the same restricted patterns of life, is the only consolation: consequently 'being different' is hated and jealously disliked . . . the Dutch way of life is good, yes the best. Consequently 'being different' is very near to 'being less good'.

Observers have seen the Dutch as reserved, stiff, orderly, deferential, seclusive, discreet, respectable, moderate, placid, sober, honest, rigid, dry, cold and righteous. De Baena (1967) has described the Dutch as 'the most conservative people in the world', the typical Dutchman as having the 'mentality of a chartered accountant', and The Netherlands as 'a bourgeois society which does not believe in eccentricity or even in enthusiasm but which is obsessed by a middle-class idea of respectability'. The Dutch sociologist Goudsblom (1967) also reinforces this picture of moderation by focusing on the legacy of bourgeois civility which stresses politeness and emotional restraint. It includes not only good manners and a sense of decorum but also self-possession, a sense of duty, and responsibility.

Unfortunately, none of these qualities is apparent when travelling on an Amsterdam tram! Daily street life and impersonal contacts in Amsterdam (as opposed to formal face-to-face encounters) seem to me to be typified, much more than in other Dutch cities, by disorder, lack of deference, rudeness and inconsiderateness. The accentuation of civility and deference strikes me as portraying something of an idealised picture of Dutch culture which gives undue attention to the dominant middle-class business and political elites while neglecting intellectuals and the varieties of working-class life-styles. The Spanish diplomat De Baena (1967) seems to be more successful than the academics at unearthing some of the ambivalences and contradictions in the Dutch character – between respectability and rudeness, between the soberness of the Protestant North and the warmth of the Catholic South, and between the Reformation virtues and a degree of nonchalance, carelessness and apathy. In brief, I feel that De Baena has at least indicated some of the historical, religious, regional and cultural differences which underlie the apparent uniformity of Dutch culture, and his musings on the 'Dutch puzzle' warn us not to take at face value popular stereotypes of the Dutch but to probe beneath the surface to those often conflicting factors which play a role in the culture of many societies.

One is on safer ground when describing The Netherlands as a small, stable, democratic and highly industrialised society (De Vries, 1973). It is noted for its small size (some 12,850 square miles or roughly a quarter of the State of New York), its population density (352 inhabitants per square kilometre compared with 217 in Britain), its geographical vulnerability (roughly a third of the land area has been reclaimed from the sea), and its political vulnerability as a traditionally non-aggressive country sharing borders with Belgium and Germany and straddling three major European rivers – the Maas, the Waal and the Rhine (Goudsblom, 1967). Following the early bitter struggle for independence against Spain, the country developed as a trading nation and colonial power which avoided serious internal conflict, which institutionalised tolerance (the Union of Utrecht in 1579 promised freedom of religion) and which opened its doors to refugees, including Huguenots, Jews, Germans and Walloons (Romein-Verschoor and Romein, 1973). More recently The Netherlands has evolved into a multiracial society. In 1974 there were roughly 330,000 foreigners registered as resident, together with around 70,000 people with Dutch nationality born in the former Dutch West Indies. Some 3 per cent of the population is foreign and about a third of this group are migrant 'guest workers' (Entzinger, 1975). Since the last war the country has absorbed 300,000 refugees from the former Dutch East Indies. There appears to be a marked absence of poverty in an economy regulated by the government in close co-operation with management and organised labour and with relatively high minimum standards of income, health and welfare.

This tiny, industrious nation, which rebuilt itself from the ruins of war, which stoically repaired its sea defences following the disastrous floods of 1953, and which lost an empire and coped with a massive flood of refugees following decolonisation, has not received much sociological attention from abroad. In particular, we are handicapped by a paucity of material on the rapid social and cultural changes of the last decade which have weakened traditional patterns of allegiance (Thurlings, 1971). There has been a noticeable preoccupation with questions of authority, sexual tolerance, and democratisation of power and even taste in terms of clothes and material possessions, yet it remains extremely difficult to decide to what extent this has effectively challenged or changed basic values (Middendorp, 1975). I acknowledge, then, that we do not have a very up-to-date picture of contemporary Dutch society and the above remarks are merely intended as the most summary outline for the reader.

In terms of the criminal justice system The Netherlands seems to be experiencing something of a reaction to its enlightened policies, in sentencing and in prison regimes, because of an increasing preoccupation with rising crime. Yet compared to other industrialised countries The Netherlands is not a conspicuously criminal or violent society. For the period 1961–5, Gurr (1969) estimated a 'civil strife index' for 114 countries which was headed by Zaïre and in which the United States came 41st and The Netherlands in the 109th position. The death penalty was abolished in 1870, almost a century before it was suspended in Britain, and the probation service traces its origins to 1823

(Smits, 1973a, p. 40). Until 1970, when a policeman was murdered during the occupation by South Moluccans of the Indonesian Embassy in The Hague, there had been no 'political' murders for almost three centuries (Goudsblom, 1967, p. 77).

The current dilemma may have arisen because a liberal justice system, faced with the challenge of rising crime, cannot retrace itself without considerable confusion. More generally, the wider society may be shocked by a smaller absolute increase in crime than is the case in more crime-ridden societies such as America. The mini-'moral panic' (Cohen, 1972) which has resulted has arisen largely because of the terms of the debate which tends to identify 'crime' with violent crime (Smits, 1974a). Since the last war, for example, the penal system has developed a fundamentally rehabilitative ideology of avoiding long sentences and emphasising resocialisation (Zwezerijnen, 1972). Certainly in comparison with other countries, prison sentences are fairly light in Holland. In 1972 the average sentence was 12 weeks and in 1974 this had risen to 14 weeks. In general, three to four years is considered a heavy punishment and also the period beyond which institutionalisation is likely to defeat hopes of resocialisation (Buitelaar and Sierksma, 1972). The total number of people detained in prison in 1972 was 2827 and of these 52 were woman; in 1971 the now infamous Attica Prison alone housed 2200 inmates (Commission on Attica, 1972). The United States has 15–16 times the population of Holland, but about 130–140 times the prison population (Van Ruller, 1973, p. 92). Official penal policy has been trying to move towards fewer prison sentences as punishment and to lighter sentences (Heijder, 1974). Neighbouring countries like Belgium, France and West Germany appear to have harsher penalties and severer prison regimes, and one commentator feared that The Netherlands would become 'an island of mildness' attracting foreign criminals (*De Telegraaf*, 26 August 1974).

The crime picture, at least as portrayed through official statistics (and with all the qualifications that surround their use and intepretation), is one of steadily increasing property crimes and steadily decreasing clear-up rates, but crimes of violence and sex offences have remained fairly constant. Between 1963 and 1971 the total number of offences against the person remained virtually static at 10,716 and 10,881 respectively. Murder and rape, for which roughly 70 and 40 suspects per year are convicted, are much lower than in other countries and remain fairly stable. Chicago in 1972, for example, had 711 cases of murder/manslaughter for a population roughly a third that of The

Netherlands (Smits, 1973a, p. 12). Indeed, a quarter of all the crimes comprised the theft of bikes or mopeds. As criminality is related to a certain extent to age, it is clearly not insignificant that in 1968 just over one-fifth of the population between 12 and 79 comprised young people between the ages of 12 and 20 (making roughly 2 million adolescents); and this group was responsible for twice as many reported crimes as one would expect if offences were distributed in proportion to the size of respective age groups (Smits, 1973a, p. 16). The specific offences which accounted for much of the rise in the figures during the late sixties were simple theft, theft with breaking-in, and vandalism.

Although the evidence indicates that crimes of violence did not in general increase conspicuously (and actually declined from 16 per cent to 3.3 per cent between 1950 and 1972 as a proportion of all reported crimes), the public debate has been posed very much in terms of violence, danger and safety on the streets. Between 1965 and 1974 the press gave increasingly more space to reports of murder, manslaughter and armed robbery (W.O.D.C., 1975), and politicians began to make exclamations of alarm about public safety. Rather predictably, police representatives also began to voice increasing disquiet about 'tolerance' and 'progressiveness' in the justice and crime sphere. For example, the retiring Chief Constable of Amsterdam called in 1974 for longer sentences, including life imprisonment (*Het Parool,* 24 Aug 1974). A number of police union leaders made strong attacks on reforms in the criminal justice system which were particularly attributed to the influence of criminologists, psychologists and sociologists (Smits 1974a, p. 15).

In effect, The Netherlands provides us with an enlightened justice system being put under strain to reverse its policies by the 'law and order' debate surrounding rising crime. In 1975, for instance, there was a critical response from conservative quarters when it was discovered that there was not enough room in the prisons and that 14,000 people were waiting to undergo their sentences. Such developments create a serious dilemma for a liberal system by forcing it to retrace some of its steps. The police too have begun to demand more manpower, improved weaponry and more backing from the courts (these themes emerge particularly in the correspondence columns of the police magazines). They are engaged in an internal debate about their role and functions and are being asked by external critics to become more liberal and tolerant yet while being faced with rising crime and falling detection rates. Two ex-policemen (Van Reenen and Verton,

1974) wrote that the police, faced by an increasingly complex society which sometimes made contradictory demands on them, were creating their own legitimacy by emphasising their impotence in order to pressurise the politicians. In a sense, then, the Dutch justice system, and especially its front-line troops, the police, are being tested by the strains and dilemmas of a changing society at a vital moment in their development. And if there was one city which best fitted the role of testing-ground for the resolution of tensions at the political, ideological and cultural levels in daily police practice, then it was the trouble-ridden and always newsworthy capital, Amsterdam.

(iv) THE AMSTERDAM POLICE AND CRIME

Amsterdam is the largest police force in The Netherlands (almost 3000 men and women) and the force that ineluctably attracts the most attention. This is partly because any innovation in cultural or criminal fashions tends to emerge first there, partly because the city is the centre for the national press, and partly because traditionally Amsterdam-mers are said to be highly sceptical of authority. The evident lack of affection for the police may also be the legacy of their dubious role during the German Occupation (*Accent*, 7 May 1977). But certainly since the mid-sixties, when Amsterdam witnessed several outbreaks of collective violence, the Amsterdam Police has rarely been out of the news. These traumatic and highly symbolic confrontations elicited from the Police a sometimes over-hard, panicky and indiscriminate reaction, and one legacy of that period has been to confirm Amsterdam as a 'troublesome city' and the Amsterdam Police as a problem-ridden force. For traditionally Amsterdam has been the cosmopolitan, free-thinking, avant-garde, politically restless centre of Holland, often resented and decried by the rest of the country. The delinquent image of Amsterdam came to a head, and reached world headlines, in 1966, the year of 'the Provos'. Between 1 September 1965 and 31 December 1966 the police recorded 270 major incidents related to 'public order' (Enschedé Final Report, 1967, p. 138, app. 2). To review that period, and to make acquaintance with the leading actors for the first time in clippings and reports, is like stepping back into another era, because, in retrospect, '66 appears to be a watershed which ushered in the voice and values of radical youth and progressive opinion (Mulisch, 1966; Frenkel, 1966; Van Duyn, 1967; Arts et al., 1973).

When the riots were over the reputation of the Amsterdam Police was tarnished and to a certain extent it still lives in the shadow of '66. More importantly it had been mercilessly exposed as the victim of a double-bind; it was damned when it enforced the law and it was damned when it did not. A deep-searching inquiry was instigated and in the political backwash of those turbulent days the mayor and chief constable were forced to resign (Van Hall, 1976). The Enschedé Commision put the Amsterdam Police under the microscope and dissected the force's internal weaknesses. What emerged clearly – and this is crucial – was the insecurity of the police in a changing society. One police witness complained:

> People don't feel that they are being backed up. The ordinary policeman doesn't know where he is going to anymore. You find the uncertainty also with inspectors and chief inspectors. You get the feeling that you are not being backed up the courts, nor by the press. The question of when and how to use weapons is an especially difficult business. . . . Nowadays we no longer know what we may or may not do; and our opinion is that the leadership also doesn't know it exactly. (Enschedé Final Report, 1967, p. 120)

The police were seen to be the uncertain servants of political masters; senior policemen complained that they did not know what to do or what was expected of them. They seemed to want guidelines and were reluctant to accept responsibility. Yet at the same time they resented encroachments on their authority. A senior officer complained:

> We have to sort it out for ourselves. From top to bottom everyone has the feeling that there isn't one guiding-line in our policy – and that policy has now to be decided at a higher level than previously. Before, the Chief Constable could lay down whatever measures had to be taken; now the business has become part of the political set-up and the Chief Constable can no longer take an independent decision. For example, before, as district chief, I could have decided for myself to remove the Provo boat: 'That thing is disturbing public order, get rid of it' – and the River Police would have towed it out, let's say, to the Coen Harbour. But now that has really become a decision which cannot be taken below the level of the Mayor. (Enschedé Final Report, 1967, p. 122)

In short, 1966 demonstrated that the policeman in Amsterdam was an actor beset by dilemmas and exposed to role-conflict. His traditional authority had been undermined and his relationship with the public fundamentally altered.

The trauma of '66 – when the authorities were remorselessly exposed as indecisive, vacillating and incompetent – led to two major consequences for the capital city and its police. In the first place, political control over the police became more overt and the police force was forced to liberalise and to become less heavy-handed. And, in the second place, Amsterdam became a magnet for the beat generation who saw it as a liberal haven in a sea of bourgeois oppression. This youth tourism combined with other factors (ease of travel, loosening of border controls, liberalisation of sexual norms, etc.) to broadcast the international image of Amsterdam as the 'swinging city' and ensured that the city was inundated with an annual invasion of young people, became renowned as lenient on the use of drugs, developed into a thriving centre for the sex industry, and provided a refuge for long-stay bohemian youth. The combination of these two features, a police force on the defensive and an increasing tolerance for deviant behaviour, gave Amsterdam the reputation of being the most difficult city for police work in The Netherlands.

For if demonstrations were the hallmark of the sixties for Amsterdam, then crime became the catchword in the seventies ('Is Amsterdam Becoming the Chicago of Europe?', *Elseviers Magazine,* 19 Feb 1977; 'Amsterdam: the Sick City', *De Volkskrant,* 9 and 16 July 1977). The two city-centre police districts – District 2 (Warmoesstraat) and District 3 (Leidseplein) – were most involved in tackling crime, and the Public Prosecutor, who was responsible for bringing criminal cases to court originating from these districts, outlined the contemporary picture:

Amsterdam is the largest court in The Netherlands. We have the largest number of criminal cases and it just keeps growing. There is a lot of pressure and we are always occupied because we don't have sufficient personnel to cope. . . .

The city-centre provides us with a good deal of work, especially in the [tourist] season. But the season lasts practically from Easter to November and at its height we get an enormous number of foreigners here. . . .

The police could use hundreds of new men. But the practice adapts to this to a certain extent in that summonses aren't written for certain cases. For example, there have been developments in applying the Drugs Act which have led to us setting a limit of ten grammes of hashish in possession before beginning to prosecute as we do not view that as a very serious offence. . . .

We are extremely tolerant regarding drug users; after all there is not much point in prosecuting some of these French and German youths whose only fate is to go insane or to die. . . . But over the last four years since I've come here I've noticed an increasing amount of violent crime, of drug cases – we had a case today involving eight kilos of heroin – and of armed robbery, although that dropped a bit last year [1974].

(Interview)

The issue of 'safety on the streets' was discussed in the city council's budget debate for 1974 ('Amsterdam: De Zorg voor de Veiligheid', 1974). Changing patterns of crime were reviewed on the basis of statistics, most of which originated from the police. These reflected a pattern all too familiar in large cities – steadily increasing 'crime', but especially theft, and steadily decreasing clear-up rates. In Amsterdam during 1969–72 the number of reported thefts (i.e. not 'simple' thefts but largely theft as a result of break-ins) doubled. In three other categories – assault, sexual offences, and crimes related to traffic – there were *decreases* over the period concerned. These are scarcely figures to disturb the mayor of a large American city.

Smits (1973b, 1974c) has argued that, as with the national figures, much of this crime concerns property offences, and particularly thefts of bicycles, mopeds and cars. In 1953, for example, there were 3876 bikes stolen compared to 14,081 bikes and mopeds in 1973. The latter accounted for a *third* of all the offences committed in the capital. In 1953 some 102 cars were reported stolen compared to 3351 in 1973, while in the same year 4637 cars were broken into and articles removed. Indeed, 90 per cent of the crime committed in Amsterdam comprises some classification of theft. What had increased was reports of pocket-picking (from 1492 to 1822 cases between 1972 and 1973). Armed robbery began to emerge in The Netherlands in the late sixties and over a third of these offences took place in Amsterdam, Rotterdam and The Hague (these offences were generally committed by amateurs and of the 50 per cent of cases which were solved, most involved a first offence: Van Bergeijk and Ovaa, 1975). Perhaps the most conspicuous rise, as we shall see later, came in the area of drugs and offences which might be related to drugs (such as shoplifting and breaking into cars). In examining the issue of 'safety on the streets', Smits (1974c) compared the figures for 1972 and 1973:

If you really want to appraise the climate of violence in a world city, then naturally you have to look at the figures for assault [573–675], theft with violence [343–408], offences under the Firearms Act [110–125] and robbery [225–214]. There is clearly a rise here. But the figures certainly do not reveal Amsterdam as in the grip of widespread gangsterdom. . . . Not incorrectly, the District Attorney, Mr J. J. Abspoel, maintained in his plea in this case [the murder of Constable Simon Landman] that in Los Angeles in 1970 there were on average 175 shootings per day between policemen and civilians. Compared to that Amsterdam is a sleepy village.

Yet one newspaper wrote of a 'wave of crime and street terror', although the mayor and the chief of the uniformed police were less convinced. The latter said, 'Amsterdam unsafe? We mustn't exaggerate this. I don't agree that it's not possible to walk on the streets at night. That's laughable' (Smits, 1974c).

The 'sleepy village', however, is an image that is not reflected in much of the press, in general conversation, and certainly not in the eyes of many policemen. For the latter particularly, the 'reality' of crime is more immediate and threatening and the uniformed men in the city-centre are differentially involved in coping with it. The daily dilemmas confronting them in 1975 can introduce us to the values and behaviour of a unique occupational group engaged in police work in a metropolitan city-centre. Hopefully their experience can reveal something about the strains and tensions of a liberal justice system being forced to question some of its enlightened assumptions and also about the social reality of inner-city life. But, in essence, this is a case study of the occupational culture and identity of the policemen in the Warmoesstraat.

(v) CULTURE IN THE WARMOESSTRAAT

'After a rough tour, a guy's dead, shot, people stabbed, you go into a bar where the guys work on Wall Street, margin clerks, "How ya doin'? What's new?" You say, "You wouldn't understand." ' (New York policeman in Terkel, 1975, p. 746)

The reality of police work is difficult to convey accurately to outsiders (Manning, 1977, p. 143). Seen from inside, routine police work is pedestrian and somewhat monotonous and the police organisation appears to be a rather dull and ineffective instrument of social control. There is a wide discrepancy between dramatic presentations of police work, particularly by the visual media, and the actual occupational activities of police patrol (Manning, 1977, p. 12). A consideration of what policemen actually do reveals that their occupational culture is based largely on the exceptional rather than the daily routine. In Amsterdam, moreover, there are elements which have weakened the police culture and which have undermined the notion of a police craft. The exclusive and solidaristic culture of Anglo-American policing (Westley, 1970; Alex, 1976, pp. 140–4) is not so apparent among the social world of the Warmoesstraat policemen.

Intuitively I feel that there is a universal police code with considerable correspondence across cultures but that within that, considerable national and local variations may appear. The American picture, for instance, seems soured by the racial element both in enforcement and latterly within departments (Alex, 1976), by a mercenary attitude to police work and perks (Maas, 1973, p. 42; Alex, 1976, p. 179; Manning, 1977, p. 151), by a high tolerance for 'easing' behaviour (ibid., pp. 154 ff.), by a condoning of police misconduct (Westley, 1970, p. 118), and by a somewhat rancorous attitude to the public and liberal developments in the wider society (Alex, 1976). Some of that sense of grievance was echoed by my respondents, and would almost certainly be voiced by some British policemen, but in general I do not feel that police work in The Netherlands engenders the extreme reactions found among American policemen with their often bitter sense of betrayal and resentment.

Basically the policemen I talked to seemed more 'privatised', less prejudiced, more able to step out of their police role, less identified with the police outside of work, and less given to crude anti-liberal statements. Most of the people whom I interviewed had served for at least a couple of years because I wanted to probe their experiences and discuss changes in policing. To generalise broadly, I would say that two patterns of recruitment emerged. The first concerned older men, now in their thirties or late twenties. These were often people who did not perform conspicuously well at school and who became semi-skilled manual or low-status clerical workers; after a number of uncertain jobs came military service as conscript or professional; parental backgrounds were often conservative, conventional, Protestant and petit-bourgeois; fathers were tradesmen, civil servants, shopkeepers or policemen. Following the military there was an inability to readjust to routinised civilian life and to work, which was often coupled with marriage plans whereby security and immediate rewards played an important role. The second pattern concerned younger men in their early twenties. These men tended to come from a wider range of backgrounds, rarely had close relatives in government jobs, were fairly well educated, did not start a trade but entered the police directly from school, had not undergone military service (being exempt because of their police function), and were primarily motivated by instrumental reasons in choosing the police over other trades and professions. The economic depression of the last few years has helped to stimulate recruitment and to make the stability and pension rights for policemen appear attractive in comparison with other jobs. Their motivations about joining tended to be mundane, practical, and even rather vague (see Alex, 1976, pp. 24–6, on the 'drift' into police work in New York).

In almost all the interviews, for example, the reason for wishing to join the police was that it offered security, a reasonable salary, an alternative to civilian life on leaving the forces, or simply the best job for someone with not very good paper qualifications. One young sergeant explained:

[Why did you join the police?]
I just think because there was nothing better. You're seventeen, still at school, and people come to tell you about jobs. More or less for the fun of it I decided to apply and before I knew it I was accepted. But before then it had never occurred to me that I might join the police. It's just that you're looking for a job, I didn't fancy office work, I might have tried the army, but I drifted into this. My father was against the idea and didn't like it one bit that I was going to join. He is from the Jordaan [a traditional working-class area of Amsterdam] and there people are a bit anti-authority. People ask me sometimes, 'What are you doing in the police?' and then I say, 'I really don't know why, certainly not from idealism, perhaps for the security.'

(Sergeant, 29 years)

An officer was asked if he thought people joined the police because unconsciously they wanted to play an authoritarian role; he replied:

I wouldn't rule out the possibility that that is the case. But I think the romanticism – if that's the right word – of the job has more pulling power than the idea of authority. But how can I defend my unconscious motives? I can imagine that if you carried out a project you would find that a lot of people, who come from 'hervormde' or 'gereformeerde' [Protestant and Strict Protestant] backgrounds where order and authority play an important role, choose for the police. I didn't notice that clearly in my family and in fact my parents were really bewildered when I decided to join. I've also come to the conclusion that the average police officer in Amsterdam is quite liberal and socially conscious, even a bit socialistic perhaps.

                                                    (Chief Inspector, 32 years)

Unfortunately, there is a serious dearth of material on this area in The Netherlands and the police culture may be much stronger in the provinces than in Amsterdam. At the Police Academy for Officers, for example, some 28 per cent of recruits had fathers who were already in the police (Hopmans and van de Scheur, 1975, p. 44), but more detailed data on self-recruitment among lower ranks are simply not available.

What did emerge very clearly from the interviews was a degree of withdrawal from the police culture and the police identity outside of work. A lot has been made of police solidarity and its incestuousness and, presumably in countries where accommodation is in barracks (as with the Gendarmerie in France: Edmond-Smith, 1974) or where police residences are provided, this will be reinforced. Some 66.8 per cent of a sample of British policemen reported to the Royal Commission Survey in 1960 that the job had adversely affected their outside friendships (Whitaker, 1964, p. 127). Hopmans and van de Scheur (1975, p. 54) reported that surveys had indicated that 35 per cent of a sample of printers had close friends in the same profession, that a similar proportion was found among policemen by Skolnick, but that the figure for a sample of Dutch policemen was only 20 per cent. There does seem to be a cultural norm in The Netherlands that close friendships are not sought primarily in the work-place. My respondents expressed an aversion to the idea of police residential communities and there were almost no social clubs in Amsterdam exclusively for policemen. However, colleagues were routinely invited to weddings and birthday celebrations, and were expected to help each other with moving house and in times of need, and on such occasions the conversation invariably remained riveted on the police.

When we get together we talk about nothing else except the

police–'then I gave him a good thump' or 'I ran my stick over his head'. Bragging about their prowess and also about their sexual exploits. What a joke! It's really juvenile as if they'd just reached puberty. I enjoy good gossip and talk shop too but I say, 'Let's talk about something else for a change', and some of the lads are sensible enough to appreciate that. . . . I have good friends outside of the police. Sometimes I see colleagues out of duty but I don't have any confidential relationship with them. As colleagues and mates they are very good, but as off-duty friends, no. But we don't use special police terms, a real police community doesn't exist here, when your duty is over everyone goes his own way and you only see each other again on the next duty day.

(Constable, 33 years)

Negative stereotypes of the policeman hold that his social-political views are conservative if not reactionary. In America the political polarisation of the sixties, which saw the police increasingly involved in public order disturbances (where their sympathies were not disguised) and increasingly the target for abuse, ridicule and violence, moved the police even further right. At times there were threats of 'police rebellions' by police unions (Juris and Feuille, 1973) who were exasperated at their 'fall guy' role in confrontations with radical students, militant Blacks and anti-war demonstrators. Lipset (1969) suggests that there are cycles of right-wing radicalism affecting the police. Status frustrations and discrepancies, which are said to generate right-wing radicalism, are not so evident in the Dutch Police with its relatively generous economic rewards and high standards of entry and training. At least that is my general impression, although some symptoms of disquiet and discontent have begun to appear. In police circles one encounters a somewhat bitter, resentful litany about freedom, tolerance and progressiveness; in essence, the 'good old days' of traditional morals have been undermined by too much freedom (in schools and especially the universities), by affluence and social security (which people abuse), and by political weakness which cannot cope with articulate militant groups and which gives in to the slightest pressure (see also Alex, 1976, on similar views among New York policemen). In short, fathers are no longer fathers, men are no longer men, and alas, policemen are no longer policemen.

In general, Dutch policemen are probably right-of-centre without being extreme. The tradition of formal political neutrality rules out open expressions of party affiliation, and the publicity given to an activist Chief Inspector in Rotterdam (a member of a pacifist party who is not slow to criticise publicly police ideology and practice) is clearly an enormous embarrassment to his superiors. He protested publicly about the behaviour of the South African Police at Soweto and supported the occupation of an abortion clinic which the Minister of Justice was trying to close (*Elseviers Magazine,* 20 Nov 1976; *Accent,* 4 Sep 1976). Eventually, however, the officer was forced to resign owing to pressure from colleagues and other officials who objected to his participation in a march to protest about the deaths of RAF members in German prisons. The police unions asked their members to observe a two minutes' silence to protest against the execution of five Spanish terrorists in October 1975; the murder of three policemen in Madrid just before caused some policemen to ignore the request while others resigned from their union (*De Tele-graaf,* 2 Oct 1975). Nevertheless it would be difficult to find such open displays of 'liberal' sentiment among British or American policemen. But the normal reaction I got in interviews and conversations was one of distance from politics but couched in 'right-of-centre' sentiments.

The ordinary policemen appear to have a low political conscious-ness, in ideological or doctrinal terms, although they are often quite vocal about general societal influences and national and local political directives which impinge on the daily practice of their craft. In Amster-dam these feelings were expressed during my research period in terms of perceptions of the town council, which is perceived as 'progressive' and as giving support to radical opinion. Thus an underlying motive of the town council, irrespective of its political colour, is said to be the preservation of peace and quiet by avoiding confrontations, by collu-sive agreements to turn a blind eye to deviance and non-conformity, and by restrictive guidelines on police enforcement. In the policeman's eyes the council is an indecisive, vacillating, left-wing group of 'do-gooder' liberals who maintain their power and influence with the voters by dubious, and devious, short-term policies in which the police are expected to play a subsidiary and subservient role. To the police-men, such politically initiated guidelines percolate down to them as largely unexplained restrictions on their freedom to enforce the law which they resent and only dimly understand, such as the relative freedom given to 'crash-pads' (squatters in derelict houses) and alter-native drug-treatment centres.

To a certain extent, salt is rubbed into the policemen's wounds in that some of the 'no-go areas' are peopled by conspicuously counter-cultural types – characterised as bohemian, dirty, long-haired, workless, etc. – who fit precisely their stereotype of the archetypal deviant. Their scepticism and suspicion is roused because they associate such people with progressive, left-wing tendencies and see dubious relationships between them and radical representatives on the town council:

> If you raid the Prinsenhof [drug-treatment centre] then you're not going to make the junkies clean people, that's obvious. But it is a phenomenon which under the guise of a social agency allows all sorts of rubbish to go on. They just let people go on injecting themselves, enjoy a subsidy with which so-called expertise is bought but which isn't there, and it's tolerated that stolen radios are bought and sold, that nothing is done about it and that the people there are protected against it: well, that's not what I call helping.

> [Isn't it frustrating then that you can't go in there?]
> That's a business which is locked up in politics. There's a trend towards helping that sort of welfare agency and to give it a degree of protection. People believe in it – let it grow and flourish in its own right, and don't let the police chase around in there, even when there are blokes there who've nicked a car and are perfectly sober. 'You mustn't go in there, because that disturbs the culture or subculture which grows there among the inmates, so stay out.' I'll buy that for the Jellinek [clinic] becau. ~ a good deal of expertise is available, but not for dumps like the Prinsenhof where there's a fake environment developed that has no right to exist. And if you are not allowed inside then that's frustrating.

> (Constable, 28 years)

Such festering sources of frustration are reinforced if we turn to the criminal justice system. Yet I suspect that more jaundiced and prejudiced views would be expressed on this area by some American and British policemen (Alex, 1976, pp. 180–4). However, my respondents, working in an allegedly 'tough' area, tended to express a fairly widespread position that police work is becoming increasingly more difficult and that policemen receive less support from the judiciary, from central and local government, and from the 'general public' (that mythical animal). A young police officer explained that he was enthusiastic about his work but that he had learned to rationalise away his frustrations:

[Do you feel powerless when faced with the rising crime in the city centre?]
If I feel that then it's the fault of those people who sit on the town council. They're always moaning about the police, 'Give them less money', or 'We don't need the police' and 'The police should not have pistols because that looks so aggressive'. So I say, 'O.K., it's your fault'. In the whole of Holland there's a tendency to diminish authority, as if it's become a dirty word and you mustn't say 'I'm the boss and you have to do it my way'. There is a general devaluing of all values and authority relationships and of the ability to take decisions. One result is that Amsterdam has become a den of foreigners and strangers, who aren't registered anywhere, all they do is nick things, and they can't be kicked out of the country because the Ministry hasn't got any money to keep the border closed. . . . But if I become frustrated then I've only got myself to blame. Then I sit at home with red eyes, have rows with my wife, hit my kids, and drop dead from a heart attack at forty-five. My work is fine, and I like it, but it's only my work, and my life is more important and so is my family. Perhaps I'm taking the path of least resistance but I do my work as well as possible – I live for my work, because I'm as fanatic as anyone, and I think it's great – but I've made up my mind not to let myself be chased over the red line so that it gets out of hand. But if it does get out of hand nonetheless then I'll say, 'It's not my fault'.

(Inspector, 24 years)

Generally there was a feeling that the liberalisation of the last years has gone too far and that somehow there ought to be a return to more traditional values which would include more support for the police. Perhaps this is a perennial lament of the policeman whose work tends to bring him into contact with the seedy side of society, which gives him an exaggerated and distorted picture of degeneracy and decay. In The Netherlands specifically the police have had to adjust to a lenient judiciary and this tolerance impinges fairly directly on to the policemen's occupational culture, although it is not something that is in their power to alter. The adaptation of the policemen in the Warmoesstraat, then, was to express regret and frustration at the 'puny' sentences – which in a sense crown their handiwork – but to adopt an almost ostrich-like posture to sentencing in specific cases in which they have been involved:

I've got the ability to distance myself from these things. The pronouncements from the courts don't interest me. My job is to nick someone and make out a charge-sheet. Then it's over for me. I once had a case of a bloke who kicked his highly pregnant wife down the stairs. He had stolen 18,000 guilders and was a real brute. At that moment I thought, 'This fellow deserves the rope'. And the chap got a suspended sentence, separated from his wife, and got 15,000 guilders from Social Security in order to start a new life on the other side of the town! When I heard that, the tears welled up in my eyes. At that moment I realised that this was something I had to forget otherwise in no time I'd be having an ulcer.

(Constable, 33 years)

Like any other worker, the policeman seeks the esteem of his colleagues and the rewards produced by good work. With police work, however, the end-product is so nebulous – has there been a victory in a minor skirmish in the 'war' against crime or has the 'moral order' been defended and reinforced? – that feelings of frustration and impotence can easily result. A major adjustment is to seek solace and security in the expectations and praise of one's colleagues. There is a common-sense reality of policing which binds policemen together (Manning, 1977, p. 142) and which awards status, dispenses praise and attributes blame. Elsewhere (Punch, 1976b) I have used the 'front-line' concept to discuss policing in the Warmoesstraat. It does seem to have utility both in describing the organisational position of patrolmen, with their considerable autonomy on the street (Clark and Sykes, 1974, p. 473), and also in alluding to an ideology of being literally in the front-line. The Warmoesstraat policemen's mentality was very much a front-line one and this may accentuate their attitudes to police work more than, say, policemen in other stations, in other parts of the organisation, or in other towns. But their predilection for 'real' police work, even if it is situationally strengthened, is echoed elsewhere (Wilson, 1968, p. 68; Banton, 1974, p. 7; Alex, 1976, pp. 11–20; Manning, 1977, p. 362).

The informal norms of the culture define what is good work. The hierachy of status accorded to cases is posited almost unanimously on the symbolic rites of chase, search and arrest. In effect, it confirms and legitimates the moral feeling that this is 'real' police work, although representing but a fraction of actual police work ('The President's Crime Commission' estimates that the chance that an officer will encounter a robbery in progress is once in fourteen years!). In the

Warmoesstraat the policemen used the following terminology to grade cases:

(a) '*A big case*'. This is where the scale of the operation demands admiration, e.g. a large amount of heroin or an expensive haul of stolen goods or weapons. But by its very nature, the bigger the case, the more likely it is that the patrolman will have to loosen his grip on it and pass it on to one of the specialised detective branches. It has, therefore, a rarity value.

(b) '*A nice piece of work*'. This is the much sought-after accolade of a case that is above the ordinary or where the policemen concerned used above-average initiative or pluck. Even though many such cases contain a degree of luck or coincidence, the men involved are credited with sizing up the situation and bringing it to a successful conclusion. This is particularly so because some policemen more than others seem to attract good cases and this confirms the belief that it is not luck but skill which accompanies good police work. The latter is said to require a 'feeling' or a 'nose' for the unusual and suspicious. This category of praise can be used either where the case itelf was interesting or complex, or where the 'haul' was above average, or where the patrolmen themselves acted intelligently or courageously. To a large extent the cases concerned involved drugs, firearms, stolen property and usually prisoners.

(c) '*An open-and-shut case*'. This is often a characteristic of (b) because it provides what policemen as workers clearly wish to see – a completed piece of work with an end-product. So much of their work has no visible end-product, or no end-product which is ever communicated to them, that they derive special satisfaction and kudos from such a case. Basically these cases involve an offence, evidence, a prisoner and a confession. In other words, the patrolman has virtually tied up the case before passing it on to the detectives and so feels that he has influenced the criminal justice system. There are no loose ends and no ambiguities (Manning, 1977, p. 241, speaks of policemen enjoying satisfactory termination to their work which also does not violate peer standards of performance).

(d) '*Rotten jobs*'. Finally there are the cases which are considered of low status or worthless. These can and often do include traffic, extra duties and 'social work' cases. Their characteristics are that they can take up a lot of time, lead to no discernible result, and rank low in the official and informal reward systems. Also included are the nasty jobs–conveying messages of death to relatives, recovering dead bodies, witnessing small children involved in injury or violent death, and evictions. On the one hand are the incidents which have an emotional impact and on the other hand are the pointless and almost degrading little jobs which devolve on to the patrolman's shoulders. He resents being used as a messenger boy, a first-aider, a handyman and a traffic warden. Above all he objects *to being used* because that interferes with his notions of himself as an independent craftsman engaged in important work. Policemen in Philadelphia referred to these cases as 'bullshit calls' (Rubinstein, 1973, p. 110).

(e) *'A limp case'*. This is one where, for instance, someone is arrested and brought to the station where it transpires that there is not enough reason to charge or detain him. On closer inspection, for instance, a dealer may be found to have only fake hash on him or such a small amount of real hash that it is not worth charging him. In other words, the patrolman has nothing to show for his work, and the fish is thrown back in the sea.

Generally, when asked to describe a 'nice case' the policemen used examples involving serious crime, an arrest, and a hint of danger:

[What is a nice case?]
Arresting a man who an hour before had shot his wife to death in The Hague. We had received his description and knew he was on his way. Then he arrived, got out of his car, looked carefully around but after two steps he was standing with his hands in the air. There was another time in a youth hostel when five Germans were going to shoot a Dutchman. He had cheated them out of something and one of the Germans was standing outside his room with a big 9 mm pistol ready to shoot. The best arrests as far as I am concerned are with people with drugs or weapons on them.

(Constable, 29 years)

An experienced constable talked about cases which had resulted in 'good' arrests:

Once I had a nice amount of heroin, or at least then it was considered quite a lot, 15 packets. Someone came out of a café and when he saw me he started to walk away from me and I thought, 'Heh, don't I know him?' So I said to him, 'Let's take a walk to the station'. At the station the bloke emptied his pockets and out came the heroin. Recently I got a kilo of hash. We were walking along the Warmoesstraat on the way to 'The Old Bakery' [youth hostel] and nearby you have those old warehouses which have been turned into flats. A young lad comes out of one of the warehouses with a small suitcase and walks off looking directly in front of him as if he's scared. I thought, 'Something is wrong here', and went after him and shouted, 'Heh, Johnny!' but he didn't look around. So I caught him up and said, 'Let's go down to the station'. There we open up the suitcase and out comes a kilo of hashish and a pile of dirty books with 2000 guilders between the pages. That comes purely from the feeling that when people are trying to hide something then they have something cramped about them. I saw that and nicked him. . . .

Another nice case was a car full of stolen radios and tape-recorders. I came to work at 6.30 one morning and just then a big Ford came out of the Oude Brugsteeg and into the Damrak. Two yobs inside. You see it and think it's a bit funny but you can't do much about it, just two blokes driving a car. On patrol we had a newspaper reporter from *Panorama* in the car. About ten o'clock we started driving along the Damstraat, and near the Oudezijds Voorburgwal I see the same car coming along the side of the canal. I said 'That car is for us!' So you put the car on the side of the road and search the yobs. One had heroin on him but threw it away and tried to stamp it into a pool of yoghurt in the gutter. I saw that and said to my mate, 'He tried to kick something in there, get hold of it', and out came the heroin. So everything goes down to the station. There we open up the boot and what do we see – about 10,000 guilders worth of stolen radios! These were nicked in Beverwijk, no Heemstede, that very night and you phone up the police there who didn't know anything about it. Then you've got it – while the case is still hot – and that's great and gives you satisfaction.

(Constable, 28 years)

Clearly this incident was magnified for the men concerned because it happened when a reporter was travelling with them and the chance that they would encounter such a juicy case on that day was extremely slim. Holdaway (personal communication) has commented that poor cases can be raised to 'nice ones' by a realisation of the importance of who is involved, and perhaps by a significant audience, or by a sexual element with young females: 'a parking ticket for a Chief Superintendent is a "nice case", a shoplifter who is a solicitor, and so on.'

(vi) THE DECLINE OF THE POLICE CRAFT

> Since the old personal radio came in, I think that instead of talking
> their way out of trouble like the old coppers did and getting by that
> way, they just pull their truncheons out and shout for assistance on
> the P.R. [personal radio]. They don't talk their way out of it at all,
> they just ask for assistance and get their truncheons out. (Holda-
> way, 1977a, p. 128)

Traditional policing was based on the visible presence among a stable
population of a uniformed, and preferably very large, policeman who
used local knowledge, experience and common sense to keep the
peace on his 'patch' (Whitaker, 1964, p. 42). This mythical old-time
copper may never have existed but he certainly exists in the minds of
policemen (Cain, 1973, p. 200; Manning, 1977, p. 143). He plays an
important role in defining good police practice and in exposing the
current generation as incompetent apprentices. It is rare to hear
criticism of the traditional stereotype in which the policeman is portrayed as an infallible mine of information on the local community, a
genial arbiter in all manner of disputes, a no-nonsense handler of
aggression, and a punctual and punctilious follower of rules and
regulations (Bittner, 1967a, and Rubinstein, 1973, particularly reflect
aspects of this image).

The central tenet of this traditional mythology is that police work is a
practical craft (J. Wilson, 1968, p. 283; Skolnick, 1975, p. 231) which
can only be learned through prolonged experience on the street for
which training and 'theory' is largely irrelevant (Banton, 1974). This
engrained cornerstone of the occupational ideology is clearly derived
from the long-standing practice of police work as a solitary function
carried out with quiet dignity in a small, familiar area without telephones:

> The district was divided into blocks and you got one or two blocks to
> patrol. You had a certain route which you had to follow and there
> were control-posts along the way. You could walk with your bike in
> your hand or else cycle.
>
> [Was it difficult on the streets?]
> No, not at all. In those days people had more respect for the police
> and the young lads nowadays have a much more difficult time. You

hardly ever heard of cases of resisting arrest then. Someone who had broken into a car, for instance, you took him by the sleeve with one hand and in the other hand you held your bike. You had no handcuffs. There was a wrist-chain but you hardly ever used that. And you had to do it all on your own. Then there were more older constables and they have a different attitude to the public. I remember men of thirty entering the training school. Perhaps ex-merchant seamen, and these blokes see things completely differently, are often more helpful and take more of an initiative. They've already learned a hell of a lot working under a boss.

(Sergeant, 39 years)

It is difficult to separate two features of the elevation of the old-time copper to a model of competence and self-assurance. One is that police work has moved perceptibly away from a traditional skill learned on the job orientation and the other is that the more old-fashioned and conservative elements employ the past to flagellate younger colleagues whom they accuse of laxity, lack of deference, unpunctuality, lack of independence and initiative, poor orientations to the less dramatic and less rewarded aspects of the job, less respect for the uniform and for rank, careless attitudes to personal appearance and to preparing charge-sheets, and a too easy-going relationship with the public. A somewhat embittered brigadier who later moved away from Amsterdam commented unfavourably on the young policemen:

The policemen in those days [fifteen years previously] were more craftsmen and from head to toe they were policemen. Previously, if you brought a prisoner to the station you knew exactly for which department he was meant, but now they come in with someone and then go and see what they can get him for. That doesn't convince me of their knowledge of the job. If I bring someone into the Warmoesstraat from the Western Docks and I want to sort it out at the station then I've robbed someone of his freedom for an hour.

(Sergeant, 38 years)

So in a sense the generation gap in the police uses traditional craft stereotypes to identify itself and a lot of mythologising definitely goes on. Such observations are extremely difficult to appraise objectively as they contain all sorts of retrospective distortions, and yet there is evidence which suggests that police work is becoming more complex and difficult and that the traditional skills of the patrolman are being undermined. There are structural explanations as to why this should be true, but an important role is also played by the emotional belief that the young generation of policemen cannot cope with, or are not trained to cope with, the rough and tumble of inner-city police work. It should be said that a 'generation' in the Warmoesstraat replaces itself in two to three years and the 'old hands' are often not conspicuously older than the newcomers but, in terms of street experience, are indisputably senior. The negative stereotype of the new hand is that he is indecisive or out of touch with the reality of the situation in the inner city whereby, traditionally, policemen acted quickly and in almost blind support of a colleague. I was told numerous stories about puerile and pathetic new boys who, with baby-face and sweating palms, had ineffectively patrolled the streets or unwittingly failed to back up their older colleagues at crucial moments. These stories may simply be a way of dramatising the distinction between inexperience and experience in a way to be found in other jobs.

In any event, the new generation of policemen are held to be of a different type than their traditional forebears in that they are said to be more instrumental, less bound to the group culture, and less able to cope with people in general and aggression in particular. When Rubinstein, for instance, writes, 'the astute man knows his corners as well as a trout fisherman knows the pools of his favourite stream' (1973, p. 100), then he is clearly referring to the experienced patrolman with intimate local knowledge. That sort of particularistic relationship with the district cannot always be assumed in Amsterdam:

> You keep getting new people and when you want to send them out somewhere then they don't know how to get there. What it comes down to is that people don't know the area and it is really incredibly important that you know the district where you work. Sometimes I feel that the work is not done precisely enough; there is too much haste and then things get missed. But the lads want to be all over the place and want to chat with everyone but they fall short in their craftsmanship.

> (Sergeant, 38 years)

Of course such observations come disproportionately from older men who experienced the 'good old days' and who may perceive the casual, long-haired newcomers as somehow symptomatic of the liberalisation in society and in the penal and legal systems which has been difficult for them to accept.

What did emerge from the interviews, however, was the discrepancy between experienced policemen's conceptions of how long it took to learn the basics of the police craft–and this was usually expressed in years (mostly three to five)–and that of younger patrolmen. The current situation in fact conspires to prevent many constables from ever getting the opportunity to learn their craft adequately. In Amsterdam and elsewhere there has been a general loss of older experienced personnel and their replacement with young men in their early twenties (in Manning's research sub-division in London the average age of uniformed men was 38.5: 1973b, p. 4). But this has occurred at all levels including constable, sergeant and chief inspector. Fifteen to twenty years ago most ranks were filled with men in their thirties or forties, but mobility out of patrol work has accelerated. The chief of the uniformed branch expressed his opinion on the matter:

> I'm also concerned about the behaviour of constables in contact with the public. Because they lack experience and weight they become unsure and through that insecurity they begin to behave a bit insolently. But it's our fault, because we don't give them enough supervision and because we send out lads of 18 and 19 in a city like Amsterdam. So that is my biggest objection to the police at the moment, that they are too rude and too uncontrolled. Yet it's our fault. Most of the lads come from the countryside and after one year's theory they go out on the street and often with a girl younger than them. Then you kick them up the backside for not doing it properly.   (Commissioner, 49 years)

The vicious circle is that most policemen agree that a prolonged apprenticeship and gathering of practical experience is essential to learning their craft but structural features make that ideal impossible to realise. The crucial features are shortages of personnel, loss of experienced personnel to other forces and to specialised services, and the pensioning-off of the post-war generation. While it is easy to use these as excuses for failures, they do seem to have had a considerable influence on policing in Amsterdam and elsewhere. In particular the uniformed branch loses its best men so that patrol work becomes a task for young men and older men with blocked mobility:

> The times have changed so much that you can't compare them. You can't send a constable out on his own anymore. A few years ago men

didn't want to take a portable radio with them on the street and now two constables have refused to go out on patrol because they did not have a radio. First it was seen as a sort of nark but now they don't feel safe without the radio. Now that I've a lot to do with pairs then I'd prefer to see a young and old constable together. Two youngsters together can lead to escalation. But because of the build-up of our force we've lost a certain age group. Also because of the specialisation which takes away experienced personnel. Now we have very young constables and very old ones and there's a big gap between them.

(Adjutant, 51 years)

The most serious drawback currently appears to be the decline both of the informal apprenticeship which is carried out by 'mentors' (who are formally responsible for training younger colleagues) and of the dominating presence of highly experienced colleagues, who provided stability, guidance and role-models:

It was like this. You had a whole lot of older colleagues who you could talk to. You were the only constable among a lot of constables first-class. You were a whipper-snapper, just there for support, and everything was done by an older copper as if you were his assistant. He didn't expect you to say anything or to interfere because what were you – a little lad who was scarcely dry behind the ears. It was just a period of only watching to see what you must not do. When I joined there were only older men of around forty with a load of experience who had spent years on the street. In those days if a constable first-class came into the canteen and there was no chair free then you had to offer him yours. If you tried that now they would all die laughing. But they were constables first-class so you had to keep your distance. They took you around by the hand and let you see things and what you got out of it was for yourself to sort out. Actually, it's like this. You keep coming against things where you thought, 'Cor, and I thought that I knew just about everything', but there are always new things. Nowadays a young constable has to learn from a colleague with not much more experience and that didn't use to be the case. If they do something wrong now, and the brigadier doesn't get to hear of it, then they never get hauled over the coals about it. Because they miss experience they become worse and worse; not that I blame them because they couldn't be any other way. There is no one who really tells them how they ought to do it. The longer it goes on the worse it gets. It really is an enormous problem.

(Sergeant, 28 years)

The whole area of the changing occupational culture of the police-man in the seventies is a complex one which clearly needs further study, and the foregoing remarks can scarcely be seen as more than speculative. But there seems to be a world of difference between Wambaugh's idealised beat man, 'Bumper' Morgan, in *The Blue Knight* (1972) and his boozing, wenching, 'hippy' policemen of *The Choirboys* (1975), and the bitter New York policemen protesting the decline in standards of traditional working habits (Alex, 1976, pp. 5, 35). Holdaway (1977a), for example, provides a badly needed revision of the standard material on British policing by documenting how a manipulative informal system has used new technology to magnify a hedonistic culture based on easing and on generating action, fun and excitement, which is in stark contrast to the 'managerial professional-ism' promulgated from above. In this section I have tried to sketch some salient features of the police occupational culture and to identify some specific elements in the Warmoesstraat occupational identity. It was argued that my Amsterdam respondents were probably more liberally minded and less solidaristic outside of work than their Anglo-American counterparts. However, there was considerable correspon-dence with them on the emphasis given to 'real' police work which was generally defined in terms of drama, excitement and successfully completed crime cases. There was a strong feeling among some respondents that the traditional craft orientation of police work was being undermined by rapid structural changes and that the quality of contemporary patrolmen left much to be desired. These themes under-lie the analysis of practical policing in the city-centre of Amsterdam which will be presented in detail in the following chapters.

3 The Warmoesstraat: Police Work in the Inner City

The Warmoesstraat, one of the oldest streets in the city, is a narrow street full of clubs, hotels, cafés, small businesses and a few old-fashioned shops in the heart of Amsterdam. At the time of the research the police station was housed in temporary accommodation. Next door, behind the builder's hoarding, one could still see the wall of the old, and notorious, station which was being demolished and rebuilt. The old building was cramped and crowded and was apparently unpleasant both for policemen and their 'clients'. The cells were in a basement worthy of Mervyn Peake; they lay beneath the water-line and smelt like an unwholesome medieval dungeon. Some men claimed to be ashamed at having to take 'decent' suspects down those infamous steps. The working conditions for the men were also not particularly edifying. At one end of the canteen was a long bench where suspects awaited their turn to be booked while, at the other end, off-duty policemen were eating their lunch or typing under the eyes of curious, scornful or annoying suspects. It was in such circumstances that an excited or aggressive suspect could receive a thick ear, or even a stripe over the face with a sabre, for disturbing the peace in the canteen. Out of such conditions was bred an attitude that perhaps the Warmoesstraat was a rough-and-tumble station where business, and sometimes justice, was handled quickly and somewhat gruffly. Certainly I was told over and over again that the Warmoesstraat was different from the other stations in Amsterdam and that:

We do things differently in the Warmoesstraat. We have to. We do things here in a manner that you won't see in other stations. You can't go on arguing with people in this sort of neighbourhood. There comes a point where you just have to say, 'Right, that's enough, on your way mister', and perhaps help him along a little bit.

(Constable, 26 years)

The only access was through the front door. On entering there was a counter on the right jutting out into a hall. A sharp right turn around the end of the counter brought one to a door which could only be opened manually from the outside, and by an automatic release button on the inside, which gave access to the cells. Opposite the entrance was another door leading by a temporary staircase to the canteen, the administrative office, the rooms of the detectives and the offices of the senior officers. Behind the counter sat two or three sergeants whose major functions were to organise the shifts, to handle the public and to process suspects and prisoners. Behind them was the communications desk. Down a passage lay a room for searching suspects, the cells, two rubber-floored cells for drunks, showers and toilets for the prisoners, and a staircase leading below to a changing-room and lockers for the men and a large, secure room with a bench for groups of suspects or for short-stay, non-dangerous suspects. As a building it was clean, functional and undistinguished. But presumably the majority of people who entered its portals were not overly concerned with the décor.

Activity appeared to go in waves so that everything would be still and quiet for a period and then, at once, the bureau would be full of people. Many were coming to pay fines, to report thefts or assaults (these were sent upstairs to the detectives), to report stolen or towed-away vehicles, to drop off the arrival and departure slips kept by all hotels in Amsterdam, and to ask for advice. These comprised 'front-of-the-counter' clients in contrast to the 'behind-the-counter' clients who were mostly in some sort of trouble. There were a number of local 'characters' whom every station seems to attract (Rubinstein, 1973, p. 174). In the Warmoesstraat there was a large, angular simpleton called 'Crazy Piet', who ran errands for the prostitutes ('They are all my little daughters', he used to say). Whenever he saw an article about the police in a newspaper he cut it out and brought it along. Whatever was happening in the station he was always accorded the time of day and any offering was placed in a large folder carrying the official stamp of the Amsterdam Police. Occasionally Piet was given a new folder for his cut-outs and this was ostentatiously stamped in his presence. He was always humoured, was never turned away, and was accorded unlimited licence in the area. 'Albert' was a dishevelled alcoholic from the Nieuwmarkt and his speciality was singing ribald songs to his own guitar accompaniment. Sometimes he was palmed off on the C.I.D. and sent upstairs to sing them something from his repertoire. One evening an Italian family were reporting the theft of their car and there were also a few other people at the counter. Albert entered and to cries of 'Sing us a song, Albert' he burst into song to the astonishment of the Italians who forgot their problem for a moment and started to laugh.

The basic unit of the uniformed branch was the shift or group. Every station had eight groups of men who worked a complicated, overlapping system of six different shifts. Each group in the Warmoesstraat had two permanent sergeants. The sergeants were the linchpin of the patrol system, responsible for allocating manpower, for processing suspects and for taking immediate decisions. Generally officers worked office hours so that in the evenings and at night the sergeant was the highest-ranking policeman available in the station. If he felt that matters were getting out of hand or that a decision was too important for him to take alone, then he could, between 5 p.m. and 7 a.m., call upon a peripatetic inspector who was responsible for major incidents throughout the town. Detectives at the district level were usually available until late in the evening and could also be called upon. But at night and at weekends detectives and officers were basically not available. In the eight hours of a shift the sergeants normally spent four hours behind the counter and four hours on other duties. Generally they were desk-bound and did not carry out very much supervision outside the station. Behind the counter one of the sergeants handled the public and the duty-roster and the other took responsibility for the prisoners and the station diary. Behind and facing the sergeants was the communications console with a double set of telephones for incoming calls, a switchboard for internal calls, a radio receiver and transmitter for the district portable radios, a receiver for the messages from the Headquarters Radio Room, a panel for showing the disposition of cars, and a tannoy system for locating people within the building. Normally one or two men sat behind this console to take incoming calls, to pass on messages to the brigadier, to check with headquarters for details of wanted cars and persons, and to work the radio. The men were changed every hour or two hours and all members of the shift took their turn behind the console. This constant changing, apart from creating confusion when messages were not passed on properly and continuity was broken, meant that no one could monopolise the position of radio operator in the station in the way that

Rubinstein (1973, pp. 69–123) describes for Philadelphia, and could not make it a source of informal power and control.

The confined space meant that there was very little privacy and people had to explain their problem within earshot of others while prisoners were brought in through the same door and might brush past waiting clients. The corridor where suspects waited was partly visible and easily audible from the counter, and the communications console was in full view of the people. Anyone who attempted to walk straight upstairs without announcing himself to the sergeant was brusquely called back (this happened to me several times when sergeants were on duty who did not know me). This counter was a boundary between 'them' and 'us' and a civilian who mistakenly walked through the door to the cells was quickly turned away. The sergeant has a strong sense of territory and resented it when the constables hung around or utilised his sanctuary for their own activities (such as typing, telephoning or eating). Suddenly he would jump and herd everyone out, telling them to take their coffee-cups and Coke-bottles with them. Similarly, the constables guarded the canteen from intruders; as everyone who passed up the stairs could easily take a wrong turning and end up in the canteen, the men quickly questioned anyone in the landing outside who did not seem to belong there. For the canteen was their inner sanctum, cut off from public scrutiny, where they could relax, eat, play cards, watch television and be themselves. It represented 'backstage' (Goffman, 1959, p. 113) where they were no longer performing, and because the discrepancy between a policeman's public and private performances is great, so is the wish to restrict the visibility of his private self correspondingly high.

'Downstairs' the sergeants ran the show. One of them was responsible for processing suspects. Practically all suspects to a crime were searched at the scene for weapons. Women, old men, people suspected of minor crimes and those who did not appear dangerous were not always searched at the scene. This initial search was 'frisking' against a car or wall. At the station a more thorough search was carried out. This was done in an empty room, with no furniture and only a shelf for possessions, and was normally conducted by someone other than one of the arresting officers. A female suspect has to be searched by a woman and a policewoman was always called from one of the adjoining districts (the Warmoesstraat is the only station in Amsterdam without policewomen). This investigation was designed to uncover weapons, concealed drugs or money, and other not immediately visible belongings and identification. It was a smelly room, pervaded by the stale odour of sweaty bodies and unwashed feet. The suspect was required to strip naked. Force was normally not necessary and the vast majority of searches that I experienced were undertaken without demur. The individual, once naked, must bend to reveal any item concealed in the anus or in the crotch and to show the soles of his, or her, feet. Every personal belonging must be handed over. This meant wallet, money, watch, ring (most of the obstinate ones respond to soap and a forceful tug), ear-rings, necklaces, handkerchief, belt, braces, socks, shoe-laces, ties, badges and brooches. These were carefully recorded, signed for by the prisoner, and signed for again on release or transferral elsewhere. Occasionally a suspect claimed that he had been cheated, that some money or a ring had not been returned to him, but generally the prisoner's belongings were processed without mishap. I do remember once a tubby, middle-aged sergeant frantically searching for the brassiere of a black prostitute who had to be despatched to headquarters less one item of underwear. But the recording of proper-ty and the return of possessions in the station appeared to be scrupul-ously carried out with no suggestion of profiting from prisoners' belongings, in contrast to Spradley's (1970, p. 144) account of the handling of tramps in Seattle who were routinely robbed by the police (but see section (iv) below). Belts, ties, shoe-laces and so on were removed for the prisoner's safety. Following a suicide in the cells of another station, where a man used his socks to hang himself, socks were also included. But the primary purpose of the search was for concealed weapons and incriminatory evidence. 'Afro' hair-styles have been used to conceal razors, stiletto blades have been taped to the soles of feet, and drugs have been carried in the anal passage. A man with a plaster on his crotch had it painfully ripped off to reveal a festering sore (*Periodiek,* Nr. 58, July 1974). A prisoner, who had just stabbed a prostitute to death and who had been searched on the street, was found to have the murder weapon on him only after he had been searched in the station and after he had had the opportunity, if he had wanted to take it, of using it against the policemen guarding him. Once a prisoner, who had been searched on arrest, was discovered with a loaded revolver in his underpants. Banknotes were frequently con-cealed in underclothes. These incidents were sufficient in the police-men's eyes to justify these mini-debasement ceremonies. They also allowed thorough investigation of the lining of clothes and the heels of shoes for concealed drugs. There was little doubt that arrest—involv-ing the deprivation of liberty and personal freedom – and bodily scrutiny were 'stripping processes' which symbolically assaulted the individual's identity and which signified his unworthiness in the eyes of the law (Goffman, 1961, pp. 14–17).

By Dutch standards the men of the Warmoesstraat have a considerable involvement in crime cases and they referred to the inner city as 'a square mile of trouble' (*Elseviers Magazine*, 21 Feb 1976; *De Telegraaf*, 16 Apr 1977). This emphasis emerges clearly from a brief comparison of reported police activity between the city-centre districts (Warmoesstraat District 2 and Leidseplein District 3) and the four outer districts (North 1, East 4, South 5 and West 6) which comprise primarily traditional and/or new residential areas, mixed with offices or light industry. The two adjoining centre districts, 2 and 3, were the busiest in terms of charges for criminal and other offences. This was also true concerning people detained, with the Warmoesstraat entertaining 435 prisoners in July 1974 or roughly 14 per day (though this figure includes a number of lost children and emotionally disturbed people detained 'for their own good'). One category which was almost exclusive to the Warmoesstraat was 'wanted' persons; in August 1975 some 82 people were held because of unpaid fines, unfinished prison sentences or broken parole, compared to 19 in the five other districts combined. The suburban districts, on the other hand, were more frequently involved in lending assistance to the public and with traffic offences and accidents. In brief, then, the busiest stations with regard to criminal offences and arrests were the inner-city stations (Warmoesstraat, Leidseplein, and to a lesser extent East, which borders the centre) while the suburban stations tend to be relatively more involved in traffic accidents and domestic assistance (Monthly Reports, Uniform and Detective Branches, 1974 and 1975, City Police, Amsterdam).

A number of features of contemporary police work in Amsterdam are worth recording for the light they shed on crime in the city-centre. For example, the total of charge-sheets in 1974 reached a peak in August with 5398 offences. A definite seasonal element was noticeable which can be related to the tourist industry. Also of importance is the proportion of 'known' to 'unknown' offenders mentioned in the charge-sheets. Roughly in only one out of six to seven offences was the suspect known to the police. To put it another way, in June 1974 there were 4172 offences where the police had no information about the identity of the perpetrator of the crime, amounting to about 87 per cent of the cases. In terms of apprehending criminals for all offences the Amsterdam Police was clearly on the losing side. If we examine specific crimes for individual districts, then breaking into and theft from cars, for example, was very much a city-centre phenomenon and the Leidseplein, with its high concentration of hotels, had 324 cases reported for July 1974 or roughly 10 per day, which was slightly more than the Warmoesstraat. In the same month thefts were recorded from 741 cars in the whole of Amsterdam, or roughly 25 per day. There was a definite seasonal fluctuation in this crime for the inner city (with the Warmoesstraat noting 181 cases in August 1974 as against 94 cases in January 1975) as the laden cars of foreign tourists were favourite targets. The Warmoesstraat also saw a good deal of the victims of pocket-picking (117 cases in August 1974) while robbery on the street was almost exclusively a Warmoesstraat offence. The station also reported more crimes involving aggression (assault and bodily harm charges) than the other districts. With regard to 'foreigners without visible means of support' the Warmoesstraat again took the lion's share of the business with 57 cases in January 1975 (and a monthly average of around 30 during a six-month period).

If we try to assemble a typical day in the Warmoesstraat on the basis of figures from the monthly reports, then we get the following picture for the summer of 1974. In any one day the patrol cars of District 2 could expect around 50 recorded orders direct from the Radio Room. The station itself might handle 40 charges for a variety of offences, might detain 14 people, attend 10 accidents, respond to 3–4 calls for assistance (doubtless a huge under-representation), have 6 cars reported broken into and objects removed, entertain 4 people whose pockets have been picked, see a victim to a mugging every other day, have 10 burglaries reported, see a victim to an assault in two days out of every three, a victim to a serious assault against life every week, at least one drunk per day, usually one penniless foreigner a day, a lost child every two weeks, and 5 people whose car has been towed away by the police (in August 1974 the Amsterdam Police towed away 897 cars because of parking offences, with a maximum of 51 cars in one day), a fire at least every other day, and rescue someone from drowning every month. In practice, incidents did not occur with clockwork precision but in fairly predictable waves with occasionally an unpredictable torrent; on some days the station was simply a mad-house. Practically every day, but especially in the summer, there was a constant stream of tourists through the station who complained in a variety of languages 'I've just been robbed', 'My car has been stolen', 'My passport, traveller's cheques and airline tickets are missing from my hotel', 'My car has been broken into' and 'I seem to have lost my wallet on the train'. In 1975 Amsterdam celebrated its 700th birthday and one weary detective finished a report with the words: 'If it goes on like this will Amsterdam ever reach its 800th anniversary?'

To police this district the uniformed branch has at its disposal 3 officers, 5 adjutants, 24 sergeants, 57 constables first class, 106 constables and 16 Marechaussees. Some of these were attached to specialised groups and the remainder were divided into eight groups ('shifts' or 'reliefs' in British terms). A sergeant decided on the daily distribution of available manpower and had before him on the desk a large roster of all personnel who were on duty. On paper he has around fifteen or more men in a group. But, in practice, he will be lucky to have twelve or perhaps even as few as ten available for patrol. Normally a couple of men were off sick or injured, were assigned to light duties inside the office following sickness, or were involved in courses such as learning to drive different types of vehicles while, during the day-time, periods of sport and shooting practice also had to be fitted in (cf. Cain, 1973, p. 74, on what she calls 'gimmicks'). Assuming the sergeant had ten men available, he would assign them to the priority beats on foot in the town-centre, e.g. the Nieuwendijk, the Zeedijk and the Nieuw-markt, with two men in a patrol car, free to roam throughout the whole district, leaving two men in the bureau for the radio and for helping behind the counter. It came as a surprise to realise how few men were actually on the street and how great areas of the District remained almost continually unpatrolled. This was amplified when operational demands were taken into account. For example, a patrol might arrest someone who had to be taken to the detectives at headquarters and for whom a charge-sheet had to be typed; that meant one pair of constables off the streets engaged in typing the report. Or perhaps a couple of prisoners had to be escorted to headquarters and two men were lost for half an hour or more on escort duty. Occasionally help was requested with special duties, such as guarding the Mayor's residence, or attending a demonstration with the riot-squad, and one or more of the group was not available for the whole shift. Particularly on Thursday evening, which was late opening day for most of the shops, a pair of men might be sent out on plain-clothes duty to watch out for shoplifters or pickpockets. The operational reality of a busy station, hampered by a manpower shortage, meant that preventive patrolling by uniformed men on the street was often more of an ideal than a reality. One evening, for instance, there was a phone call asking for assistance at a fight in a café: the sergeant had no men available to attend it and had to shrug his shoulders and say, 'They'll just have to sort it out for themselves'.

At seven o'clock one morning there were three constables on duty, but as none of them was a qualified driver the sergeant had to keep them inside and the district was totally devoid of mobile patrols. A sergeant explained the problem facing him as station-sergeant with responsibility for assigning patrols in the district:

> You have a patrol function and an assistance function. You always have to bear the latter in mind and keep three or four men inside in case something suddenly crops up. In the evenings you may have a reasonably large group, say eighteen or nineteen men, and you can place a couple of posts and send a couple of lads out in plain clothes – 'You two go and hang around the Beursplein, there's been a lot of cars broken into recently'. But when you have to start a night shift with six men, plus perhaps two from another district, and you're supposed to guard the whole of the Second District, well that's hopeless. You practically can't fulfil your assistances and certainly can't do much in preventive terms. So as duty-officer you just don't have enough men and its a disappointing and frustrating state of affairs. You have a couple of lads who've just come in after two or three hours on a case and they've just sat down to eat a slice of bread and you have to call them up, 'I'm sorry lads, but you have to go out again'. They'll do it, and they'll accept it as normal, but it's obviously not very pleasant. Perhaps you rely on the goodwill and capacity of the lads too much and that can weaken their input.
>
> (Sergeant, 36 years)

Generally the sergeants were on good terms with their men and the relationship was easy and relaxed (critics of the Amsterdam Police say too relaxed). For most of the time I was there the men did not have to appear downstairs for roll-call and there was almost no evidence of formalism. A more critical picture was painted by a sergeant who generally found that the manner of working in the station left much to be desired, and who conveyed something of the casualness which characterised the Warmoesstraat style:

> My first priority is that I like to work in an orderly way. Not with a hubbub and everyone going his own way but with a bit of order. It's getting a bit too relaxed, the way the police works at the moment. I believe that there ought to be a bit of discipline but you have to go a long way to find it nowadays. Perhaps it comes because some sergeants don't like to say anything, I don't know, but they give

everyone a free hand and then you get some pretty funny things going on. A couple of patrolmen walk in to the station with a prisoner and put him in a chair in the corridor. One of them strolls across to the telephone and the other goes to the cupboard to look for a photo of the suspect. They don't say anything to the sergeant and he says nothing to them. That's not right. If I'm station-sergeant and they bring someone in then I say, 'What have you brought him in for?' . . . There is less respect for us and we have only got ourselves to blame because of a lot of small things. I feel that if you patrol in uniform then you ought to look well turned out and not stroll with long hair because if you look like a scarecrow then you lose people's respect. Soon they'll be coming on duty with red shirts and white socks under their uniform. One came the other day with grey socks. That's something you needn't have tried before because you could go straight home for the regulation socks. But then you hear people saying, 'We'd better not say anything because we have such a shortage of personnel'. I'm not sure about that. If we would just begin to do what we are supposed to do then I think that the shortage wouldn't seem so bad.

(Sergeant, 38 years)

(ii) PATROLLING THE CITY-CENTRE

At the end of a night-duty on a cold, wet March morning, the strains of the 'Marseillaise' were heard echoing down the empty Warmoes-straat. A few men wandered to the door and were greeted with the sight of a young lady, in a long gown and with bare feet, marching towards them singing at the top of her voice and holding aloft a lighted candle. The candle flickered out and the apparition turned sharp right, entered the station, and, having cadged a light for the candle and a cigarette, proceeded on its way.

(Field Notes)

The Warmoesstraat station controls a district that contains several traditional working-class areas, such as the Spaarndammerbuurt and a part of the Jordaan, and a sparsely populated industrial area containing the Western Harbour. But a disproportionate amount of its energy is focused on the city-centre which is made up of public places such as offices, restaurants and places of entertainment, a notorious red-light district, and a decaying inner-urban area. The population and life-style is quite unlike a suburb of Amsterdam or a smaller Dutch city. There are still a few of the old original inhabitants, but mostly the population is a fluctuating one of day visitors from out of town, commuters, tourists, students, 'gastarbeiders', young people, Chinese and Surinamers. The number is swelled by runaway girls and boys, deserters, illegal immigrants, and criminals attracted to the city as a hide-out. The city-centre is thus a melting-pot of ethnic and deviant groups and contains anonymous physical spaces suitable for crimes such as picking pockets and breaking open cars. The Warmoesstraat is also situated in the centre of the red-light district. If one stands in Dam Square, looking back up the Damrak to Central Station, then the 'warme buurt' (the warm area) lies in the square mile to the right of the Damrak. It comprises narrow cobbled streets, tightly packed houses, and picturesque humped bridges over the tree-lined canals. Like Soho it is a colourful mixture of cafés, sex-shops, porn-clubs ('erections guaranteed or money refunded' boasted one, and 'non-stop, live porno with real hard fucking' claimed another), Chinese restaurants, bars, clubs, discos and, pre-eminently, prostitutes. The girls, who range from the gorgeous to the grotesque, usually sit provocatively in a window or stand engagingly outside a door. At night the streets are crowded with buyers as well as just window-shoppers, and, especially at weekends, the area is busy until four or five o'clock in the morning.

With 2000 registered prostitutes, with sex-shows catering for all tastes (one offered a choice between 'The Hard Porn Show, The Life Show, The Real Fucky Fucky Show, and The Super Fucky Fucky Show'), and with porn-shops displaying sailors' comforts, obscene monks, vibrators and rubber penises, flimsy nighties, whips and stocks, and aids such as 'Adam's Success', 'Erekta Prompt', 'Erecto Fix' and 'Retardin Cream', sex has become an industry which attracts many foreign and domestic tourists. A stripper explained that tourists now thought of tulips, windmills, clogs *and* 'live shows' and that some visited Rembrandt's 'Nachtwacht' in the morning and then went to see 'a couple having it off' in the evening (*Haagse Post*, 4 June 1977), while a policeman said:

> People come up and ask you 'Where is the red-light district?', 'Can you recommend one of the girls for me?', 'How much does it cost?', and 'Are the girls clean?' They ask why we don't do anything about it and if you feel like it you explain it or else make a joke of it.
>
> (Constable, 28 years)

Informal argreements between the Mayor, the Officer of Justice (or 'Public Prosecutor') and the police have created a sort of 'normative' ghetto in the red-light district. It seems to be a distinctive feature of Dutch society that deviance is tolerated if it is confined within certain areas and provided it conducts itself in an orderly fashion and that it does not threaten to spread to respectable areas where it will shock 'decent' citizens. Within a few hundred yards of the Warmoesstraat, for example, are brothels, gambling houses, drinking clubs, live pornography, street prostitution, reception centres for drug addicts, houseboats, youth centres and derelict houses full of squatters. All in some way broke the law but the police turned a blind eye. The officer in charge of the Warmoesstraat explained:

> For donkey's years there has been a policy that all sorts of things can happen in this area. If soliciting gets really bad here then we do something about it but meanwhile it's cracked down hard elsewhere. Also the Chinese gambling houses are accepted here because of the social role of gambling in Chinese society while there is enforcement against ordinary gambling dens. . . . There is an informal agreement between the station and the Prinsenhof [treatment centre for drug addicts]. You can scarcely call it official because what goes on there is unlawful. But this is something that isn't on paper; it's just an agreement with the people in charge that if we have to go in there we'll do it with their co-operation . . . and they ask us not to let a couple of policemen wander in umpteen times a day because that is hopeless. Their work is disturbed and neither of us gets anywhere.
>
> (Chief Inspector, 48 years)

The patrolman from the Warmoesstraat, then, works in a deviant community and has an audience and clientele comprising junkies, drug dealers, Chinese cooks, transvestites, transsexuals, homosexuals, sailors, lesbians, ponces, prostitutes, university students, students of the Hare Krishna and the Children of God, 'guest-workers', dossers, alcoholics, porn-club owners, bouncers, begging gypsies, Latin American pickpockets and shoplifters, predatory Surinamers, and tourists of every nationality.

Like San Francisco (Becker and Horowitz, 1971) the inner city of Amsterdam contains a mosaic of life-styles. These are geographically divided into territories. The Chinese community, for example, has several restaurants in the Binnen Bantammerstraat and extends, with more restaurants and several 'for Chinese only' gambling dens, along

the Zeedijk. One can enter an unmarked door in the Binnen Bantammerstraat and find an opium den with oldish men in shabby suits lying
on low rush-matted beds smoking long pipes of opium. Or be warmly
received (with a policeman as guide) in a gambling den where voluble
Chinese surrender small fortunes on seemingly infantile games. Behind these activities exists a thriving marketing industry for distributing heroin. In the middle of the Zeedijk is a piece of 'old Dutch glory',
as the men call it; a sort of no-man's-land, it comprises a few bars and
houses where some of the original underworld characters of 'de wallen'
[the old city] still live. The Chinese have been steadily expanding their
influence and have moved further along the Zeedijk. The Surinamers
used to operate at the other end of the Zeedijk, near Central Station,
and around the Nieuwmarkt, but with police pressure on their two bars
in the Nieuwmarkt (''t Winkeltje' has been closed and 'De Cotton
Club' can only sell soft drinks) they are now concentrated around
'Emil's Place' near the Prins Hendrikkade. They specialise in pickpocketing, drug-dealing (often with fake substances), muggings and
knifings. The Nieuwmarkt is also something of a mini 'skid-row' for
alcoholics. Nearby are two reception centres for Dutch drug-addicts
who account for thefts from cars and the breaking open of parking
meters. The Oudezijds Achterburgwal is the hub of the sex industry
with girls in the windows and with clubs. Central Station is a meeting-
place for dossers, pickpockets and homosexuals hoping to pick up
young boys. At night it attracts the flotsam of the city who hang around
the hot-dog stall and who often get involved in scuffles. The Haarlemmerdijk and Nieuwzijds Voorburgwal contain several bars and restaurants catering mostly for Antillians from the Dutch West Indies
and for North African guest-workers. The latter deal in and use
hashish and occasionally settle a dispute with the gun. The Damrak is
the stamping-ground of international pickpockets and passers of false
cheques. Somewhat scattered and more diluted than previously is a
community of artists, academics and journalists (some of whom have
moved away because of the lack of safety on the streets). The city-
centre is characterised by 'street life' whereby social life takes place
partly in the open and where people define themselves as belonging
somewhere in the lattice-work of territories; people are assigned to
groups according to 'clothing, apparent ethnicity, demeanour, sex,
age, companions, location, and plausible destination' (Suttles, 1968,
pp. 15 ff.). Traditional and transitory subcultures exist side by side, in
constantly changing combinations, and the inhabitants and the police
share many assumptions about life there.

Patrol work in this colourful area can briefly be characterised by two features. The first was a feeling for the special atmosphere in the district which bound the policemen closely together, and second was the lack of preparation and guidance for patrolling this unique community. In an area which allegedly contained 60 per cent foreigners the policemen were scarcely likely to identify with a Surinamese dealer or a German junkie, so they were thrown very much back on colleagues as a reference group. Affiliation with the group or shift was said to be particularly strong in the Warmoesstraat compared to other stations. In 1976 reinforcements were brought into the area because of manpower shortages and to combat increasing street crime; the policemen from other districts rarely felt at home in the Warmoesstraat, e.g. a constable from a suburb said of his duties there:

> I can do without it myself. It's lousy work. Also there's a completely different mentality among the policemen here. Much harder and more aggressive. But I think that it has to be. Such an area demands it. But personally I would have a lot of difficulty adjusting to it.
>
> (*Elseviers Magazine*, 21 Feb 1976)

An inspector who had just come to the station also had a rather negative picture of its style:

> It's a bit Wild West. There are some people here who think they have got their own police station. Especially with some of the younger ones there's an attitude of 'I'm the boss. Complaints? Don't give me that rubbish. This is the place where you can get a thick ear.' The atmosphere is rough, undisciplined and lacking in polish. I notice a symptom here of, bang, straight away draw your pistol.
>
> (Inspector, 54 years)

But the rapid turnover of personnel and the wastage of men to other forces has served to undermine the traditional cohesiveness of the group:

> The turnover is incredible. You just get to know the mentality of the group and get tuned in to each other and then you lose four or five men and get new ones, and the spirit changes in the group completely. We had a group, for instance, which was a solid unit where no one could come between us. We were working really well. But then you

get four or five new lads and then you need a good couple of months
before it is a unit again.

(Constable, 26 years)

Nevertheless, mutual reliance within the groups appeared to be
stronger than in other districts. A new sergeant remarked:

There is an enormous difference between the groups and it is
stronger here than in other stations. But group spirit is very strong
and as an outsider you can't get between them; a group is a group,
and that's it. Group D, for example, is only interested in the drugs
problem and they forget they have other tasks. They really go after
the stuff. Some constables don't know any better and become so
influenced that they think that is all there is to police work. . . . We
have people in some of the groups who dominate and slant the group
in a certain direction. And it's not difficult to influence the younger
lads because they can identify with the group and do what the rest of
the group does and that means drugs in Group D. The atmosphere in
the group is often set by one man and that is naturally a bit
dangerous.

(Sergeant, 28 years)

Patrol work has to be learned and the individual's style and profi-
ciency depended on several factors – the self-identity of the district, the
collective style of the station and the group, the sort of supervision a
man received, the type of public he met, and his own personal
characteristics. One man was quick to learn, decisive, and emotionally
detached whereas another was perhaps uncertain, slow on the uptake,
vacillating, and emotional about his new experiences. There were as
many adaptations as there were individuals, according to the men
themselves:

Everyone performs differently, that's a part of you, you all look the
same but there are distinctions. You know Felix, with the mous-
tache? He is a typical example of people who try immediately to take
control of a situation by shouting or by handing out a thump. You
have some people who will let you grab their tie. Take Joop, the
Limburger, you can casually pull a couple of buttons off his coat on
the street and he'll just go on grinning and then walk away. You try
that with someone else and he'll start fighting. There are some

people who prefer to shout rather than hit and straight away give someone a flea in their ear. I've got my own style, a bit special, with a certain feel for humour and my own manner for approaching the public. Not everyone agrees with me but there is no one the same. Paul, for example, tends to challenge people more quickly than me on the street because he comes from a sporty background, he was in the marines and his father as well I think, but still he's good to work with on the street. Eric is sometimes a bit of a twit but he's always ready to stand up to someone and René is the same. But none of them is a Frits Oostman [the interviewee's fictitious name] and we are all different.

(Constable, 28 years

In brief, the social reality of patrol work in the Warmoesstraat was dependent on the station's norms, group affiliation and personal identity, which combined to form a variety of working styles.

A noticeable feature of patrolling at the time of the research was the lack of co-ordination and guidance for the men on the street. A critical adjutant saw this short-sightedness as endemic to the police organisation:

I also consider it sad that young constables come to the Warmoesstraat where so many problems are heaped together. All sorts of groups, anti-social types, prostitutes, Turks, Surinamers, and so on. Along comes a constable with a training that comprises the Hunting Act, Work Act, Criminal Law Book and Criminal Procedure. Then it's 'off you go', you're introduced, and then 'sort it out for yourself'. And they're confronted with problems which in fact they know nothing about. Station Singel (in District 3), for instance, has a lot to do with homosexuals. In that case young constables should receive continued training over the problems which confront them. There were newspaper articles about discrimination against Surinamers. There was absolutely no guidance whatsoever available for the constables on this problem. That was not just a blatant mistake but deadly dangerous. Exactly the same situation with the homosexuals. The lads knew three words for them but otherwise nothing. Yet every day of the week they were involved with such people. And then it's a shortcoming on the part of the police that these lads don't get further instruction. It's always a miracle that it continues to come off all right because in fact we sit waiting for the first accident.

(Adjutant, 52 years)

When a constable was asked if he received sufficient guidance from officers, he replied:

> I've never noticed any guidance or else I don't see it as guidance. You are your own boss inside and out on the street, and nobody comes to tell you to do it this way or that. A sergeant could say to watch out for this or that but it's never happened to me. You get in the car and you go for a drive and there's no system in it at all. . . . I've no idea if the officers could do more, I just don't have any contact with them. We live in our own little worlds. I'm just so used to it I don't know if it could be done differently.
>
> (Constable, 26 years)

A sergeant expressed the opinion that this social distance between officers and men was partly responsible for the restriction of sergeants to a supervisory role:

> When I became sergeant I thought, 'Now I'll never go out on the street again', but I managed to get out quite often during my three months training period. But now that I've settled in here I discover, to my own stupid surprise, that I get the chance to go out now and again and I don't do it. And I must say that really being station-sergeant is a load of old cock. You're nothing more than an expensive porter and any young constable could do his job. I feel that the sergeant's place is on the street, with his men, working as a group, so that they can rely on you. I believe that the problem with us sergeants, why we don't go outside, is that we feel left in the lurch by the people over us. They do say from above, 'The door is always open', but you don't run upstairs every time something happens. There's a thick wall between us, which you can't break through. They would like us to get through it but we have to do it together. I don't know what the answer is because I also don't expect them to spend all day downstairs sitting around to see if I'm doing it all right.
>
> (Sergeant, 28 years)

The duality of this response – the awareness of a communication gap together with a desire to be free from restrictive supervision – is doubtless typical of most hierarchical organisations (Rubinstein, 1973, p. 17).

Perhaps an extreme example of this gulf came from an inspector who had been trying to exert more control over the situation:

> What I find objectionable about the present system is that the
> people in the canteen see you as a sort of troublesome insect who
> watches them to make sure that they do things all right and who only
> says something when it goes wrong. That comes from the system. As
> long as you stick to a system where officers are a select group, who
> are separately trained, then that distance will always remain. . . .

[I often hear the lads say that they scarcely see the officers?]
> Of course it could be better but the guilt lies with both parties. For
> instance, if something is going on downstairs or something impor-
> tant is happening on the street then I expect them to phone me. I'm
> not here as decoration. But most of them [sergeants] don't do it; they
> say, 'We don't need the governor around, we'll sort it out for
> ourselves, it won't go any better if he's around'. But I want to know
> what is going on, if there's a shooting or a fight or the constables are
> in trouble. For instance, there was the shoot-out among the Chinese
> and I was sitting here on my own, but no one asked me to help. I read
> the daily reports and brought them downstairs and there were four
> sergeants with about thirty prisoners. I said, 'What's going on?' and
> they replied, 'Oh, don't you know sir? A shoot-out with two dead,
> four wounded, and thirty prisoners.' No one had called me! That's
> wrong. I demand that they let me know and they'd better get used to
> it.

(Inspector, 54 years)

To summarise briefly, patrol work in the Warmoesstraat was characterised by an area exhibiting a mosaic of life-styles, by a degree of
dependence on the group, by a variety of working styles within a
pattern often characterised as 'hard', by a lack of preparation and
guidance for the reality on the street, and by a considerable gulf
between operational men and supervisory personnel.

(iii) DANGER AND EXCITEMENT

Two cornerstones of the policeman's occupational culture are, as was
seen in the previous chapter, the element of danger (Tauber, 1967)
and the relishing of excitement (Banton, 1974, p. 7). Both factors play
an important part in the world picture of the Warmoesstraat police-

men. One particular night service can illustrate the seriousness of certain situations and how this was laced with excitement, speed and the brandishing of weapons:

It was a Friday night and just past midnight when a call came to the station that three American cars were parked on a bridge over a canal and that the occupants were possibly armed. Several constables jumped into a VW minibus and began to complain on the way that half Amsterdam would know by now as the location had been given over the radio instead of via the station. On arrival there were only two cars with youngish men and girls in them. 'Step out and put your hands on the roof', said a constable, conspicuously drawing his pistol. 'Why, what's all this in aid of anyway?' said the driver of one car. He was dragged out and unceremoniously pushed against the car – 'I asked nicely, lads', he protested. No weapons were found and the policemen carped that the third car could have taken off, warned by the radio, or a gun could have been dropped quickly into the canal. To emphasise the grumblings about the radio there were two press cars *waiting* nearby for the incident to unfold. Later we were cruising in the patrol car when a call came through. At once the car took off with blue light flashing, siren blaring, tearing through red lights, swerving the wrong side of traffic islands, screeching around narrow corners causing passers-by to leap for safety. Two men in plain clothes had stopped a suspect – a strongly built, well-dressed Turk with dark curly hair and a grey tailored suit – and he had reached for the glove compartment of his car. Fearing accomplices (three more Turks had been mentioned in the original tip-off) they radioed for assistance. On arrival the Turk was standing legs apart, hands on top of his car, being searched by one policeman while another held a pistol at the back of his head. At 1.40 a.m. under street lights it looked totally unreal, except that the automatic in the man's glove compartment was real. The suspect was handcuffed and put into the cramped back seat of a Beetle and his legs were persuaded into the right place with a few perfunctory kicks. On the way to the station one constable held a pistol to his ribs, saying, 'If you try anything I shall have to put a bullet in you, is that clear?', while the driver scolded him for carrying a gun and shouted, 'Where do you think you are, Cyprus? Well, you can't run around shooting people here.'

We then cruised around waiting for the accomplices until the call came that they had been sighted on the Prins Hendrikkade. This time there was no siren but just the screech of tyres to announce our arrival. The Turks seemed amazed at half-a-dozen armed policemen surrounding them and one said in response to 'Put your hands above your head' that he'd only been buying a packet of chips, and to reinforce his point he held out a full packet of mayonnaise-covered chips. The next second chips were raining down and his hands went up very quickly.

Back inside the station there came a report that a Black man carrying a machine-gun in a suitcase had entered a club. Suddenly everyone was jumping over the counter and sprinting down the street with pistols drawn to search the club. But it was a Surinamese club with a thick wooden door and a small window protected by a metal grille. Willem banged on the door and demanded entry. The policemen, some in plain clothes but all carrying drawn weapons, entered and began to search the premises while the mainly Black members carried on dancing to the reggae music. But the suspect had already left. Later a Surinamer answering the description (he had a plaster on his face where someone had tried to hack his ear off in an argument) was seen driving a car and the patrol car swerved in front, the red 'stop' sign was left on, and the men jumped out with drawn pistols. The man was asked to get out of the car but a Black woman was allowed to stay inside. One officer placed his pistol at the back of the man's neck and said laconically, 'You won't make a run for it, will you, sir? Otherwise I shall be forced to shoot you. You do understand that?' The suitcase referred to in the tip-off was in the boot but it only contained a curved ornamental knife. There was no sign of the machine-gun. The men apologised to the man for the inconvenience, one of them putting his hand on his shoulder in a friendly manner, but he did not appear to be put out and had a short conversation with them. Then one of the officers went around to the car window and apologised to the woman ('She was a decent woman', he explained later). Just before dawn there was a call concerning armed suspects in a red Citroën in front of Central Station. The car took off in an endeavour to get there first and we saw a patrol-car from another district also racing to get some of the action. Several cars arrived simultaneously and the Citroën was surrounded by armed policemen who dragged out the occupants, two young Italians. There were a lot of people hanging around, some of them keeping warm in telephone boxes and some buying coffee and chips from a van, waiting for the first trains. A curious crowd gathered and a young drunk, his raincoat smothered in mayonnaise from a scuffle, staggered into the arena complaining about some mishap and was swiftly propelled out of it again by a policeman as the car was searched. Some packets of powder and pills in silver paper were discovered, indicating that the Italians were probably waiting to make a sale, but no weapons were found. On the way back to the cars a nondescript, studious young man stepped in front of the officers and asked them something but he was rudely pushed aside. When we returned later to the station the man, who was from the press, was sitting behind the counter. Two officers had decided to look at his car because pressmen in Amsterdam follow the activities of the police throughout the night and there is little affection for them. In the car of this inoffensive-looking man at five in the morning was an enormous alsatian dog, a short-wave radio receiver tuned in to the police waveband, an illegal transmitter, a bayonet, a long saw-toothed knife, a rubber truncheon, and his wife.

(Field notes)

This was an especially active night in my experience, but the men of the Warmoesstraat would hold it to be symptomatic of the increasing tension of their job caused by a widespread willingness to use violence and to carry a weapon. A man with nearly twenty years' experience in the drugs squad lamented the 'good old days' before drugs became a big, and potentially violent, business:

It used to be fairly relaxed. Och, the lads with hash were really quite sweet, completely unaggressive. But now there's much more aggression. Perhaps Malaysians who have concluded a deal. Then you discover they're walking around with loaded pistols in their waistbands. You're all in plain clothes so you don't take any chances and move in with say fourteen men with drawn pistols just in case they think you're the competition trying to muscle in on a deal. You used to put someone in the car without thinking. Now you use the American style for everyone – against the car, legs wide open, hands over the head, and a careful search. I say to them at the training school to look first for weapons even if its an arrest for drugs. Because its not much use to you to be lying in a coffin with a wreath on it being taken from Headquarters to the Eastern Cemetery while everyone says, 'He was a good lad'.

(Detective, 52 years)

In practice, policemen in Amsterdam are rarely exposed to the level of danger in some American cities (cf. *Police Review*, 20 Sep 1974). But just before my research commenced in the summer of 1974 a constable was shot dead and his colleague seriously wounded, during an attempt to arrest two armed foreigners. In May 1975 there was a shoot-out in a Chinese gambling house between rival factions of the Chinese underworld in which twenty-five shots were fired, two people were killed and four were seriously wounded. In another incident, gang warfare was prevented by a raid on a Chinese gambling house, where an armed group was preparing to attack a rival gang, in which nine firearms were seized and over forty people arrested. Several 'executions' have taken place openly in the district which were related to power struggles in the Chinese community. At a time when their use of violence was increasingly under scrutiny, the policemen felt that aggressiveness around them, and against them, was increasing. The police unions have increasingly called for better weapons (*De Volkskrant*, 12 May 1976) to protect their men. A side-effect of this emphasis on danger and excitement was that enforcement in the Warmoesstraat could be edgy, prematurely aggressive, and even panicky.

I've been with colleagues who have completely messed up a situation out of pure fear. They've over-reacted and don't know what they're doing anymore. That's deadly dangerous. So at a group meeting I said, 'Let's talk about it. If there are colleagues who suffer from fear – sweating palms and knocking knees – then let's chat about it because I don't want to be dropped in it by a panic-stricken cop who reacts blindly in a dangerous situation.' But no one wants to own up that they are frightened.

(Constable, 33 years)

On another occasion the same constable was watching a violent and destructive fight in a bar, waiting for it to subside so that he could arrest the trouble-makers outside, when he decided to ask for a back-up car to hang around the area for 'eventual' assistance; the result was a speeding patrol-car with blaring siren which warned the fighters who took to their heels. This was seen as an unnecessary response by 'siren-happy' youngsters. Holdaway (1977a) has also highlighted this emphasis on speed and excitement in a British force. The widespread use of vehicles has clearly undermined the conventional wisdom of experienced British policemen who used to tell new boys, 'Remember, son, you always *walk* to a fight' (B. Devlin, personal communication).

Some men in the Warmoesstraat argued that the haste and the jumpy response was related to an underlying fear. A sergeant tried to specify this concealed element among the policemen:

[What did you experience in your three months training period?]
On three occasions I had someone covered in blood at the counter. One had his skull split open with a billiard cue, another had been stabbed and blood streamed out of his mouth and swum around in his shoes, while another bloke came in with a knife wound and collapsed in front of the counter. That was three times one behind the other. But there were lots of arrests for possessing firearms and for drugs. It's an extremely busy station where you have to stay on your toes. You can't afford a mistake. You're involved with so many dangerous people who've often been in trouble before. I'm always amazed that so few colleagues get injured; that they're not knifed or shot. The mentality of the constables here is harder, their style of work is different; they are harder, tougher, and you don't see that in other stations. . . . My feeling is that, when you first go on the street, you're unsure and frightened, in case it goes wrong or you get injured. Suddenly, that feeling seems to go and you're not frightened for anything. But after a certain period that feeling comes back and suddenly you're frightened for something. For a lot of people it's a trauma. They get the feeling that they must get away and they're not prepared to fight against it. They've all got such a big mouth, that they can tackle anything and laugh about it, but at any moment of the day you can be confronted with something and you have to be ready for it. And that they want to get out of uniform shows me that they can't cope any more and have lost their guts. A lot of lads leave Amsterdam and especially from this station. But it's strange; you never talk about being frightened, or about fear. But I'm certain that it's often a question of fear. But a policeman won't easily admit it.

(Sergeant, 28 years)

The occupational emphasis on danger and excitement played an important symbolic role in the world of the Warmoesstraat and may be responsible for occasionally hasty and reactive enforcement while also perhaps contributing to a degree of stress and fear among the policemen.

(iv) BRUTALITY, DISCRIMINATION, CORRUPTION AND THE WARMOESSTRAAT'S IMAGE

The public image of the Warmoesstraat is almost exclusively negative. It is probably the one station in The Netherlands which practically everyone knows by name and it is associated with accusations of brutality, discrimination and corruption. The research period coincided with a relatively quiet time in between a spate of complaints by Blacks about ill-treatment and a widely publicised series of corruption cases. Perhaps this accounts for the fact that I experienced the station as predominantly calm and routine and quite unlike its negative stereotype. I witnessed very little violence and also formed the opinion that corruption did not play a role in the uniformed man's life. Indeed, when the corruption cases broke, they were confined to accusations against detectives and plain-clothes men involved primarily in the so-called 'victimless crimes', principally drugs and vice, and/or in relation to Chinese people. Although the number of arrests to date number only eight, which hardly compares with the scale of cases in London (Judge, 1972, pp. 154–86) or New York (Knapp, 1972), they have revealed the possibility of policemen dealing in drugs, 'planting' drugs, using drugs to pay informants, possessing illegal weapons, accepting payments and entertainment from leading figures in the Chinese underworld, and extorting money from brothel-keepers (*Nieuwe Revu*, 28 Jan 1977; *Haagse Post Extra*, 'Heroine', 1977; *Accent*, 14 May 1977). But the daily life of a uniformed constable, paying a guilder less for his Chinese take-away meal because he was in uniform, was far removed from the twilight world of plain-clothes drugs and vice enforcement. However, the recent press revelations are useful to set next to my original positive picture and have also continued to keep the negative image of the Warmoesstraat in the headlines. This undoubtedly increased the self-consciousness and isolation of the policemen there who viewed the outside world, the press and much of the public as unco-operative and hostile.

For as long as anyone can remember the Warmoesstraat has had a reputation as the station where you can get a thick ear. Rudeness and insolence are also said to be characteristic of enforcement there. The rudeness is not one-sided, however, and the policemen also receive provocative remarks and insulting behaviour. Many Amsterdammers are suspicious of the police and roundly abuse them when given a chance. For instance, a sixty-one-year-old woman was being given a ticket for a traffic offence when she began to shout at the constable, 'Drop dead, you idiot. You're a stupid arsehole.' A young constable was supervising a demonstration of taxi-drivers when one of them called out, 'You're a layabout, a big prick and an arsehole.' A man was reported as calling two patrolmen 'dirty rotten stinking stupid yokels and dirty bleeding pimps' (from the Station Diary). In another case there was a traffic accident where a witness had alleged that a woman had been driving but that she changed places with a man before the police arrived. Because the woman had no driving licence and the man was suspected of being under the influence, both were taken to the station. There a constable told them to 'shut their faces' when they started to talk; the woman asked if she could go to the toilet and was told, 'You can piss in your drawers'; the man asked if he could smoke his pipe and was told, 'Don't dare to stick that pipe in your gob because then I'll shove it in one go down your throat'. A complaint was laid against the constable and he replied in his own defence that the man was very recalcitrant, refused to sit down, and began to shout,

... that I was a fascist. In addition, the Police was worse than the N.S. and the N.S.B. [Fascist organisations] in the war. Three times he screamed that his brother-in-law, who was an adjutant in the police, had told him that the personnel of the Warmoesstraat was only scum. Holland was supposed to be a free country but countries behind the Iron Curtain were freer than here.

The constable admitted that he had used the alleged words against the suspects and was reprimanded for his conduct (Archive, Warmoesstraat Station).

But since the early seventies the Warmoesstraat has become almost a by-word for violence, particularly in relation to Surinamers. Bagley (1973b, p. 14) reproduced some of these allegations, e.g.

... this nephew, who protested, was punched on the nose. Inside the police station Roy was kicked down a short flight of stairs into a cell, where about seven constables kicked and stamped on him. He was also beaten with the usual rubber truncheon. He was made to undress in order to be searched, now stark naked he was again beaten with a truncheon. As he knelt down to avoid further blows the end of the truncheon was prodded into his anus.

More recently, a young Surinamer interviewed by a reporter pointed to the station and declared:

> You're brought in there and thrown into a cell with three policemen around you. They kick you until you can't breathe any more. Then they shout at you: 'Dirty blacks, don't you ever wash, you're monkeys, you're not really people.' If you answer back you get a kick in the crotch. Or a wooden stop in your mouth. You would think that the days of slavery were back again in that station. They say to you, 'We'll make sure that your race is rooted out. Piss off to your own country, you rotten niggers.' (*Elseviers Magazine*, 21 Feb 1976)

In 1973 some twenty serious complaints of mistreatment against Surinamers and others were investigated by the State Detectives but did not lead to any prosecutions against policemen, although the Minister of Justice used the term 'vigorous enforcement' to character-ise the Warmoesstraat (Smits, 1973c). Following a number of inci-dents over the last year a lawyer demanded that the entire uniformed branch in the Warmoesstraat should be suspended and replaced with military police (*De Volkskrant*, 6 May 1977), while a junior minister had called the Amsterdam Police a 'dangerous dog which ought to be kept on a line' and stated that he would not himself dare to enter the Warmoesstraat (*De Telegraaf*, 6 Apr 1977).

I never witnessed collective violence against suspects and most of the men denied that such systematic mistreatment had taken place. The one occasion where clearly 'illicit' violence was used was during a riot when, in plain clothes and under cover of darkness, a number of policemen followed the riot-squad and took the opportunity to beat up young men who were in the forefront of the crowds. These youngsters were knocked down and worked over with rubber truncheons and, in one case, 'nunchaku' sticks. That was the most serious transgression which I witnessed. Rubinstein, on the other hand, recounts several incidents of systematic violence, one of which involved a man accused of assaulting a young girl of four years:

> Any squad member who wished was allowed to beat the suspect from the ankles to the armpits with his stick. Men came in off the street to participate in the beating and then returned to patrol. Before he was taken down town, the suspect had been severely battered, although he had no broken bones. (1973, p. 183)

Generally, however, excessive violence was not condoned and unnecessarily aggressive policemen were not respected in the Warmoesstraat in my experience. At the same time, 'normal' but illegal violence
was accepted in certain cases. There was the euphemistically entitled
'calming-down slap' which was scarcely perceived as violence. A
young policeman also explained how he first assaulted a prisoner
inside the station, following an affray:

> When I came back to the station I had to first go and sit down. I
> always thought that I would never thump anyone in the station. But
> in the same disturbance I'd seen a yob kick a copper in the balls.
> Later I saw the bloke in the station and thought, 'I've seen it for
> myself so he can't possibly deny it', and said, 'You're the one who
> kicked a constable in the balls'. And he answered, 'It wasn't me who
> did it' with a laugh, 'ha, ha', just like that. A flame shot through me
> and I gave him a thump. Afterwards I thought, 'How could you do
> that?' But because of the whole situation beforehand it had got to
> the stage that I could thump someone inside the station. Not that it
> was so terrible, because it happens more often. But I realised that I
> could get into a white-hot rage.
>
> (Inspector, 24 years)

One way of rationalising excessive violence was to translate it into
'normal' behaviour, with which most people are presumed to sym-
pathise:

> If someone gets thumped here then he has earned it because no one
> likes to hit someone. You hear about people getting a thump that is
> not justified but that has not happened when I've been around. We
> have kicked people down the stairs but then it was someone who had
> tried to knife us or who had spat in our faces, and we're not accepting
> that. But I consider that a normal human reaction.
>
> (Constable, 26 years)

Generally, excessive violence by policemen in The Netherlands is
critically highlighted by the press and not condoned by the courts. The
Public Prosecutor in Rotterdam demanded a suspended prison sentence for a constable from Schiedam who twice used unnecessary force
against suspects (*De Telegraaf*, 8 June 1977), while a heavy fine was
also demanded for a State policeman who had accidentally shot a
civilian in the face during a chase (*De Volkskrant*, 22 Sep 1976). In the

Warmoesstraat the alleged excesses of a few years ago seemed to have been ironed out, but there remained at times an aggressive and even provocative stance. Suspects were pushed into chairs, had cigarettes pulled out of their mouths, and were shouted at, while, especially at night, half-drunk and recalcitrant clients were 'shown the door'. One night, for example, a man drove through four red lights and, when he was stopped, the policeman walked towards his car with his hand under the flap of his holster. He came back to the station to lodge a complaint about this and was simply thrown out. One respondent talked of a period when a particular group were known as 'fighters':

> Group F used to have Felix, Tom and Piet. They would come on duty in the evening and six of them would go to the Zeedijk and stroll along pushing people out of the way. If someone didn't get out of their way then Tom would poke two fingers in his eyes because he was a karate man, Felix might kick him in the balls, and Piet would think nothing of breaking his arm – and that's happened in those days. Next morning the cells would be full, say thirty men, and all for 'causing a disturbance'. But by the time the detectives had finished perhaps there was only three suspects over. The rest were let go.
>
> (Constable, 33 years)

This may be exaggerated, but what sounds authentic, given the Warmoesstraat mentality, is the following account by the same policeman (which was probably not the sort of incident likely to happen if I was standing around behind the counter):

> You have Sergeant Jansen as station-sergeant. A useless character. He really talks unnecessarily crude to people at the counter, including ordinary clients. So some half-drunken bloke wanders in in a happy frame of mind and asks the way. The sergeant makes some facetious remark and a couple of coppers laugh at the sergeant's humour. The man at the counter mumbles on about not being helped or something so the sergeant starts shouting at him to piss off. By now the man refuses to piss off and starts to get aggressive. So the coppers feel that they can join in, encouraged by the sergeant, and also start abusing the fellow and laughing at him. The sergeant orders the man to get out but he refuses, so he shouts, 'Lock him up for trespassing', and two constables jump over the counter and grab him. The man resists so with a kick and a thump and a push he's rushed through the door to the cells, banging his head on the glass on

the way through to make a nice star in the glass, his clothes are pulled off to search him, and he's thrown in a cell. If I see the charge-sheet I think, 'this looks a bit suspicious', and the more I talk to the suspect the more sympathy I get with him. But there's a charge-sheet with signatures on it and you can't tear it up.

(Constable, 33 years)

It could well be that gross violence has been damped down by pressure from above, by press scrutiny, and by the removal of notorious 'fighters', and that this sort of semi-conscious verbal aggression leading to 'justifiable' physical violence has taken its place.

It is perhaps also the case that people were inclined to complain against the men of the Warmoesstraat because they felt their case might be strengthened by the station's reputation. At a meeting in 'De Brakke Grond' theatre in 1972, Surinamers were advised to complain against the police in the Warmoesstraat whenever they were arrested in the hope of influencing their cases (F. Bovenkerk, personal communication). People in the area were said to know when individual policemen have their duty and they waited until they were off-duty to put in a complaint. Prostitutes sometimes complained that they had been sexually assaulted in the cells – so that now some policemen refuse to attend to a prostitute in a cell on their own on the grounds that it was necessary to have a colleague to support any disclaimer against an accusation of improper behaviour – and suspects also alleged that money has been stolen from them (*Elseviers Magazine*, 21 Feb 1976). My feeling was that stealing from a suspect inside the station was quite difficult, compared to on the street, because searching was done more or less under the scrutiny of others. The routine of counting suspects' money to the last cent gives a sense of scrupulous attention to property as well as covering the men concerned in searching from accusations of theft. But recently a policeman from the Warmoesstraat received a fine, a suspended prison sentence and was dismissed from the force for trying to steal 200 guilders from a suspect while he was being searched in the station (*De Telegraaf*, 25 Mar 1977).

Such publicity, along with the corruption cases (which at the time of writing have not yet come to court), have revealed a criminal element within the Amsterdam Police. Reports on the American police over the years have traditionally exposed glaring evidence of gross brutality, widespread incompetence, in-built illegal practices, deeply engrained corruption and the insidious hold of political graft (Sherman, 1974; Dodd, 1967). This picture is doubtless true of only certain departments, and yet it serves to abase the police in the eyes of the public and to demean his own work in the policeman's eyes. Rubinstein writes persuasively of the negative effects of malpractice among policemen in Philadelphia:

> The patrolman is obliged to violate the law, degrade people, lie, and even shame himself in his own eyes in order to make arrests he knows are meaningless and he suspects produce money for others. This not only tends to make him cynical about the law and the motives of many people he knows, it also makes him think of himself as a special kind of fool. . . . The real cost is the degradation of the job, the destruction of morale, the erosion of discipline and supervision, and the breakdown of clear standards of what constitutes 'good work' which allows some policemen to become criminals in every sense of the word. (1973, p. 401)

Rubinstein goes on to mention policemen who run businesses when they are supposed to be on duty, who have become drug-addicts in the course of their work, who rob drunks, and who routinely collect pay-offs. Such routinised deviance was simply not evident in the Warmoesstraat, at least in relation to the uniformed branch. The policemen always paid for cigarettes, meals and sandwiches when I was with them. Several cafés and Chinese restaurants in the area, which were heavily patronised by policemen, gave reductions and some bars offered free drinks or drinks 'on account' to well-known patrolmen (officially all bars in the area are out of bounds). Some men, however were extremely wary of the Chinese because they would tuck parking tickets into the take-away parcels, take a token price for the meal, and then expect the tickets to be cancelled. Generally the men with whom I worked were wary of attempts at corruption and distanced themselves from it. I never once heard, for example, of patrolmen taking money for not giving traffic tickets (even though they could accept payment of a fine on the street – provided they had a receipt book in their possession – so that money did pass hands between policemen and the public outside the station). Profiting from illegal sources of income arising from police work did not appear to be a widespread part of their working culture.

One also heard occasionally of men coming to work smelling of alcohol or of driving off-duty while under the influence of alcohol. But the general opinion was that it was foolish to jeopardise a secure job and there was very little consumption of alcohol on duty. When offered a drink the patrolman would often refuse, with an excuse that they had to go to an urgent call or report back to the station, or just accept one beer. The 'easing' practices reported by Cain (1973, pp. 58–62) and by Manning (1977, pp. 151 ff.) were not apparent in the Warmoesstraat, partly because the policemen would spend a considerable amount of time inside the station (Holdaway, 1977a, pp. 125–6, also argues that easing has moved inside), and also because of the nature of the area which was not always receptive to the police. There was, however, one occasion on a wind-swept dreary night when two patrolmen asked me if I wanted a coffee. We then entered a tiny cubicle of a projectionist in a pornographic cinema and gratefully drank scalding coffee while watching a man on a crowded bus, speeding down a German motor-way, ejaculate over his girlfriend's face. Such moments were, alas, rare.

In practice, I would say that my Amsterdam policemen generally behaved tolerably well in the light of what we know of some American and British forces (Reiss, 1968). I do not believe, for instance, that many policemen in the Warmoesstraat were taking the law into their own hands. The opportunities for doing so were much more limited for beat-men than for detectives but, apart from that, sadistic violence, corruption, planting of evidence and gross racial prejudice did not appear to be the norm. Certainly, people were kicked and slapped, and were intimidated by the display of firearms, but systematic beatings or collective violence were not observed in six months' full-time observation. Nor did there appear to be a highly developed informal culture of 'easing' or of deviant-criminal activities among the uniformed men. Nevertheless, there are numerous complaints of unnecessary force, crude language and discrimination against the Warmoesstraat, and it remains the most notorious and newsworthy station in The Netherlands. This undoubtedly plays a role in the occupational identity of the patrolmen who work in a colourful, deviant community which also promises elements of danger and excitement. These themes will be explored in more detail in the following chapters where the interaction on the streets, the involvement in assistances, and the handling of crime in the city-centre enable us to view the predicaments and dilemmas facing the policemen of the Warmoesstraat in daily police practice.

4 On Becoming a Policeman in the Warmoesstraat

(i) GAINING EMOTIONAL DISTANCE

Controlling and manipulating encounters with citizens is the staple of police work. And the inner city of Amsterdam probably provides a wider range of people than most cities because it contains many nationalities and the full spectrum of social class from respectable upper professionals to criminal outlaws and social outcasts. Our interest in this chapter is focused on how the often young and inexperienced policemen of the Warmoesstraat learned to cope with their occupational world. The earlier discussion analysed the occupational culture and portrayed the atmosphere in the Warmoesstraat, and in the next three chapters those themes will be related to concrete situations and to how the policemen perceived those situations. In particular, it is hoped to uncover what the policemen themselves consider important in terms of handling people, how they learn to control themselves and to gain control of precarious social engagements, and the significance of these micro-encounters for a broader analysis of the dilemmas of police work in the centre of Amsterdam.

In analysing occupational socialisation in the Warmoesstraat, I view police work simply as *work*. That means that to a certain extent a policeman's performance can be seen as a reflection of his work milieu and of definitions by significant others who set levels and standards, who enforce the definition of mistakes, and who are able to construct the 'social reality' of work (Manning, 1977, pp. 13 ff). For example, Holdaway (1977a, pp. 129–31) has written of the 'economy of arrest' whereby British policemen patterned arrests to bring themselves financial benefits and Rubinstein (1973, p. 168) also mentions how patrolmen in Philadelphia could postpone an interaction to benefit themselves:

A patrolman sat in a car one evening pondering whether he should take a corner [the haunt of a gang of youths]. 'Tomorrow night we lock them up. Yup', he said, looking at his pocket shift calendar, 'that will give us four hours' overtime.'

One day in Amsterdam we were called to a car that was blocking someone's exit from a parking area:

The citizen began to complain about all the illegally parked cars in the district and pointed to a row of cars in a 'no waiting' zone. 'Just look at that', he said. 'That's just where I don't want to look', replied the constable. Together we bumped the offending car out of the way. The new constable said to Jan, 'Are we still going to put a ticket on it?' and Jan replied, 'You bet we are. Do you think that now we're here we are going away without doing anything. Besides, that's really asking for it, parking in the middle of an exit.'

(Field notes)

This brief interaction can only be understood in relation to the hopeless parking problem in Amsterdam (*De Telegraaf*, 23 Mar 1976), the selective inattention of the patrolmen to faulty parking, the irritation at having a member of the public endeavour to define work for them, the sense of reasonableness in judging tolerance limits for widespread traffic offences, the policemen's resentment at being involved in traffic duties at all, and the feeling that, having exerted themselves, they should complete the encounter with a ticket. This simple incident was guided by a number of particularistic and universal norms which guided the policemen in selecting and approaching work and which they swiftly internalised.

The policeman must learn, largely through trial and error, to handle people and also to handle himself. He has to develop a feeling for appropriate behaviour towards superiors, colleagues, and different types of public and also when to enforce the law, to exercise discretion, to turn a blind eye, to turn his back, to hit and to shoot. For instance, an important role was played in the occupational socialisation of policemen in the Warmoesstraat by the verbally transmitted folklore of the station and the 'war stories' of the older hands. At a slack moment, around four or five in the morning, a sergeant might ask one of the constables to make coffee and someone would start recounting horrible accident or decomposing bodies stories. Usually the sergeants, with their longer service, could cap any grisly yarn and would warm to the subject – usually over their sandwiches – of maggots, smells, messy suicides and bodies half eaten by animals. This usually led to the theme of 'the good old days' when policemen were policemen and villains were villains. One heard of legendary policemen possessed of almost mythical qualities – be it huge size, immense strength, utter crudity, or total insensitivity – the like of whom no longer existed and whose passing left the field open for young, colourless whipper-snappers who could never emulate their feats. The men listened with respectful interest about the days when justice may have been rough and heavy-handed but at least people showed *respect* for the police. With such folklore and nostalgic myth the policeman's culture was transmitted from one generation to another and in this manner the fag-end of many a dreary night-shift was made tolerable.

But, more importantly, this lore confirms images of good police work and implicitly prepares the constable for unforseen circumstances. For the training does not adequately prepare for the initial immersion in patrolwork with its anxieties and new responsibilities in real, rather than simulated, situations:

My first station was in the Linnaeusstraat. The experience was overwhelming and really shook me. I kept a notebook of my experiences during the day and all the cases just shattered me – a fire, an accident, a break-in, an abandoned baby, and in the very first week a delivery of a baby to a girl somewhere in the back of an attic four floors up. And my mate said, 'You stay here and I'll fetch a doctor!' And I wrote all this up in the evenings and I found it shattering, the action, the activity, and I had a bit of trouble sorting it all out at first.

(Constable, 33 years)

One experienced respondent explained that he had learned to distance himself from situations encountered at work in order to preserve his emotional balance:

[Can you shake off the things that happen at work when you get home?]
Yes, I shake them off, certainly, because I sleep very easily. You must learn to separate your personal feelings from your work as a policeman. We really experience a lot of ugliness here – deaths, suicide, theft, robberies, vandalism, and lots of other nasty things which make life disagreeable – but if you start to take all that personally then you'll soon be away from the Warmoesstraat and

sitting in the Valerius Clinic [Mental Hospital]. But I don't think about it when I go home. Then I drink a glass of wine or a gin with my wife. But that's not the same as saying that I'm insensitive to it, not at all. Because as a policeman you musn't become mentally insensitive. You have to be human, that's incredibly important, and you have to stay human towards your family which for me is my wife and my cat because I haven't got kids. It's not the case, for instance, that if I see a junkie lying dead in an hotel room, that the thought doesn't pass through my mind, 'Jesus, that's a young fellow with all his life before him and now suddenly it's been broken off by that rotten stuff'. You see, a civilian who experiences that will talk about it for weeks but during my time on motor-bikes I must have attended forty or fifty fatal accidents. One night duty three young blokes flew out of a bend at nearly 200 kilometres an hour and the car rolled over and hit a lorry and trailer. There were brains all over the street and their limbs had been ripped off their bodies. When you see that a lot goes on in your head. At the same time, I set it aside as quickly as possible because if you keep thinking about it then you'll never have a good night's rest again and you'll be waking up with clammy hands, thinking you can see limbs lying around you. That's not for me. So you begin to protect yourself mentally as a policeman but you learn that with experience.

(Sergeant, 36 years)

The policeman often becomes involved in emotionally charged encounters with citizens, which are perhaps uniquely stressful for the participants, but which he accepts as normal events and as everyday occurrences, and he must learn to protect himself by distancing himself from unpleasant scenes or by developing a somewhat callous or cynical viewpoint (Manning, 1977, p. 236). Once I went to a suicide where a young man had hanged himself in front of his girl-friend's door following an argument; one constable said, 'Shall I stay by the body', and the other replied, 'Why, it's not going to walk away, is it?' Nevertheless, specific events could still have the impact to disturb a policeman, and this was said to be particularly true of accidents involving children:

My second fatality was a little kid of two or three. He ran out of some woods into the path of a moped and the boy on it couldn't do a thing. But that little lad lay on the cycle path with his brains next to his head. You give the ambulance an escort and drive like a madman through the town. You hang around the hospital and after half an hour you get to hear that the kid is dead. That's something you never forget. You can't eat for a day or two and you take about a week to talk it out of your system. Sometimes you go to a bar after a knifing and there's a body lying in a pool of blood. But that little kid affects you much more because it has nothing to do with crime. But with someone who has been stabbed in a bar you say, 'He came here on his own account, and that's the risk you take. He shouldn't have gone there.'

(Constable, 28 years)

In another incident a constable received an urgent call to go to a knifing. On arrival he discovered that two young boys had been watching *Ivanhoe* on the television, that they had begun to play with two swords which one of their fathers had brought back from his time in the East Indies, and that by accident one boy was fatally wounded:

And then you get the aftermath. I had to fetch the mother because she worked in a shop. In fact we were going to tell her at the station but she wanted to know in the car and the detective with me let the cat out of the bag. She threw herself around my neck and I had to stop the car. That really shakes you up. After that I had to get the father – we didn't have so many cars in those days and you did almost everything with one car – and I told him too but he stayed calm until he saw the mother and then five coppers were needed to calm him down. Then I took a brother-in-law and a sister to the hospital to identify the lad in his ice-box. After that I reported to the duty-sergeant and I was completely shattered. I started to cry, and I did the same at home, and I'm not the soft-centred or kind-hearted type, but if I think of it now then the tears come to my eyes because it was a kid involved. I've been to loads of shootings and knifings but they concern people who've asked for it whereas this was just a young kid.

(Sergeant, 36 years)

New and inexperienced constables had to feel their way into their new roles, and strike the right emotional balance, and many of the respondents reported initial difficulties in handling people and in finding the right words or the appropriate display of confidence. An experienced mentor told a new boy, 'When you are in uniform and you step out of the car then the person who gets out has to exude a self-confident impression and civilians should think, "Now something is going to happen"' (Hopmans and van de Scheur, 1975, p. 19). But that self-confidence is not achieved instantaneously:

[What was the first experience on the street like?]
That was really strange. I can still remember exactly my first ticket. It was for a car which had parked a little bit on the kerb. I thought, 'Hallo, that's for me', but I was incredibly nervous, my hands were sweating. But after that it went more easily.

(Sergeant, 36 years)

Several men recalled that it was dealing with their very first case which was the most nerve-racking:

[What was it like alone on the street for the first time?]
It's exactly the same as when you've passed your driving test and go for a drive on your own for the first time. I was a bit nervous but I didn't have any trouble. My first ticket was for someone who cycled without lights. But it felt so unnatural, I was very nervous, and stood shaking in my shoes. I was glad when it was over. I had the same feeling when I sat downstairs for the first time as duty-sergeant and had to send the lads out on duty.

(Sergeant, 28 years)

These initial confrontations reveal that, while intensive anticipatory socialisation had taken place in training, there was nothing quite like the real thing and that the role of law-enforcer, with its overtones of gravity and propriety, has to be learned in encounters on the streets:

You went out with the idea you had learned a lot and that you knew everything. I thought, 'I'll nick the first thing that comes along'. And along came someone on a bike riding on the wrong side of the street, but he was a real cocky Amsterdammer. I knew what I was supposed to say but suddenly had a big lump in my throat. But you have to learn that with practice. I'd say that half of what you'd learned in training was forgotten within a month or you couldn't use it or you didn't need it, or very little happens related to it in this area.

(Constable, 26 years)

There was an enormous discrepancy between officers and sergeants on the one hand and constables on the other hand as to how long that learning process should take, with the former speaking of a matter of years and the latter talking in terms of months. This selective perception arises partly from the fact that a sergeant has had, say, twelve or fifteen years' experience and is conscious of how long it took before he felt secure in the role of patrolman and before he appreciated fully all there was to learn.

I got the impression, however, that the average young constable tended to have a somewhat inflated conception of his ability to master the work. This could simply have been the surface bravado of insecure young men, self-consciously feeling their new power and presenting a confident face to older colleagues, or else it was simply that a young policeman is so busy learning and assimilating that he just does not perceive the lengthy and complex apprenticeship ahead. A twenty-year-old constable, who had only been six months in the station, expressed this myopic confidence:

I don't think a mentor is really necessary here in the Warmoesstraat. If you're a bit independent, and I think I am, then you don't need anyone. You keep an eye out for yourself to see what's up for grabs. If you rely on the old hands who are dyed in their ways then you can get a one-sided picture. You have to see for yourself what happens. You can learn from experienced people and you can also learn a lot from your own experiences. If I need something for a charge-sheet then I look it up in the book or find it out. Maybe when you're new and you come to an accident then you watch what the other bloke does and what he writes up in his book. But you become independent incredibly quickly. It goes pretty quickly. I'd say it takes around three months to settle in.

(Constable, 20 years)

This contrasts strongly with an experienced sergeant's perception:

[How long does it take before a constable is sure of himself on the street?]
That depends very much on the individual; one man needs six years and the other twelve years. But if a constable is well intentioned and likes his work and spends a lot of time on the street, then you can say around four years.

[How many people in your group have spent four years on the street?]

Not one. They really have insufficient experience.

(Sergeant, 36 years; my emphasis)

Indeed, an inspector added a proviso that the learning experience was accelerated in the Warmoesstraat, because of its varied and high work-load, so that elsewhere the learning was likely to be even more prolonged:

> [How long does it take for a constable to become a good policeman?] At least five years but that depends on where he does his duty and what his attitude is. We have the advantage in the Warmoesstraat that we get the more successful people because it's a difficult district. And we get the people who come out on top after the training and the training sub-station. I can imagine that three years intensive beat work, with good supervision, in the Warmoesstraat is worth as much as five years in District 6 [West]. (Inspector, 50 years)

It is extremely difficult to assess accurately the divergences of opinion about the length of the learning process which are clearly related to perceptions of the decline of the police craft. On the one hand the length of time spent on uniformed patrol work in the Warmoesstraat has definitely declined, and yet the amount of work done and the range of experiences available now can mean that a constable matures more rapidly in police terms and that the dissatisfaction with young policemen arises from externals such as appearance and discipline. It could simply be that older hands do not recognise that police work has changed and that the stable, patient, long-serving and accomplished beat-man has disappeared (if he ever genuinely existed). In early 1975 two young policemen joined the group (one was just twenty years old and he became the youngest constable in the station). Just over two years later there is only one other constable with more experience than them in the group and they are themselves 'mentors' for new boys. The twenty-two-year-old now behaves with all the ritualised cynicism and panache of a veteran. In fact, the uniformed personnel in the Warmoesstraat replaces itself within three years and as the new, young police patrol the area, wags call out, 'Heh, does your mother know you are working around here?' (*De Telegraaf*, 16 Apr 1977). Elsewhere there is talk of increasing stress among policemen (*De Telegraaf*, 23 Mar 1976, reported that the Hague Police were going to research the stress factor and some American policemen speak of 'battle-fatigue' symptoms: Punch, 1976a, p. 33), and it could be that young policemen engaged in an accelerated learning cycle find it more difficult to accommodate to fear, violence and suffering than was the case with the more leisurely moral and emotional career in earlier periods. Some of the verbal and physical aggression, which is held to be the hall-mark of the Warmoesstraat, could arise from such inner tension and frustration. But as Manning (1977, p. 261) states, policemen claim to have seen 'everything' and it is not easy to get them to talk about fear and insecurity.

(ii) LEARNING TO EMPLOY SUSPICION AND VIOLENCE

As well as having to learn a degree of emotional distance and perhaps a measure of cynicism, the policeman is said to acquire an in-built suspiciousness (Sacks, 1972; Skolnick, 1975, p. 45, reproduces part of a field manual which lists behaviour that should arouse a policeman's suspicion). This is generally held to be one of the main planks in his occupational ideology and working personality; 'the working environment of the police is not only charged with emotion and suspicion, it is often, in the eyes of the police, hostile and unco-operative' (J. Wilson, 1968, p. 27). He also has to learn to anticipate danger and to respond with violence under appropriate circumstances. The best discussion of the norms of secrecy surrounding the use of police violence is undoubtedly Westley (1970), while Rubinstein (1973) gives a graphic account of the instruments of violence used by contemporary American policemen. Both recount relatively extreme situations compared to the Warmoesstraat, although some of their insights sound as if they would have almost universal validity irrespective of local and cultural differences (such as Rubinstein's important perception of how the urban policeman approaches and views 'symbolic assailants'). Earlier, however, we saw that the Warmoesstraat had, by Dutch standards, a tarnished reputation for crude violence. Here attention will be turned on the common-sense assumptions which mediated norms surrounding, and the use of, violence in the Warmoesstraat.

   I intend to relate this theme from the previously reviewed academic literature, highlighting suspicion and violence, to the manner in which the policemen in the Warmoesstraat developed styles for approaching people and under what circumstances and with what considerations they learned to employ violence against them. For it is argued that the policeman's ideology is geared to potential violence and aggression so that he unwittingly brings with him a persona and attitude which make interaction with the public stressful and conducive to a mutually reinforcing cycle of aggression and counter-aggression. There is doubtless an element of truth in this, but in a way the interaction is more complicated than that because the policeman comes to the situation armed with not inconsiderable legal powers, with socially sanctioned weapons, and with an array of techniques designed both to allay violence and yet to anticipate it. The contradiction in his behaviour is based on two principal dilemmas. Firstly, that the policeman enjoys extensive legal powers to interfere with other people's liberty but that he is restricted from fully employing these by common sense, occupational norms, and community notions of justice and reasonable behaviour. And secondly, as we have seen, his work is largely peaceful, unproblematic and routine; yet he protects himself against the unexpected by carrying a built-in mental reservation that to treat situations as routine is to fall into a false sense of security and to disarm himself for the day when the routine explodes into the unanticipated and the dangerous.

Furthermore, as Rubinstein (1973, p. 267) has so vividly depicted, the policeman's principal tool is his body and this can cause him to adopt unconsciously certain physical poses and to be alert to certain body cues which may affront a citizen. Some element of tension, if only mild embarrassment, probably attends most interaction with the public: 'You can always *arouse* a sense of guilt, especially in a respectable man. Almost everyone feels guilty about *something*. And you can work on that' (MacInnes, 1969b, p. 547). This will be especially true of police-initiated activity and of behaviour related to control functions (Rubinstein, 1973, p. 269). The simple power of being able to watch people, to scrutinise them covertly or stare at them openly, contains an implicit violation of the unwritten rights of others in our society. MacInnes (1969b, p. 494) writes: 'And then, all coppers *stare*. Nobody else in England, except kids and coppers, *stare*.'

In the course of his work the policeman becomes suspicious about known individuals, types of people, specific buildings, means of concealing weapons, and so on, which he brings to interaction with people in general. If, for instance, he is warned about a stolen Volkswagen Variant seen in the area he may look out for all Variants even when they have a different colour and a different registration number than that originally given. Wambaugh's (1974, p. 186) reconstruction of the murder of a policeman in Los Angeles includes the apprehension of one of the suspects by two patrolmen who checked his stolen Plymouth although he had changed the number plates. He may pay especial attention to behavioural cues from the occupants of the car: is the car being driven normally, do the occupants seem conscious of police scrutiny, and so on. A description of a suspect wearing a certain coat or hat may cause him to stop and search all people with a similar coat or a similar hat (Rubinstein, 1973, p. 290). If colour is mentioned then any Black person in the vicinity of the incident can become a legitimate suspect because colour is one of the few factors that policemen take seriously (they consider most eye-witness accounts or descriptions useless). When called to a break-in, *anyone* in the immediate vicinity may be considered a suspect. The patrolman is also scanning people for furtive glances and unwitting signals of guilt. Laurie described a plain-clothes patrol in London:

> It seemed to me that we were very conspicuous: two large young men walking slowly, looking keenly about them, going nowhere. I put this to my companion. 'That's part of the point: you stand out as law, but the only people who notice are the villains. You watch their eyes because they are watching for you. I can smell them, I feel them in the pit of my stomach.' After a few days' practice, I saw what he meant: the ordinary pedestrian becomes almost invisible, but those who were up to no good flashed their uncontrollable code of fear to us. They were too alert. However hard they tried to suppress it, their anxiety to spot us made them glow as if they were outlined in neon. (1972, p.151)

The implication is that the policeman's own transmission of body cues and sensitivity to body cues is reflected among 'police-wise' criminal elements but that they may be considered inappropriate by ordinary civilians and conducive to emotionally charged interaction (Sykes and Clark, 1974). For example, although a policeman seldom becomes involved in fights, he tends to sum up carefully the physical assets of all the men he approaches (Rubinstein, 1973, p. 272), monitors a scene momentarily before entering it, adopts a self-protecting stance (right hand free to reach for his stick, body at an angle to avoid a kick in the groin), manoeuvres himself into bars and houses with an eye to keeping an exit clear, and is alert to signs that an opponent may be carrying a weapon. Even when he is not specifically warned about the possibility of armed suspects he may be running his eyes over someone for hints of concealed weapons – a bulge in a pocket, a heavy plastic bag, a stilted gait, and so on. Some men look first at a suspect's hands to see if they bear signs of karate exercises so that they can be prepared for a sudden karate blow or kick. And not surprisingly, he looks for signs of sudden movement (Rubinstein, 1973, p. 247).

Policemen use and are faced with violence far less than their popular stereotypes suggest (Cain, 1973, reports observing only one physical attack in twenty weeks of field-work). Most of the men I met had never fired in anger and could count on one hand the number of times they had used their truncheon. Few of them had ever been wounded on duty or been in serious difficulties. They admitted mistakes easily and were not particularly embarrassed about having been hit. At times they almost seem suprised by their involvement in suddenly threatening situations, as if all the mental preparation for them still foundered on a sort of disbelief that it was happening to them:

[How often have you used your truncheon?]
Very little, perhaps three times, because I always try to sort it out first with my hands *or my feet, then I kick out fairly quickly.*

[Have you been in close situations?]
Not much. I've got practically no experience and perhaps in all these years [five] I've had to fight four times. There were times when I didn't expect it. Once on a Saturday morning, it was fabulous weather, you stroll nicely along and the next minute you are fighting. There was a Black sleeping in a car in the Geldersekade and I woke him up and asked him if the car was his. No, it was not his. So I said, 'Well, you'd better get out then if it's not yours'. But he wouldn't get out so we pulled him out and he began shouting. So we said, 'Shut your mouth otherwise you'll get a ticket for sleeping in a public thoroughfare'. Although that wasn't our intention at all. Then we decided we'd have to take him to the station but he resisted with all his might so there we were, fighting in the Geldersekade. We got help with a van and three or four men although in the meantime we got him under control but he was punching and kicking. We were covered in mud because it was near roadworks, the road wasn't surfaced, and the mud was as slippery as ice. A year before that there was a young bloke, I think from Groningen, who was urinating in a doorway. It was also Saturday morning and also nice weather funnily enough. We said, 'Heh, is that necessary? Pissing in a doorway? Then it goes down into the people's basement'. But he began with 'Shag off', etc. So we said, 'Right, now you're getting a ticket'. 'Och', he said, 'Drop dead', and took up a karate stance and said 'Let's see if you can take me'. He was still half-drunk from the night before, a

young troublemaker. But always stupid things like that.

(Constable, 26 years; my emphasis)

The use of feet and kicking, as mentioned by this respondent, was often considered advisable in order to avoid injury to one's hands.

Violence and physical prowess were not conspicuous topics of conversation in the canteen and ability to fight was rarely mentioned; willingness to fight when necessary, and especially in mutual support situations, was, however, a pivotal tenet of the patrolman's unwritten code. Rubinstein (1973, p. 301) echoes this view:

His success is measured by his capability in controlling people, but his failure is not measured simply by defeat – although defeat is always humiliating – but by errors, failures to act when necessary, and an unwillingness to take the calculated risk everyone who uses his body as a tool must finally accept as a way of life.

Moreover, there were well-defined rules for the regulation of violence and the use of weapons. In theory, bare hands should not be used to strike people but the truncheon must be employed and a written report detailing its use must be submitted after the event. Once there was a call to a fight in a café and Paul, a new man, pulled out his truncheon and went in first; Hans, the old hand, shouted, 'Put that thing away or we'll have to write a report!' In effect, the number of times a policeman has to use a truncheon may bear little relation to the number of times he has been in fights; some men are contemptuous of the short rubber truncheon, some are too lazy to write reports, some consider the drawing of a stick counter-productive, and some only use it when it is really necessary (reporting the use of a truncheon is generally automatic as it anticipates any comeback or complaint by a suspect or enquiry by a senior officer). Several men in the Warmoesstraat had purchased longer, heavier models than the regulation issue:

[How often have you used your truncheon?]
Not so often, about ten times. Mostly I use bare fists, you're not supposed to, but it's a human reaction. The truncheon is a worthless thing, it's like liquorice stick. Here in the city-centre a lot of policemen have their own truncheon, more or less illegally. Because if you have a truncheon then a person has to feel it when he gets hit.

(Constable, 29 years)

Rubinstein (1973, p. 290) maintains that in Philadelphia many men go through their career without ever using a weapon and that some men resign the first time they are forced to hit someone with their stick. And if 'headbeaters' and 'headhunters' were relatively rare there, then this is more likely to be true of Amsterdam where control of violence – legally, internally and informally – is more closely practised. Nevertheless, the use of violence and one's own emotional reaction has to be learned in real situations and, in tight corners, guidelines on the use of weapons could fly out of the window:

[Do you keep cool during a fight?]
Yes, I can control myself all right. You do hear about people who see a red flash before their eyes and I said, 'That's not going to happen to me', and it hasn't exactly. When there's a punch-up you stay fairly calm, you grab one of them and keep looking around so that no one can come up and get you from behind. But when I came to Amsterdam there were the forerunners of the Nieuwmarkt [action group] and they had occupied a housing office. A couple of colleagues were molested and there came a call 'colleagues requiring help', so we went there with a brigadier and seven men. And the people simply attacked us, with chair-legs. It was an incredible fight with hard punching, it must have lasted five or ten minutes, and we were simply defending ourselves. You weren't hitting to drive them off but to defend yourself. Then I saw them kick a colleague in the balls and they tried it with me so I just thrashed a couple of them. Before I used to hit on the arms or shoulders, but not on the head. But there I hit them in the middle of the face, and as hard as possible, not because you really intended to hit them but more because you thought 'get them'. That incident was a sort of psychological barrier for me because now if I get real troublemakers and I have to use my stick, then I don't hit them on the arm but right across the face and then one blow is enough. Then I realised that you could still get into a white-hot rage . . . and in certain situations I'm prepared to cause someone considerable pain. I also believe that I could shoot someone if it's necessary. But you have to find out all these things through practical experience.

(Inspector, 24 years)

Furthermore, a sergeant explained to me that seventeen years previously he had entered service as an inexperienced constable and that at a time when police violence was more readily condoned, he had used violence in order not to appear different from his colleagues:

[Were the policemen tougher in those days?]
It's difficult to say but I think there was a certain amount of aggression amongst the police, you know. As a young constable you listened to stories in the locker room. There were always stories with 'Then I put a stripe on him' or 'Then I gave it to him'. That was when we still carried a sabre – I never used mine, great big thing, and I was a bit frightened of it – but there were people around who used it practically every night with, you know, 'We really hacked at him and he was covered in blood'. The civilians we had to contend with weren't exactly sweetness and light but still the stories were told with a certain pleasure. . . . On another occasion we arrested two young blokes who were involved in a break-in. We went up on to a roof with drawn pistols and arrested them. Good, there we are before the counter. I can remember the other policeman, an older man, and I had perhaps only six months' duty. So I keep my eyes on the old copper and think what he does must be right. The sergeant asks one of the suspects his name. The suspect says nothing. We'd learned in training that a suspect is not obliged to answer so I thought, 'That's the end of that'. Then the older policeman gives the suspect a thick ear, before the counter, with the suspect handcuffed. You see it happening before you, heh. Asked for his name again. The man still says nothing. So I feel that I have to give him a clip on the other ear. And afterwards you realise that you've done the wrong thing by hitting a suspect who is not obliged to answer. And it goes to show how important, incredibly important, it is who you first go out on the street with.

(Sergeant, 36 years)

For a number of reasons, I gained the impression that such arbitrary violence was less common and less condoned informally now in the Warmoesstraat than previously. But the use of violence by a colleague was generally seen simply as one of many personal characteristics, and a negative opinion on his use of violence did not in any sense prevent him being fully accepted as a colleague:

[Some constables say that they've only used their truncheons a couple of times.]
There are some who use them more often. That's because of the way they go about things. They provoke a certain aggression and then

they're forced to use their stick. They can't do anything about it, that's just their way of approaching things. They are excellent colleagues but you notice some strange things. I've got my eye particularly on one of them at the moment. But they don't get any guidance from the brigadier and they don't hear anything if they go too far. But the hitting that goes on in this area is nearly always justified.

(Constable, 32 years)

In addition, the men themselves learned to judge situations and soon developed a sober attitude to disturbances which they could not handle. There tended to be a negative stereotype of colleagues who rushed in unthinkingly to situations because they could hurt themselves and involve others unnecessarily in danger. Also there was an obvious risk that a group of fighting people would turn on the police and most patrolmen deliberately sought to avoid this:

[What do you do when there is fighting?]
I never threaten them like saying 'You'd better piss off', because then they can explode against you, and I don't fancy that. If there are a lot of them fighting then you jump in between them and it usually works out all right. I think the uniform does make some impression on most people.

[Is there a lot of aggression against the police?]
Not so much in a fight but more with an arrest. There's a good chance that passers-by will come straight away to help the man out. That happens a lot. Last year at Christmas we nicked a drunken driver and were going to take him along to the station. A car comes along with three big blokes in and when they see us they jump out of the car and immediately start to attack us, 'Let the man go, it's Christmas!'

(Marechaussee, 27 years)

In general, there was a feeling that violence had changed in the area and that knives and guns had taken over from fists (cf. Rubinstein, 1973, p. 324). For example, an experienced constable maintained that mass violence in the area had actually decreased over the years but that the element of danger had increased:

The biggest difference between 1958 and 1975 is that there used to

be far more punch-ups in those days. Suddenly an enormous fight
would break out, sometimes several times in one evening, and it just
seemed to happen spontaneously. Perhaps you had as many as two
hundred people involved. You just don't see that any more, now it's
always these tiny little affairs. But at the same time there was
normally never any weapons used; then there was hardly ever a
knife or a pistol used. It was always bare knuckles and almost never
with a weapon. It happened mostly along the Nieuwendijk or the
Zeedijk. Then we went with everyone available, eight or ten men,
and rushed out the door. You'd have a whole group of policemen
with drawn sabres running down the street. The people disappeared
down alleyways and you really didn't need to do very much. It was
scarcely necessary to hand out a good thump. The people ran in
every direction and within a couple of seconds they disappeared as
soon as they saw us coming. Then you had the whole Nieuwendijk
cleared. There was not a soul to be seen.

(Constable, 50 years)

Another man explained that violence in Amsterdam was highlighted
negatively by the press whereas in a smaller town where he had worked
the authorities condoned the use of violence by the police. This could
mean that relatively less violence in Amsterdam received more attention than elsewhere and that this publicity acted to a certain extent as a
brake on excesses.

In The Netherlands wooden sticks (like the night sticks in America
or the truncheons in Britain) are never used, longer sticks are used only
in riots, and devices such as the black-jack and lead-loaded sap gloves
(see Rubinstein, 1973, pp. 281 ff.) are forbidden. There is not a great
deal of emphasis on close-combat in initial training and after that no
training at all. Sport is compulsory until the early thirties but contains
no self-defence techniques and is devoted to general fitness. Generally
the younger constables were or had been keen on sport; and a small
minority in the Warmoesstraat were fanatical karate students. But
there is a world of difference anyway between training and street-
fighting, where the 'Queensberry' rules do not operate:

The first week I was on duty we arrested a bloke in the Nieuwendijk.
We had to drag him all the way to the station because he resisted and
we didn't have any portable radios then to ask for help. On the way
we kept being attacked by his friends but we fought them off, it was a
hell of a long trail, but they kept coming back at us. Just before the

station they seemed to give up. Then someone called me and I looked around and someone straightaway punched me on the chin [the wound required six stitches]. It was an enormous great bloke so I kicked him on the knee and whipped out my truncheon. He shouted, 'No, that's not fair, that's mean'. Yet the yob had a special ring on for fighting! My colleague came back to help and we included the yob in as well.

(Constable, 29 years)

But throughout my research period I witnessed remarkably little violence (though frequently the consequences of violence). In six months there were precisely three occasions when unnecessary force was used by patrolmen and on only two occasions were policemen assaulted. It should be added that there were countless encounters replete with the threat of violence, but normally the policemen were able to control these situations. One evening, for example, Hans seemed nervous and wound-up, having just returned to duty after an illness:

We were patrolling in plain clothes when about twenty-five yards from the station a Black asked me if I wanted to buy hash. I got him talking in English and he pulled out a piece of hashish. Hans came back and handled him brusquely, pushing him up against a wall, and searching him at pistol-point. When the Black protested he received a smack across the face with the hand holding the pistol although I could not see if the pistol had been used to strike the man or just the hand. The suspect was taken to the station but did not have enough hash – it was in any case fake – to justify detention and was released. Inside the station the suspect was handled routinely. On returning outside there was another Black standing on the same corner, where the first suspect had been detained, and he was talking to a White man who rapidly walked away when we approached. Brusquely the Black was pushed into the doorway and searched. He protested and demanded that the policemen identify themselves. Hans pressed the barrel of his pistol against the man's temple and said, 'Is this enough identification?' Inside the station Hans was continually aggressive and threatening to the suspect, who lost his temper. He claimed to be an American on holiday: someone said, 'Welcome to Amsterdam'. Hans threatened to take him downstairs to the cellar so that they could fight it out but the sergeant, who was watching, told him to take it easy. The suspect was shaken up and had blood on his lip but had not really received any hard blows: it was an unedifying scene of pushing and squabbling. Again there was not sufficient evidence to hold the man and he was released. Frightened that he might complain about Hans's behaviour I chatted in an apologetic manner with the suspect before he left the station.

(Field notes)

I had not interfered with the situation when it occurred, although I felt that it was getting out of hand, because I was unsure what to do or say and waited for someone else to make a move. Afterwards there was mild disapproval about Hans's behaviour, though evidently a reluctance to interfere while the incident was in progress as it was witnessed by three or four other policemen, and he later asked me my opinion. I explained that he seemed worked up and that the aggression in the two incidents had been, in my opinion, unnecessary. He agreed with me. Later we saw the man in the area and Hans asked him to come for a beer but, after first accepting, he went away muttering to himself. On another occasion there was a commotion outside and a woman came into the station with a badly bruised eye claiming almost hysterically that her husband, who was an alcoholic, had just assaulted her in the street. She said that this was the last time she was taking this and was prepared to make a statement.

We set off on foot and caught him up in a side-street. When apprehended he took a swing at one constable but was easily restrained when each constable took an arm. On the way back to the station one constable suddenly hit him on the side of the head. At first I thought this was some form of primitive justice for having struck a woman but, in fact, he had been trying to twist the fingers of both constables. When being searched he suddenly started swearing and smashed his watch on a shelf in a rage. The constable gave him a quick punch on the side of the mouth and crushed him up against the wall saying, 'Do you need another one? Haven't you learned?' Willem turned to me with a smile as if to say, 'It's nothing'. No visible damage was done to the suspect and he explained that he didn't hit him hard and had no intention of hurting him but was just 'calming him down'. The suspect was classed as 'difficult' and to stop *him* getting violent they used a degree of physical intimidation. Faced with a difficult client who was beginning to lose his temper, the two policemen used a small amount of violence neutrally, and almost with the demeanour of an adult admonishing a naughty child.

(Field notes)

Compared to most major American cities, there was relatively little use of firearms by policemen in Amsterdam. They were obliged to shoot at the range or simulator four times a year and use twelve rounds each time. It is nothing like what is required for expert marksmanship. Also the use of firearms was strictly controlled, more so than in other countries. I suspect that illegal use of firearms was rare in Amsterdam as almost every incident that involved shooting by police was attended by close public scrutiny in the press. But accidents and improper use are likely to increase as weapons are increasingly drawn, though not necessarily fired, because the policemen were prepared to take fewer risks as the number of armed criminals in the city-centre allegedly increased. There were times, however, when most danger seemed to come from colleagues; there was a hole in the floor of the Warmoes-straat where a policeman accidentally fired his pistol when de-cocking it, and Henk told me that once he was checking a break-in, when he was still undergoing probationary training, and his nervous mentor nearly shot him in the back by mistake from less than 10 feet! Additionally, the policemen themselves may be in a state of height-ened tension when carrying a weapon or when approaching suspects who may be armed. One man got his career off to a flying start by almost accidentally shooting a suspect:

My very first night duty I nearly shot someone dead. Not intention-ally though! Suddenly there was a call that a man had been seen creeping into a school. My mentor was a constable first-class, fifty-three years old, a really great bloke, and we went into the school to carry out a search. The school had separate toilets, all the toilets were in rows, and you had no idea what you might come across. I saw my mentor pull out his pistol and I did the same. I'm not usually frightened, but if you walk through a dark school at night with a drawn pistol then it's a bit exciting – I mean it's not as if you're sitting at home eating fish and chips. Suddenly I pulled open a toilet door. Nothing. Another door. Again nothing. Then the next door, with your pistol in your hand and your finger on the trigger, and there sat the bloke. I shit myself. I felt a muscle-cramp shoot through my finger and, dammit, if the thing had been cocked then the bloke was a goner. But I jumped out of my skin.

(Inspector, 24 years)

Generally the policemen entered the buildings to trace a break-in with drawn pistols and would undo their holsters if there was may reason to be suspicious when making a car-stop. And, whatever the objective picture, there was no doubt that the policemen perceived themselves as increasingly likely to be assaulted or threatened by a civilian:

> You used to get resisting arrest only sporadically but now everyone knows that enforcement is fairly slack. People brush it off now by saying, 'Och, he'd just had a few beers' or 'Oh, you just stay for questioning and then you can go home'. Often nothing comes of the case or it's let off with a fine. What it comes down to is a policeman gets a smack in the face for 60 guilders. And they say that to you openly, 'I can thump you for six "tientjes" [10 guilders]'. We used to have the sabre and people were really frightened of it. You used it flat, except in riots and then you used the sharp edge, but it is 8 millimetres thick. If you hit someone on the neck with it you couldn't see a thing, not even a scratch. But the regulations over the use of weapons have become much stricter. In those days if you got a thump then you'd earned it and you never heard any more about it.
>
> (Sergeant, 38 years)

With regard to violence, I never felt that the men were typically looking for aggressive outlets. They were prepared for it, they sometimes welcomed it, but they did not go out of their way to initiate it. For instance, one night we were patrolling in the car. The crew were hoping for something interesting and were overjoyed to get the message to attend a fight in order to lend assistance to another patrol-car. But on the way they were diverted to an accident and bemoaned their luck. They radioed the control room, 'We are only available for serious business', and the ironic reply came back, 'Proceed to the Victoria Hotel where a car is blocking an invalid's parking space'. We heard another car being directed to a fight and just heard the whoop of delight from the crew before they were cut off the air. Lending assistance at a fight was considered potentially more interesting than, say, taking down the particulars of minor accidents between two cars (see Holdaway, 1977a, pp. 128–9, on 'the fight'). Often on arrival at a bar fight the actual fighting was over and the policeman's job was merely to settle everyone down, interpret conflicting stories and take statements. Sometimes the miscreants had disappeared, at other times they had already made it up and were the best of friends again, or sometimes the participants were so drunk that a straight blow was never aimed.

The common-sense reality of suspicion and violence as occupational tools were rooted in perception of the inner city and the role of the police in its social life. For example, the feeling that violence in general was becoming 'mean' and that it was more likely to involve weapons played an important role in the Warmoesstraat mentality. Under certain circumstances this could give an edgy, provocative tone to enforcement with perhaps an over-readiness to display firearms, although they were used relatively infrequently. Police-initiated violence was mediated by a feeling of 'just deserts' and of people 'earning it' which could justify provocative behaviour towards some individuals and groups (see below, Chapter 6), and which was shared to a certain extent by people in the area. Above all, the use of violence and suspicion had to be learned and the policeman had to internalise cues signalling danger (J. Wilson, 1968, p. 39) and norms concerning support for colleagues in difficult situations. Peer-group norms played an important role in defining behaviour and, furthermore, a policeman's use of violence and suspicion could depend on the style of the group or shift to which he belonged.

(iii) STYLES OF WORK

Initially, I saw the policemen in 'my' group as being very much alike, but as I got to know them better I began to notice individual styles of working and a variety of adaptations to the work situation. Eventually I knew the biography of each man and could begin to relate it to his specific style. The men themselves spoke of the Warmoesstraat style, of group identities and of personal characteristics, and continually related behaviour on the streets to one or the other of these distinctions. They certainly did not see law-enforcement as based on impersonal and universal norms of conduct but rather as subject to spatial, temporal and individual considerations. It would be an exaggeration to say that there were as many styles as there were policemen, but there was a considerable variety in motivation and behaviour which should make us cautious about generalising unduly concerning police conduct. At the micro-level each encounter has a degree of uniqueness which needs to be appreciated – every participant has a story and makes a claim to be treated differentially – while recognising that the ways to give a ticket for speeding are not limitless. But the policemen's own diagnoses of colleagues' behaviour reveal a good deal about the norms of the informal occupational culture and the appraisal of appropriate behaviour on the part of co-workers.

For example, Hans outlined a period when he worked in the

sub-station of the Warmoesstraat, in the Spaarndammerstraat, and virtually sketched the policeman's ideal work environment. He mentions autonomy, fun, small and cohesive groups, and individual specialisms:

> In the Spaarndammerstraat we had small groups and no boss so we decided for ourselves what we were going to do and it worked like clockwork. You went with pleasure to your work and you were motivated when you went out on the street. We had a great time – we threw buckets of water and drenched each other, smashed windows, and messed around like a bunch of kids, but it was healthy and well meant. The senior constable present was acting duty-sergeant and we had groups of four or five – I can remember going into a night duty in the North with one sergeant and I was the only constable, but that really is irresponsible. Each of us had a specialism. I knew everything about the law on lorries and how long drivers could spend at the wheel. It's a complicated law but I knew it inside out and in my time I made out some beautiful charge-sheets and quite a few of them were for crimes as well. Jan was the expert on mopeds – give him a frame number and he could tell you everything you wanted to know about a moped. Jac was very involved in youth groups and got to know a lot of gangs personally. He even went out of his way, especially with one gang to establish better contact with them. If I came across a gang of youths and there was some difficulty or something I wanted to know then I just called Jac. But for a couple of years now I haven't had that sort of motivation in the Warmoesstraat and I can't say I look forward much to my work.
>
> (Constable, 33 years)

For some of the older policemen the 'fun' had gone out of police work as a high turnover rate broke up group cohesion, as their work became more subject to control from sergeants, and as the new lads neglected a range of specialisms in favour of an undue concentration on drugs and crime.

The shift system meant that my group, the E group, worked closely with the overlapping shifts of the D and F groups. Each group had a highly specific identity although these too changed over time. Group F were said to be 'fighters' and 'shouters', and tended to arrest people for 'causing a disturbance'. In Chatterton's terminology (1976b, p. 119), Group D were 'snatchers' because they had a high arrest rate and especially for drug cases. This group was known as the 'opium' group (from the Opium Act under which most of their cases fell) and I asked the sergeant to explain this nickname:

> The lads just aren't interested any more in traffic. You know what it is? Heroin has become a sort of fever with these blokes. People used to talk about the gold fever but they've got heroin fever. But I must say they bring a lot in; sometimes a kilo or one and a half kilos. You don't see that so much with the other groups. In a way it's not the sergeant who shapes what goes on in the group. I'll tell you this, [constable] van Zelm has influenced them all. It's really like this, a sergeant can say what he likes but today's policeman is an individualist and tries as much as possible to decide for himself what he's going to do on the street. You try to direct them in a certain direction but it more or less has to fit in with their ideas because if it isn't, and you're not standing right behind them, then they just won't do it. But as far as I'm concerned van Zelm has inspired the whole group, and, to a certain extent, decides what goes on and not the sergeant. . . .
>
> (Sergeant, 36 years)

This quote also reveals the extent to which a group could be influenced by one powerful personality and how difficult it was for the sergeants to control what happened on the streets. One sergeant listened to yet another horror story about something that had gone wrong outside and began to shout and gesticulate in mock frustration, yet with a clear hint to his men, saying over and over again, 'I don't want to know what's going on on the streets! Don't tell me! I don't want to know!'

My group were more inclined to be 'negotiators' (Chatterton, 1976b, p. 119) and applauded their own ability to exercise discretion, in contrast to groups which were perceived as unduly aggressive, too 'fanatic', or too anaemic. The men in Group E went in for a wider range of cases – though they had a predilection for '26-ers' (from Article 26 for driving under the influence) – but the group identity disguised considerable individual variation within the group. Herman, for instance, was the joker and was inclined to be loud and coarse. Once we controlled a car at night in a deserted industrial area and a courting couple surfaced; the man said, 'Do you want us to move on?' and Herman replied lasciviously, 'No mate, get nicely stuck in'. A former prostitute who ran a snack-bar said, 'You always know when Herman is on duty. Then there's always something happening in the area. But the way he passes remarks at people and laughs about them! I don't know how he gets by without having his head kicked in.' Herman was never lost for words and was inclined to get involved in escalatory verbal battles:

One day a young drunken man staggered towards a foot patrol with a large wet patch on the front of his light-grey trousers. The patrolmen were conversing with a couple of men and Herman said something in a derogatory fashion to the drunk. The drunk steadied himself and began an escalating round of abuse which started to attract attention as he shouted, 'Do you know what you are? You are a prick, a great big prick'. Herman laughed and replied, 'You're absolutely right, I know it, I'm a prick'. But now the man was into his rhythm and his abuse became more strident, persistent and colourful and he began to abuse Herman's mother, father and his paternity. Still smiling, Herman told the man to move along and that he had said enough. The man continued to bellow. With a fixed smile, indicating role-distance to the bystanders, Herman began to push the man away but now the drunk wanted to fight. After about ten minutes of this the patrolman decided to walk away because otherwise they would have to lock the man up. The drunk ambled after them and when they stopped further up he caught them up, shook Herman's hand, apologised, and said, 'No hard feelings'. Herman laughed it all off but he had almost talked himself into the situation of having to fight with the man and arrest him.

(Field notes)

Bert was young and covered his inexperience with a certain cockiness and conspicuous display of role-distance (Goffman, 1961). He was easy-going and inclined to use discretion whereas Anton, who had started at the same time as Bert, was rigid and somewhat inflexible:

Once Jan had been sitting inside for a couple of hours doing nothing and was desperate to get out. He was sent out in a car with a newcomer, Anton. The three of us stepped outside the station and immediately saw a young man cycling erratically the wrong way down the Warmoesstraat which is a one-way street. Anton stopped him, smelt his breath, and ordered him to leave the bike and walk home. The man refused and Anton threatened to take him inside and book him for being drunk on a bike [under an article normally applied to car-drivers and almost never used for cyclists]. Jan pleaded with Anton to let the man go so that we could get out on patrol. I also added support to Jan's plea. But Anton was adamant

and took the youth inside where the brigadier talked the cyclist into
seeing reason and proceeding by foot.

(Field notes)

Henk was a stable, mature figure who believed in correct behaviour
and showed displeasure when some of the younger men blasphemed.
Johan was the grandfather of the group who had spent nearly twenty
years in the Warmoesstraat. He was huge and ambled sedately around
wearing the long majestic overcoat which most of the men had
swapped for a short car-coat or a leather jacket. It was said that he
never became rattled and had only been known to lose his temper on
one or two occasions, with terrifying consequences. If we stopped to
talk to someone or answer an enquiry, then Johan would just stroll on
unconcernedly until we caught him up. He collected matchboxes and
would swoop down on discarded boxes to add to his collection. There
were a couple of streets which were 'his'. Amid the parking chaos of
Amsterdam his streets stood out as an oasis of correctly parked
vehicles, because he regularly went around 'sticking' tickets on faulty
parkers. When he went on holiday his streets reverted to their natural
disorder. He rarely said anything, distrusted the portable radio, preferred walking to driving, and was the only policeman allowed on patrol
alone. In the canteen he stood out as a sort of genial mastodon, or a
vestigial survival, among the young, long-haired constables who
treated him deferentially. Once I said to him, 'Busy?' and he replied
sagely, 'Och. You can make it busy. But the result is exactly the same.'

Bram was perky and cheerful and walked quickly and jauntily with
his hands in his pockets as if he was hurrying somewhere rather than
going out on patrol. In the car he would glide through road junctions
and cover his face with his hands in mock despair when he failed to give
right of way to other vehicles. He would say amicably 'Hi, pickpocket'
to a Surinamer, shout 'Wash out your ears' to people who did not get
out of the car's way, or glide up behind people and then rev up the
motor or blow through the microphone causing them to jump. He was
an expert at opening locked cars and carried a couple of wires with him
in case people locked themselves out of their cars. Hans was an
impulsive buccaneering character who would have fitted the style of
Bittner's skid-row policeman. He knew lots of people in the area,
received lots of tips, got himself involved in risky private ventures
which brought him into conflict with the sergeants, could talk the
hind-legs off a donkey, and was a caustic and perceptive analyst of the
Warmoesstraat scene. He was inclined to get himself into scrapes by

taking impetuous decisions which he later regretted. He was a colourful character – humorous, generous and articulate – but he became
increasingly isolated as his contemporaries left whereas he refused to
apply for the Detective Branch. The new boys were portrayed by him
as lacking in finesse and their unsubtle behaviour clearly pained him,
especially when it interfered with one of *his* cases:

> One evening we controlled a Frenchman with a radio receiver and
> transmitter in his car. I thought maybe that's legal in France and it's
> built into his car so he's not going to take it out for a trip abroad and
> it doesn't make much sense us confiscating it. But my partner
> insisted on contacting H.Q. purely for information. That means the
> other cars can hear and straight away a car pulls up and the P.C.
> shouts, 'Trouble?' I say, 'No, it's O.K., nothing's happening'. Then
> another car pulls up, two coppers jump out, and one jumps into this
> French bloke's car and starts poking around. I said, 'Look, you can
> hop it, when I need help I'll ask for it'. When I go to a fight it's nice to
> know that another car pulls up, two coppers jump out, back me up
> but then they can wait at the nearest corner until I really need them
> and not rush in straight away. 'This was a request for information
> and doesn't require you to rush in like a bull in a china shop. I prefer
> to handle my own cases in my own way and I'd be grateful if you
> would depart rapidly'. Then I'm accused of being aggressive and
> uncooperative.
>
> (Constable, 33 years)

There were differences in the way they walked and drove. Some men
rarely ever hurried because they argued that speed rarely made any
difference to settling a case and that it only increased the chance of an
accident. Henk, for example, was a careful driver and never rushed to a
call but took it comfortably without fuss, using the siren and lights but
sparingly. Hans, on the other hand, was more impulsive and threw the
car around. Generally, the men were excellent drivers who could size
up a situation quickly and change their mind swiftly. They become
experienced at taking particular corners, at going the wrong side of
traffic islands and at using cycle paths when the road was blocked with
traffic. On one occasion we received a call that Surinamers were
plundering a shop. In heavy traffic we hurtled down a two-lane road
with cars scattering to both sides. On reaching the Haarlemmerplein
we were caught in three lanes of traffic at a traffic-light with a bunch of

cyclists on the cycle path. Immediately a second patrol-car pulled alongside and the driver sized up the situation, whipped between us and the car in front, and stumbled over the central reservation. Our car instantly followed and the two cars careered off through a red light and against the traffic flow. But the birds had already flown. The wild driving is potentially dangerous for the crew and for other cars, although in my experience the drivers were usually in control of their cars and were rarely reckless (though Tom wrecked a patrol-car and damaged three parked cars one night when he failed to negotiate a bend in wet weather during a high-speed chase). But a call for a crime in progress or a colleague in trouble always elicited an electrifying response (cf. Rubinstein, 1973, p. 98) and a display of advanced driving skills which sometimes made me glad that the Amsterdam Police is only equipped with 'Beetles'!

Generally the patrolmen approached people in a formal and polite manner as a question of tactics; this gave the patrolman the initiative in the encounter in that an impolite or cheeky response revealed the 'moral' character of the individual and cued the policeman into an appropriate response. Of course the interaction is far more complex than that and the policeman's demeanour may unintentionally provoke the 'wrong' response. But as a matter of technique some of the men in the group adopted a scrupulously correct style and Henk explained his approach:

> If you approach people in a correct manner then the people are usually also correct with you. You can easily avoid trouble by sticking to the rules. Also you should not put your notebook on someone's car roof if you're writing him up, although I see it happen time and again. I smoke but if I have to get out of the car then I leave my fag behind and absolutely never appear on the street smoking.
>
> (Constable, 32 years)

Some men also begin to specialise and try to build up expertise in a certain area. This is an individual initiative because pressure, if there is any, is for a wide spread of cases to show that one is an all-round policeman, although informally (as we shall see later) 'pinches' for drugs and weapons rank high. Henk, for instance, had also caught the enthusiasm for lorries:

> After a few months in the station I'd had a good look around. In the evenings a stroll around 'de wallen' [red-light district] is all right now

and then but I felt like doing something else and I thought about lorries. I started carefully asking questions here and there and visited the traffic inspection unit and a man there explained to me the whole background to the regulations. A lot depends on what the driver is carrying and he needs, apart from his driving licence and log-book, a string of licences. If a lorry carries goods for its own firm, like a painter's van which carries ladders, then it has to have a licence for that. So there are all sorts of licences and, of course, a lorry which makes runs abroad has to have a document granting permission to carry goods over the border. Lorries musn't be overloaded, the name of the firm must be on the van, there must be a first-aid box, and there has to be a work-book with all the times for driving and rest periods written up. You can also look at technical things. But I enjoyed doing it and many of the drivers had never been checked out and scarcely knew themselves what they were supposed to have. And they were always very friendly and co-operative and you never have any trouble. That's in contrast to people in private cars who are always in a hurry. And if his papers are not in order and he gets a ticket then it is the boss who pays. I suppose it's a question of taste. Some of the lads think it is great to stroll through a district and take on anything that comes their way whereas I find that if you have a hobby-horse then it's easy to look out for it.

(Constable, 32 years)

In effect, behaviour was perceived by the policemen in station, group and individual terms. The policemen were generally prepared to admit mistakes and also to praise one another for good work. No one liked having his competence questioned and this was never done before the public and rarely done before others. Mostly it was a private admonition offered as advice. A mistake, owing to faulty judgement and/or lack of experience, which affected other colleagues was discussed more openly with the implication that the group could draw a common lesson from it, the individual was implicitly sanctioned not to repeat it, and no character defect was implied. A colleague who was said to be frightened, unstable or unreliable was more likely to receive silent informal social control than an open or collective warning. To be approved it was not necessary to be an exceptional policeman with many arrests (Rubinstein, 1973, p. 110). A good copper was more likely to be someone you could rely on, who pulled his weight, who did not brag, and who was neither too aggressive nor too soft; in other words he was a congenial and reliable colleague who could handle trouble and who knew how not to cause it. Frank, for example, was an unpopular outsider who eventually left the force:

> I simply refused to ride with Frank. He let you down at critical moments and was dubious with money in the area, not paying for things, playing one-armed bandits and demanding the winnings, and that sort of thing. But then others got to hear about it and also started to moan about riding with him. I went to the sergeant and said, 'I categorically refuse to ride with Frank. Under no circumstances will I step into a car with him'. So it had to come out and we discussed it at a meeting and he was posted elsewhere and went eventually to another force.
>
> (Constable, 33 years)

There were also a number of policemen in the station who acted like 'midnight cowboys' and were brash and assertive. They had close relationships with shady characters in the area, were prone to flash their weapons around (there was a rage for snappy holsters which could be clipped into trouser-bands and which promised a 'quick draw'), were dismissive about the general failure to tackle criminality in the area, and were 'bolshy' towards the sergeants. One man spent a good deal of time in the Chinese community. He became involved in a highly dubious episode when he seemed to be acting as a sort of unofficial bodyguard at a Chinese reception and intercepted two armed men who managed to get away, throwing a maching-gun under a car in their escape. Eventually he was transferred to another district and left the police, having first sold his story to a magazine (*Nieuwe Revu*, 28 Jan 1977).

But this handful of men, although they probably represent the Warmoesstraat style *in extremis*, were not generally accepted by the other patrolmen, who thought their style was 'risky' and who saw them as 'cuffers' who were too quick with their fists or feet (Chatterton, 1976b, p. 119). In short, the social and occupational reality of the Warmoesstraat was complex and varied and belied the uniformity of the outside stereotype. There were a variety of individual and group styles which allowed permutations in methods of working. A couple of men had 'easy numbers' looking after the provisions, a sergeant had got his exam for promotion by almost never going out on the street as a constable but sitting inside studying (Manning, 1977, p. 149, speaks of a constable who spent so much time inside that he became known as the 'station cat'), some of the older men were said to be 'burnt out' and performed their duties ritualistically with little or no motivation, while others were 'fanatic' and highly motivated. But the most respected colleague was not the high-flyer but the stable, reliable, average worker.

5 Street Encounters

(i) ENCOUNTERS BETWEEN POLICEMEN AND CIVILIANS

Research in American cities conveys a picture of police–citizen contacts as being largely generated by citizens rather than the police, as concerning a high proportion of transactions unrelated to crime, and as being most usually handled in a routine and businesslike manner (Reiss, 1971). In order to see if these conclusions were also valid in Amsterdam I kept a record over a period of four months (August 1974 and January–March 1975) of 'significant' encounters observed between uniformed policemen and members of 'the public' in the centre of Amsterdam. Two basic categories were not recorded: the numerous people who asked the policemen for information, and passing admonitions to cyclists and pedestrians. The former category was so frequent on foot-patrol in the summer period that it would have enormously inflated the number of contacts and enhanced the picture of the policeman's 'social' role. This sort of tourist information, which was always given politely and most often in English or German, might be sought fifteen to twenty times in a two-hour patrol along the Damrak and surrounding area. I did not consider such contacts significant and left out these short, trivial and basically information-giving encounters (similarly for people who asked the time, or for the nearest toilet, etc.). An almost universal phenomenon in Amsterdam is the contempt that cyclists have for the law, and many young people cycle without lights or consider themselves exempt from observing traffic-lights. The policemen's attitude to this was usually one of weary indulgence; they either shouted sarcastic remarks through the loud-speaker – 'Doesn't the girl with the red hair appreciate that traffic-lights are also meant for her' or 'Would the gentleman with no lights on his bike be so kind as to walk the rest of the way home' – or casually wound down the window and said, 'Get off and walk, you're a big boy now'. If they were in the patrol-car and saw someone cycling towards them without lights, then they forced him to stop by blocking his path to reinforce their point. If

117

all these contacts were written-up they would inflate the total of offences and also the number of cases where the police exercised discretion. But again I discounted these cases if they were merely passing admonitions but wrote them up if the policemen stopped someone and questioned him or her. Similarly, pedestrians who took no notice of lights regulating pedestrian crossings were normally viewed with a blind eye. In any event, I made a judgement about whether or not a contact was significant in my opinion and hence under-reported the actual number of encounters. To be significant, then, an encounter had to engage the policeman's attention and lead to some formal interaction.

In the four months' period I witnessed 447 encounters involving 816 people; there were 28 groups consisting of more than 5 people and 19 of these were counted separately because of their large size. In keeping with the slow pace of social life in a red-light district during day-time, most contacts occurred in the evening and at night. The twelve hours from 6 p.m. until 6 a.m. contained 61 per cent of all contacts and the period from 6 a.m. until 12 noon was the quietest of the four six-hour periods with 16 per cent of contacts. In 40 per cent of the cases the police initiated the encounter – and this is appreciably higher than American studies where the police were shown to be almost entirely reliant on citizen mobilisation (Reiss, 1971) – and in 60 per cent a member of the public mobilised the police. A number of factors explain the relatively high level of 'pro-active' policing (in contrast to 'reacting' to citizen calls) in the Warmoesstraat district. Firstly, there were a good deal of foot-patrols which received no direct messages from the Radio Room, which handled most emergency calls, and who could easily stop and question people. And, secondly, a city-centre and a red-light district attract many people on foot for shopping and entertainment and people perambulated throughout the district until the small hours of the morning. For the patrolmen, activity was initiated principally by checking a vehicle (32 per cent), by a more or less chance encountering of an incident in the street (14 per cent), or by deliberately entering a situation off their own bat (6 per cent, excluding vehicle checks). To a large extent, then, self-initiated activity focused on the checking of papers or people in a car or on a moped, and frequently this was done because of suspicions about the drivers or occupants of a car or in the hope of stumbling upon a possible offence.

With regard to citizen calls to the police leading to a response, the majority were in the form of telephone calls to the Radio Room or, less frequently, direct to the Warmoesstraat which were then relayed to the patrolmen by radio. Roughly a third of encounters were initiated by a civilian phoning the police. Citizens also approached patrols or flagged down a patrol-car (9 per cent) and less frequently called personally at the station to ask for police action. The policemen were also involved in small numbers of contacts arising from automatic alarms, escort duties of prisoners, and lending assistance to colleagues. Generally the contacts lasted for just a few minutes. The majority (69 per cent) took 5 minutes or less. About 1 in 10 of the encounters lasted up to a half-hour and there were 19 cases (or 4 per cent of the total) which took longer than a half-hour to handle.

Two-thirds of the encounters took place in the open and usually on the street. Roughly 1 in 10 occurred in a private dwelling while smaller percentages were in commercial premises, cafés or restaurants, places of 'entertainment', hotels, and public buildings. In most of the incidents there was no active audience. Somewhere in the background of most encounters there were one or two people who glanced curiously at the incident and then moved on, but I defined 'audience' as a group who were close witnesses to an encounter and who thereby were involved, if only as passive spectators, in it. In that sense, only 20 per cent of the encounters had a public audience in the vicinity of the contact and 80 per cent did not. In effect, the police and the participants generally carried out their transactions without interference from bystanders. Of those cases where there was an audience, I estimated that the majority were calm or passive, serving merely as a group backcloth, that in 19 per cent of the cases the crowd was actually helpful to the police and in only one case was open hostility exhibited towards police officers.

I also attempted to categorise the general attitude of the participants in the encounter towards the policemen. In just under half of the cases the people involved were calm or passive (48 per cent), displaying little or no response or emotion. The next largest category (23 per cent) involved people who were positively helpful in their reaction to a police presence. Only in a small number of cases did the police elicit a negative response. Some 7 per cent of participants were perceived by me as being 'unhelpful' while a further 3 per cent were considered to be 'hostile/aggressive'. Or, taking these categories together, the policemen encountered a degree of lack of co-operation in 1 in 10 of the encounters. In addition, however, there were 13 per cent of cases where individuals were emotionally worked up and agitated and these incidents usually had an element of tension in them for the officers as well. A small number of people were too incapacitated to have any attitude to the encounter, some remained aloof and detached, some were 'stoned', disorientated, or in some sort of trance-like pose, and only a tiny handful of people (1 per cent) were considered to be 'deferential'.

In most cases (70 per cent) the policemen's attitudes to the civilians encountered in the incidents were judged by me to be straightforward and 'businesslike'. Just over a tenth of the contacts were handled sympathetically and a smaller proportion (about 6 per cent) with good humour. In a small number of cases (3 in all, or 1 per cent of the total) officers used a belittling or sarcastic manner, in 2 per cent of contacts they adopted an 'authoritarian' tone, and in 9 per cent of incidents they were considered 'brusque'. The latter category generally involved shouting and shoving and an abrupt, forceful manner. I did not rate any of the incidents in the 'hostile/provocative' category, by which I meant a one-sided aggressive attitude on the part of policemen which was designed to provoke an opponent into counter-aggression or which might be construed as an unreasonable response to hostility from a member of the public. However, such behaviour was observed outside of the four-month period and has been detailed earlier.

In roughly half of the encounters an offence appeared to have been committed, although this was not necessarily committed by the people involved in the contacts as some of them were victims of an offence. But in just over half of all the contacts there was no offence involved. In the great majority of cases no one was arrested or detained in the station and in only 17 per cent of all incidents did the contact eventuate in an arrest. In short, these two aspects of encounters are evidence that the daily work of the policemen in the Warmoesstraat involved a good deal of contact with people which was not necessarily concerned with an offence and that roughly four-fifths of their contacts with the public did not involve an arrest or detention of a suspect.

Predominantly the contacts in the street were with males (80 per cent) rather than females (20 per cent). And, most frequently, the policemen were concerned with young people. For instance, 45 per cent of all participants were estimated to be under 25 years and 75 per cent under 35 years. Looking at it another way, only a quarter of all participants appeared to be over 35 years and 6 per cent to be over 50 years of age. A fairly typical pattern emerges, in fact, of (young) policemen being largely engaged in contact with young males. If we look at the number of people involved in the encounters then the contact was with a single individual in 45 per cent of the cases and with two people in 27 per cent of the cases. Normally the policemen were in pairs and, as such, were outnumbered in roughly a quarter of all encounters, with 6 per cent of all cases representing crowds of more than five direct participants.

As one might expect, the majority of contacts was with people of Dutch nationality. In fact, 65 per cent of all participants were Dutch (as far as I could tell), 25 per cent were foreign nationals or ethnics, and 10 per cent were Surinamers or Antillians. The foreigners were spread over 29 nationalities. Numerically, the most frequently encountered nationalities were Germans (18 per cent of all foreigners), Americans (14.5 per cent), French (12.5 per cent), Britons (6.5 per cent) and Chinese ethnics (6.5 per cent). It is not possible to state accurately what proportion of the foreigners was composed of guest-workers, but the three following nationalities contribute greatly to the guest-worker colony and there is a good chance that that was in fact their occupational status, namely Moroccan (6.5 per cent), Turkish (4 per cent) and Tunisian (1 per cent).

Here I have attempted to quantify somewhat crudely the nature of the interaction between policemen and civilians. It is hoped that this reinforces the view of police work, even in a colourful area like the red-light district of Amsterdam, as relatively routine and 'undramatic'. In general, the contacts which I observed during the four-month period were short, businesslike and unemotional. Indeed, over a half of the encounters were not concerned with an offence and five-sixths did not eventuate in someone being arrested or taken to the station. The vast majority of incidents concerned young males, while roughly a third of all people involved were not Dutch ethnics. A quarter of all civilians concerned were foreigners spread over a large number of nationalities. Although a minority of cases involved people who were emotionally excited, it can hardly be said from this evidence that the daily, routine encounters of the policemen from the Warmoesstraat that I observed could be considered dangerous, exciting, stressful, or concerned with complex criminal cases. Furthermore the policemen handled most cases in a straightforward, neutral manner while, in turn, most citizens were reasonably co-operative. Indeed, the policemen's own perceptions of working in a dangerous environment with a hostile public can hardly be confirmed by these data. For example, some form of physical restraint was employed in only 4 cases and handcuffs were also used in only 4 incidents. The daily reality of police work in the city-centre may have been more concerned with, say, young foreign males than would be the case in a suburb or smaller city, but the range of cases revealed the 'all-round' task of the police which was clearly not confined to crime and dramatic incidents.

(ii) THE POLICEMAN AND HIS PUBLICS

Earlier I drew attention to the sometimes bizarre and motley cavalcade of figures – which would be considered 'out of place' elsewhere – that inhabit the inner city and that form a backdrop to police work there. Dealing with a broad range of people and a variety of life-styles becomes normal and routine. I recall having a long conversation with a sergeant in the station while behind us a drunk was crawling around on all fours, vomiting and grunting like a wild animal. On another occasion there was a demented bellowing booming out from the cells. Eventually the sergeant became worried about the prisoner's health and called a doctor. The prisoner was a drunken Englishman who had been found attacking parked cars in the town-centre and who had fought the officers who arrested him, getting a punch in the mouth in the process of detention. On arrival at the station most of his clothes had been destroyed in the struggle. When we went to the cell to look at him we were greeted with the sight of a fat, naked man of about thirty with black curly hair and dried blood caked on his lips who was sitting on the end of the rubber bench, and who was shouting 'Fuck! Fuck! Fuck!' at the top of his voice while making vigorous 'V'-signs with both hands. Eventually a couple of flat-mates turned up and said that it was most out of character because he was such a quiet lad in the flat. But this behaviour, which was 'out of character' for the man, was considered part of daily life in the inner city and was viewed impersonally by the policemen involved. They became almost immune to a background of snivelling, puking, boisterous, pleading, threatening, arguing, crying clients. They might arrive to find congealing blood splattered over the counter from a walking-wounded case, or pass some sorrowful-looking man having a blood sample taken by the doctor for a drunken-driving case, or see a scarecrowish junkie, his emaciated face covered in spots, quietly sobbing to himself as he was charged. But for them it was simply work (some policemen are even said to refer to their uniform as their 'overalls': Hopmans and van de Scheur, 1975, p. 19).

But that does not mean that the policeman treats everyone the same, or that he views all citizens as similar. Rather he subtly but largely unconsciously changes his performance to fit situated encounters (Chatterton, 1976a, p. 114) and, in a sense, it is simplistic to talk of the 'police and the public' for the policeman has several publics (Westley, 1970, pp. 49–108). The concern with 'police–public' relations (Belson, 1975; *De Tijd*, 28 Nov 1973) obscures the fact that the police are differentially involved with social groups and that the public scarcely exists except as a useful reference point when justifying police activity (Cain, 1977, p. 9). In general, an old woman is freest to take liberties with the police (Sykes and Clark, 1974, p. 6; Rubinstein, 1973, p. 235). She is partially protected by two status factors, sex and age, which generally guarantee immunity, whereas the reverse works to the detriment of young males who often suffer amplified negative discrimination in their relations with the police (Piliavin and Briar, 1964). Such norms are based partly on a reflection that enforcing the law against elderly females is seen by the public as the least legitimate of police behaviour and by the patrolmen as likely to elicit the most negative response and practical difficulties, such as their restrictions on force when faced by a violent older woman, and partly on the policeman's appraisal of old women as a 'morally' acceptable category. For the policeman simplifies his task of adjusting to an endless procession of individuals by parcelling up society into recognisable groups; and he does this both on common-sense factors – sex, age, race, clothes, etc. – and also on their place in the moral hierarchy of people who conform to or threaten his ideological jigsaw of what is right and proper for the specific territory he patrols. People are graded according to the sort of work and the problems they present the police with and also according to the extent that they challenge the policeman's 'moral' convictions.

In the red-light district of Amsterdam, for example, the policemen exhibited a tolerance and acceptance of behaviour that would be frowned upon or sanctioned elsewhere. In turn a higher level of tolerance for deviant behaviour can allow it to be more open and conspicuous (Becker and Horowitz, 1971, p. 7). Homosexuals offended the policeman's masculine ideology and yet were tolerated because their behaviour was unproblematic for him. Their behaviour was accepted and only sanctioned when it palpably involved juveniles who might then be questioned about their age and identity; but the conduct of homosexuals in the city-centre rarely aroused comment and was hardly ever a cause for police activity (Rubinstein, 1973, p. 182). Prostitution has been for so long an accepted part of the scene in the area that the policeman scarcely questioned it as a phenomenon and generally felt well disposed to the regular girls. Through daily acquaintance, the garish sexual displays ceased to be of much interest. The prostitution, the gambling, the pornography and the sex industry were normally not of practical value to him and could not provide him with work except through incidental by-products, such as fights and payment problems. People drawn to the attractions of the district were regarded almost neutrally, or as sources of amusement, and if they became victims of a crime or a con-trick then there was a tendency to adopt an attitude of 'What do you expect if you come here?' The policeman's hierarchy of characters, partly predetermining his attitude and response to various groups, went something like this: old people, women and children, helpful respectable males, helpful 'villains', friendly 'rough' acquaintances and prostitutes, unhelpful 'respectable' males, disrespectful youths, obstinate foreigners, unpredictably dangerous clients (drunks, junkies and the mentally disturbed), and predictably dangerous clients (armed with knife or gun). But this is the barest taxonomy which does not reveal the full complexity of categories with which the policemen worked and which might influence their interaction with someone.

More generally, policemen elsewhere have been noted as developing 'anti-public' attitudes. Westley (1970) speaks of policemen viewing the public as an 'enemy' and Manning (1977, p. 264) notes the derogatory slang used by the Metropolitan Police when describing people; elsewhere (1973b, p. 26) he argues that people are seen by policemen 'as stupid, fallible, greedy, lustful, immoral and hysterical – such views provide policemen with resources for hours of stories and jokes. Man is seen as a translucent Machiavelli, easily uncovered by insightful probing or police action. *Fellow policemen* are viewed in much the same fashion' (my emphasis). Blau (1955), however, argues that such statements indicate peer-group solidarity against clients rather than representing actual behaviour because he found no correlation between welfare workers who make anti-client statements in interaction with colleagues and their attitude to the client in practice.

In the Warmoesstraat this attitude was reserved particularly for the archetypal Amsterdammer, who was held to be volubly and spontaneously against authority. The stereotype was frequently couched in negative terms and this was accentuated by the fact that many policemen were not themselves from Amsterdam. Additionally, it tends to lace interaction with a certain tension whereby enforcement is rarely accepted at face value but more frequently remarked upon:

An Amsterdammer can't take any authority. As soon as you enforce the law he'd rather open his mouth to ask 'Is this necessary?' and so on. Because here they love nothing better than a disturbance. But in general the people are anti-authority and anti-police and if you have to take action then they always pass some remark.

(Marechaussee, 27 years)

Even a young police officer who had been born and bred in Amsterdam reproduced a sceptical picture:

I'm an Amsterdammer myself but an Amsterdammer is difficult and awkward. A real Amsterdammer likes to make a joke and he'll call a constable 'colonel', but that same Amsterdammer can also jump on your neck. If you say, 'Heh, get off and walk' to a cyclist without lights in say Haarlem then he'll get off and walk. But in Amsterdam they pretend not to hear you and if you catch them up then they don't co-operate. If there's an incident with injuries and a crowd gathers and you say, 'Come along now, get back on the pavement', they just don't do it. They just stand there. Then you just have to push them out of the way but as soon as your back is turned they go back to standing in the middle of the road. So Amsterdam is a difficult city with a difficult public.   (Inspector, 24 years)

In the Warmoesstraat the policeman's interaction with his publics was partly shaped by certain features of patrol work which differ from many existing accounts of uniformed police work. Previously police work on the street was largely an individual and a solitary task. But in Amsterdam, since the riots, working in pairs became first standard and then required. Older policemen were sometimes scornful about the dependence of younger colleagues on a partner. But permanent pairs are not used in the Warmoesstraat, partly to emphasise teamwork and partly to prevent a pair getting too involved in the entrails of the underworld, and a constable has to learn to work with everyone else in the group. No one has a fixed 'beat', unlike the classic 'fixed points system' (Chatterton, 1974), the recent 'Unit Beat Policing' system (Holdaway, 1977a, pp. 123–4), or the beat system described by Rubinstein (1973, p. 180) in Philadelphia where in dense parts of the city a beat comprises five square blocks. This meant that patrolmen were not responsible for a specific territory and all the men and all the groups were used indiscriminately within the entire district. Clearly this undermined the intimate contact and personalised knowledge which was the essence of the old system:

You got to know the beat much better than now. These days the beat is much too large. We knew exactly where every family lived and which families caused trouble. You hardly see the people any more but then you used to have more time. Now you ride along and in a flash you're off again. The district was divided into blocks and these were pretty small. If you had a beat with one block then you would walk or cycle through it a hundred times. I mean after two hours you could probably count the cobble-stones. The Kattenburgh block was only three streets and the Kattenburgh square. And you had to realise that these people knew not just my name but also my personality. They knew exactly that one constable was like this and that another constable was like that, and 'If you see that one you'd better look out', you know what I mean? That's what it was like. They knew every constable personally and his personality inside out. Often they used to call you 'uncle'. But then you used to have a core of permanent residents who were born and lived there.

(Constable, 50 years)

In practice, the inner city was intensively patrolled on foot compared to other parts of the district so that potentially detailed knowledge of people and places could be developed. But while district boundaries were the first social parameters to be internalised by the patrolmen, the geographic knowledge of the district took years to accumulate and might never be completed. The city-centre is a warren of alleyways which are often not accessible by car and each one has its own name. A newcomer would soon gain a social map of the major arteries and crucial trouble-spots and then slowly fill in the detailed picture with time and experience. Generally, a patrolman who had been to an address located it in his memory and had no difficulty in relocating it and in giving an account of the people there. However, it could happen that neither patrolman in the car knew a specific address and neither had a street-reference book on him. If it was urgent they could ask the radio-operator for help or else they could set out in the general direction and drive around looking for it. Sometimes the men could not remember the sequence of canals (old hands had a rhyme to help them with the names) or did not know which side of the canal had even numbers and which side uneven numbers. It was maintained that increasingly many patrolmen did not have a detailed social knowledge of the district apart from the inner city, and it was clear that they often did not know the people involved in encounters. This was reinforced to a certain extent by the fact that they were forbidden to enter the red-light district in their free time, although some of them ignored this rule. But there can be little doubt that the organisation of patrol work did not always enhance detailed and familiar knowledge of people and places in the area.

(iii) SITUATIONAL DEMEANOUR

It should also be mentioned here that patrolling (at least for the men with whom I worked) was generally a passive, anticipatory activity with often little attempt to make contact with people. I felt that the majority of patrolmen exchanged their private personality for their public image automatically as they left the station for the street. They did not seem to concern themselves much with where they were going or what they were going to do. When they had been assigned a beat and were outside they began to give the question some thought. In the day-time, for instance, two men might get into the car and without saying anything head off to the Western Docks. As if wishing to escape the confines of the inner city they would seek out the long stretches of road, the impersonal spaces around factories, and the deserted areas at the back of the docks. In the evening, and especially at night, they would hang around the inner city hoping for a call. But the whim of the driver or his mate dictated the route unless the men were keen on generating activity or wished to keep their eyes on someone or something special. There were a number of fixed points which almost automatically they would inspect while cruising around. Casually glancing around, they talked to each other and smoked, looking for a Surinamer dealing on the Dam, someone tinkering with cars in the Beursplein, a Chinese dealer in the Zeedijk, a pickpocket in the Nieuwendijk, a group of muggers in the Nieuwmarkt, and so on. There were parking lots and garages, back-streets near hotels, and thinly populated canal areas where cars were frequently broken into at night, and these would be traversed. Other social features of the area would casually be taken in as they roamed around – prostitutes and their clients, alcoholics, homosexuals in public urinals, erratic drivers after closing time, a shooting club (to check licences for firearms), people sleeping in telephone boxes outside Central Station waiting for the first train, closing time at cinemas, the Salvation Army hostel, lock-up garages, derelict houses, houseboats, a student restaurant, and so on. Patrolling was not a predetermined plan to initiate activity but was mainly a semi-conscious scrutiny of the social horizon while awaiting a call or an incident.

But, largely unconsciously, the policeman develops a detailed but rarely articulated cosmic map of what is 'right' and 'normal' in specific areas of the inner city; sometimes behaviour is condoned in one part of a street and sanctioned in another part of the street (cf. Rubinstein,

1973, p. 151, on 'situational demeanour'). His mental map is an ecological kaleidoscope of norms and expectations surrounding acceptable and unacceptable behaviour in specific areas, particular streets, certain corners, and in or around known clubs and bars. Norms of universal enforcement founder on these minutely specified yet largely unrehearsed norms of particularistic, localised activity. Roughly, people in the neighbourhood were divided into three major groups. Firstly, there were legitimate street users (Rubinstein, 1973, p. 196) – above all, residents, shopkeepers, public service employees and tradesmen. Secondly, there were 'disreputable' groups who belonged in the area – the prostitutes, the alcoholics, the hippies, etc. – who were part and parcel of the local scene and who rarely challenged the policeman's presence. But, thirdly, there were the illegitimate street users – the dealers, muggers, pickpockets and car thieves – who were in conflict and competition with the police and who explicitly challenged their control and authority.

For groups and places, then, the policemen tended to develop with experience a sensitivity to notions of 'normal' behaviour so that behaviour tolerated in one place could be disallowed in another because it violated their notions of what was right in that place. One end of the Zeedijk belonged to the Surinamers and one end belonged to the Chinese. A group of Surinamers standing outside 'Emil's Place' or 'Atte's Club' aroused little attention; these were their haunts. But if the group stood two hundred yards further away, near the Chinese restaurants and gambling houses, then it spelt trouble with the suggestion of inter-group conflict and perhaps a fight or shoot-out related to the drug trade between the two ethnic groups. On one occasion some of the Surinamers moved to a new corner and were reported to be molesting passers-by. A group of policemen went to move them and fighting broke out (see below, Chapter 7). The Surinamers went back to the Zeedijk and conceded the corner. The Nieuwmarkt area is a mini-skid-row and drunks and alcoholics are a familiar sight; they inhabit a café there, sit on walls, and congregate on benches. An old alcoholic, in poor condition, with a couple of bottles in his overcoat pockets, could stagger around in the area, urinate in corners, and sleep on benches. If he did precisely the same on the Damrak half a mile away, he would run a much higher chance of being arrested or moved along.

Time related to place also played a role in defining normality and was rooted in notions of what a place was used for. To a certain extent street crime takes place in the evening, under the protective cover of darkness, and suspicions are aroused by behaviour at night which might be overlooked in daylight (Rubinstein, 1973, p. 165). But increasingly there are reports of crime – muggings and theft from cars particularly – occurring in broad daylight and in full view of bystanders. Generally, however, someone standing near or looking at certain buildings at night – a bank, a chemist's, a jeweller's, etc. – was regarded with suspicion whereas it was difficult to impute ulterior motives to someone engaged in the same behaviour in day-time because he could be there for any number of legitimate, and superficially indecipherable, reasons. Implicitly, notions develop that a Black woman alone on 'de wallen' is soliciting, anyone walking slowly around the Beursplein (but especially at night) is a car-thief, a Surinamer standing alone on the Damrak is trying to sell drugs, hippy-looking types standing opposite a Chinese restaurant on the Zeedijk are junkies, and so on. Bars, restaurants, hotels and businesses tended to be given a reputation by which the policemen could order behaviour appropriate to them and his own relationships with them (Chatterton, 1976b, p. 116).

The inner city also contains many people who come alive at night and go to ground during the day. The Warmoesstraat, for instance, was known as an 'evening and night' station because the red-light district flourishes in the dark. The day-shift was usually dull and uneventful. The deviant patterns of social life in the inner city, compared to other parts of the district, meant that perceptions of 'lateness' differed radically from residential areas (Rubinstein, 1973, p. 261). One of the policemen used to say emphatically:

> Anyone walking around 'de wallen' [red-light district] after two o'clock at night is a suspect. I don't care who it is or what they look like. You wouldn't look at them twice in the afternoon but as far as I'm concerned they're all suspects after two.
>
> (Constable, 33 years)

There are people wandering around 'de wallen' at four, five or six in the morning but in itself that arouses little interest whereas it might be conducive to an inquiry from policemen in other areas. (The Metropolitan Police tend to question anyone about after midnight or one o'clock, according to Manning, 1977, p. 177, and some American cities have curfews for juveniles.) The way the patrolmen approached someone and the language they used was partly dictated by location and partly by demeanour cues:

You notice in the Warmoesstraat, especially because the public consists mostly of drunken layabouts, whores and thieves, that the policemen are a bit rough and easy-going. If you address the public then it's likely to be 'Hey, granddad, you'd better piss off now'. It's a bit gruff and crude but the people in the surroundings don't expect anything else. For instance, I don't say to a tart, 'Mevrouw, your dress appears to be open', but more likely, 'Hello my girl, you've really got the goods on display today then', but that's the language they use themselves and you slip into it automatically as you arrive at the station.

(Inspector, 24 years)

The repartee of inner-city life with its debunking tone was localised to the extent that policemen accepted familiar and even insolent forms of address in the red-light district which they would regard as an offence in other environments. Obviously someone the policeman knew personally could take more liberties. After two hours walking around 'de wallen' a foot-patrol might pass the bouncers, the prostitutes and porn-shop assistants several times and allow them a ritualised intimacy. But increasingly a constable did not get to know these people as individuals – unless he had been involved with them previously or they had a known criminal record – but as faces, and this situation is replicated by Rubinstein (1973, p. 216); he writes of the beat-man in Philadelphia, 'Most of the people he sees on his sector are not known to him personally. He is obliged to rely on his notions of local behaviour and of the legitimate use of public places and on the behavioural cues people give him when they come into his presence in making judgements of what they are doing.'

In effect, the policeman continually and half-consciously adjusts his response to the different individuals and categories, allows some people to make more demands on him than others, permits some people to take greater liberties with him than others, and enforces the law more readily against some transgressors than others:

If someone calls me a prick then I'm not insulted, that doesn't worry me. I have arrested someone who called me a prick but not because of what he said but because it was an annoying bloke and he had to feel it. A thousand people can say 'prick' to me and I'll ignore it but if someone says it, and for some reason I won't permit it, his behaviour or his whole attitude, and because he's earned it, then I'll nick him. But he won't get a thump, I don't sell my thumps cheaply; only when someone has really earned it. Someone with a big mouth gets a big mouth back. You see, the mentality of the Amsterdammer is that he is brought up more freely, knows how to wag his tongue, and his choice of words is not restricted. It's never troubled me because I've trained myself to answer back. I just took the first one who tried to talk to me like that and answered back in the same style until I'd out-talked him. And I must say it gets better and better if you just go out on the street with a bit of confidence. But you have to approach everyone differently. In my choice of words I've become freer, somewhat cruder, but if you say 'Oh darn it' to a duchess and 'Goddam it' to a dock-worker then you won't have any trouble. I've learned thay my tongue is a good weapon, often better than your pistol, but you have to talk exactly the same as the man you're speaking with and then you get immediate contact. If I talk to a ponce from the countryside with an affected voice and following the 'van Dalen' [dictionary] then he won't understand a word. So I let someone start the talking and then I listen to his voice and answer back just like he does.

(Constable, 33 years)

Frequently, the presence of a social audience was held to be crucial. Abuse and threats which could be tolerated in private by a policeman became unacceptable when an audience was witnessing the event:

There was a demonstration against building the underground and there were people all over the place. Suddenly I noticed a woman of about forty, wanting to be trendy and marching around all day shouting with the rest, in the middle of the mob and she stood right opposite me and shouted 'S.S.' So I went for her, even if it was going to cost me my hat and my jacket. I was going to get her for that one word and if she only spent a couple of hours in the station then at least I've made her smile on the other side of her face. . . . Sometimes you go to arrest a man and his wife begins to scream, 'You pigs, you've only got guts against old men and children', and then she begins to attract twenty or thirty people and they all begin to shout. Immediately you grab the woman and throw her in the back of the car otherwise you'll never get out of there. But you've got to let them see who you are even though in different circumstances you'd just let the woman go on screaming. You mustn't lose face, you are the police, and they've got to see that you are in command. . . .

(Constable, 28 years)

As conspicuous costumed actors in the social scene, the policemen felt that they could not accept everything. They tended to make a judgement on the individual (is he or she drunk, or hysterical, or on a trip, so that their abuse emerges less from personal volition, as when they are sober, and their 'moral' character is weakened in the eyes of bystanders) and on the situation – is it in public or private, is there an audience, are they losing the verbal battle, and so on. In such interactions there is an individual alchemy comprising the characteristics of the participants and the unique development of the situation. Each incident begins with new actors and improvised lines, and yet the recurring predictability of cases tends to predetermine the script. The policeman is often playing a familiar role, unless he is inexperienced or not in control of his emotions, whereas the citizen, unless he knows the routine and is 'police-wise', may feel uncomfortable at being stopped or questioned and betray this in unintended ways:

> But often citizens will not embrace their roles, not only because they are irregular performers, but because they are commonly reluctant performers, and this is true even when the encounter is citizen-initiated. In fact every civilian participant displays some of those very properties which are important not to display in focused interaction – embarrassment, lack of poise, distraction, failure to take proper turns at speaking and disregard of spacing rules. . . . And even if the actors are composed, the occasion of the meeting is often such as to embarrass the citizen, for in a certain sense, to be a victim, is to have been made a fool, and to broadcast it publicly is to disclose one's foolishness. (Sykes and Clark, 1974, p. 2)

But as Suttles (1968, p. 184) argues, this sensitivity to situated perceptions of social life is not confined to the police but is shared by most of the residents (in this case with reference to a slum in Chicago) who make judgements about the location, movement, clothing, apparent ethnicity, demeanour, sex, age, companions and plausible destination of gangs:

> For instance, if a Mexican group is seen around Sheridan Park, people assume they are looking for trouble. When the boys enter a store, the management immediately takes precautions against shoplifting. If a group of boys are seen 'hanging' in a dark alley, it means they are drinking. If the boys approach a girl, they are 'on the make'. When they 'hang on the corner' they are just 'wasting their time'.

In discussing police work on 'skid-row', Bittner (1967a) depicts how conceptions of location, culpability, coercion, privacy and property were rooted in common norms related to keeping order in the area. Rubinstein (1973, p. 194) also writes of policemen viewing 'bums, winos and deadbeats' as having no privacy so that their rooms and persons can be searched at will although generally they are left alone if found in their 'normal' places. An 'urban nomad' who falls under the suspicion of the police can sometimes extricate himself simply by changing his style of walking to convey a sense of purpose but, once apprehended, whether or not he is a drunk is irrelevant for 'he became a drunk' (Spradley, 1970, pp. 82, 124). In the red-light district of Amsterdam too, police work was mediated by a complex unwritten code which helped to define notions of place, time, legitimacy, belonging, privacy, situational demeanour, etc., which were rooted in the specific cultural norms of cosmopolitan inner-city life.

(iv) KEEPING THE PEACE

A sixty-year-old man was discovered by a sales-girl on the first floor of the Bijenkorf department store with his trousers open, muttering endearments to a window-dummy ('You're a sexy bit of stuff, a nice piece of meat'). When the store detective arrived the man was on the point of ejaculating. He was taken to the Warmoesstraat and became one of the many people who are brought to the station to decide what should be done with them but who end up not being charged with an offence. This diffuse category includes lost children, people who attract attention by 'strange' behaviour or who may be under the influence of drugs, a man walking down the street in 'Adam's suit', an under-age runaway, a mentally disturbed girl, a man playing the guitar for money in the street, a youth distributing pamphlets who refuses to talk to the policemen, a Belgian military deserter giving himself up, a Frenchman behaving oddly in Central Station (he was probably 'flipped' and a psychiatrist was called), a women refusing to pay for a meal (she was well known and the psychiatrist said it was not worth while coming to see her so she was sent on her way), a hysterical young woman who attacked her father with a screwdriver, two fourteen-year-old boys found talking to homosexuals near Central Station, and a man found sleeping in someone else's car whose strange behaviour and oddly coloured face caused the duty-officer to pack him off immediately to the Binnen Gasthuis Hospital.

Such cases, culled at random from the Station Diary, represent the infinitely varied rag-bag of duties performed by the police, or thrust upon them, which might loosely be classified as 'social welfare' functions. Several studies (Cumming et al., 1965; Punch and Naylor, 1973; Brown and Howes, 1975) have documented the 'social' component in police work which, because it goes largely unreported and unemphasised, conspires to make of the police a 'secret' social service (Punch, 1978b) whose obligations in this grey area between legality and illegality remain unspecified and submerged. Recently, however, the distinction between law-enforcement and the social-work functions of the police has been said to be arbitrary and difficult to distinguish in practice (Chatterton, 1973; Shearing and Leon, 1976). Bittner, for instance, has appropriated the suggestive term 'peace-keeping' to describe the order-maintaining functions of the police, in contrast to enforcement on legalistic lines, and he states succinctly that 'peace-keeping appears to be a solution to an unknown problem arrived at by unknown means' (1967a, p. 701). It is not possible to expand at length on all the ramifications of the debate surrounding this concept. Here, it is used in building up the picture of police work in the city-centre of Amsterdam to indicate what policemen do and what their views are on the important but largely inarticulate function of literally 'keeping the peace'.

The characteristics of cases in this area are that they are frequently imposed upon the police by outsiders, that they are grudgingly accepted if not actually refused (or redefined into 'non-events': Manning, 1977, p. 284), that they consume a good deal of policemen's time (Black, 1971, p. 1090; Reiss, 1971, p. 71), and that a coincidental conclusion may determine whether or not the case is defined as law-enforcement or peace-keeping. In the following incident, for example, the report was concluded as 'assistance rendered' whereas it might well have ended in serious injury and criminal charges:

> I had my pistol out once but didn't fire it. That was when a Surinamer stood behind a door with an axe and said he was going to smash my brains in. I think he was thrown out of his parents' house and had come back to find out where his child was. He had taken a social worker hostage and wouldn't let her free until he'd found out about the child. But it was all sorted out in the end and we didn't charge him with anything.
>
> (Constable, 20 years)

There is evidence that some British policemen take a derogatory view of their 'social welfare' task (Holdaway, 1977a, p. 135) while some American policemen are said to consider it as 'shit work' (Manning, 1973b, p. 15) which distracts them from 'real' work. An American patrolman, when asked to check on the whereabouts of a missing girl, remarked, 'That's the way it goes; every time you begin to do some real police work, you get stuck with this stuff. I guess ninety per cent of all police work is bullshit. All most people want is a shoulder to cry on' (Reiss, 1971, p. 42). Similar sceptical views were expressed by some of my Amsterdam respondents who saw many interventions in the private troubles of people as futile while they resented the fact that effort expended on such cases went unrewarded by the formal system. But, above all, 'social welfare' incidents frequently did not possess the characteristics – a good prisoner, a clear outcome, unambiguous enforcement, and accompanying informal praise – which attended 'real' police work and the accolade of a 'nice piece of work'. Manning (1977, p. 289) summarises what is probably a universal norm in this area: 'The striking thing about order maintenance methods is how little they are taught, how cynically they are viewed, and how irrelevant they are thought to be in most police departments.'

In the Warmoesstraat there were specific norms about coping with behaviour that 'disturbed the peace' in the red-light district together with a more general involvement in classic social-welfare functions which might concern 'peace-keeping' but which also simply meant rendering assistance to people in need. With regard to the latter, some of the cases were open-and-shut demands for help of a mechanical kind, e.g. a man's boat has worked loose from its moorings and the constables assist in recovering it, a family notices a strong smell of gas and patrolmen pass a warning to the Gas Board (three times before there was a response), a flat is flooded due to a broken water pipe, a hole appears in the road which might be dangerous for traffic or passers-by, a lorry loses its load, a chimney has fallen in the street, a water-tap has been left open, a sewer is overflowing, oil has been spilled on the road, a house is on the point of collapsing because of subsidence, branches of trees have been blown into the street, and demolition work is creating danger for pedestrians below the building. Under these circumstances, some people call the police first because they do not know who else to call or think that the service is not available outside of normal working hours. The police are also involved in cases of old people falling out of bed and not being able to get back in again (Laurie, 1972, p. 92), in attending fires and road accidents, in helping people locked out of their homes or cars, in taking care of injured or stray animals (once a llama was injured while being transported to a circus and the elephant keeper of the Artis Zoo was called out to assist), and in aiding people in situations involving sudden death or sudden birth (at 12.40 a.m. one night patrolmen assisted at the delivery of a baby girl weighing 2.8 kg to the wife of a French barge skipper who had moored behind Central Station). Such incidents were largely unproblematic for the police although they were sometimes performed grudgingly. Much depended on the status, predicament and response of the people involved (lack of gratitude, for instance, might sour the transaction) and, at times, a call for help might provide some light relief:

> There was a call in day-time to a foot patrol that a bus-driver required assistance across from Central Station. The problem was a little, grey-haired old lady of about eighty, who refused to get out of the bus. She had got on in Amstelveen, given the driver ten guilders, and asked for Vlaardingen. He assumed that she intended to catch a train at Central Station for Vlaardingen. 'Well granny', asked one constable, 'where are you off to then?' She replied that she was going to see her parents and wanted to surprise them. 'Parents?' remarked the constable with a smile. He suggested that she might already have reached the age of seventy but she insisted that she was thirty-seven. From documents in her handbag it appeared that she was staying at an old people's home. A patrol-car was called to take her back. Gently she was eased out of the bus and into the back of the patrol-car. There she picked up one of the policemen's hats from the back seat and put it on. Laughing, the crew put on the siren and drove off into the busy traffic along the Damrak with the old lady waving regally out of the window.
>
> (Field notes)

But, in essence, the police were drawn into peace-keeping by people involved in interpersonal disputes or in behaviour which neighbours or passers-by considered out of the ordinary. A man has constructed a rudimentary wire fence carrying 220 volts of electricity to keep out the neighbour's cats; a man has been urinating through the letter-box of an attractive woman living nearby ('but the sexual excitement aroused by this act is not shared by the woman'); a woman complains that the interference on her television is caused by the electric train-set of a twenty-two-year-old neighbour; and civilian drivers of the police towing truck called for assistance with a fifty-year-old shopkeeper who was preventing them removing his illegally parked car. There were eight tickets under his windscreen-wiper together with the note, 'Ha, ha, traffic wardens. Inside you can get free pens and there is still a lot more room on my windscreen'. The man refused to identify himself to the police and was taken to the station among shouts of 'Fascists' from the huge crowd that had gathered (after he was released, the man phoned the station to make a complaint about the behaviour of the constables). These cases from the Station Diary concern basically private squabbles which have got out of hand and whereby one or both of the parties is emotionally worked up. Often involving family members, neighbours or acquaintances, these disturbances arise from unusually long-standing differences of opinion which suddenly escalate and lead to a police presence. They symbolise the inability of some people to solve their own frictions and problems which, for some reason, move from the private to the public sphere.

A middle-aged woman was being troubled by an elderly man, who had previously lived in the flat, and his female companion. Helped by neighbours, the besieged lady began to throw water over the heads of the troublesome couple who retaliated by smashing two large windows with a hammer. The inhabitants of the block charged after them and, following a chase and a scuffle, the man received a bloody head wound. The patrolmen arrived and packed him off to the Wilhelmina Gasthuis (Hospital) in a taxi. The original complainant then refused to prefer charges because she claimed that the detectives in the Warmoesstraat were corrupt and under the thumb of the underworld. An eighty-five-year-old man was threatening to set fire to a neighbouring flat with a bottle of petrol because a Chinese family was plaguing him with persistent loud music. The patrolmen conciliated between the two and asked the home beat officer (derogatorily referred to by the men as the 'beat sister') to keep an eye on the situation. A husband went back to fetch the children from his former wife but instead received several blows from her new man. In response to a call to a fight, two patrolmen discovered 'five women, apparently lesbians, deeply under the influence of drink, of whom several were completely covered in blood'. One of them, a forty-five-year-old woman with a head wound, refused to give any personal information, did not want to make a statement, and declined help from the Health Service. The constables dejectedly reported that they were given no opportunity to arbitrate.

People call out the police in situations where the people themselves are frightened to do or say anything, where they hope the presence of uniformed policemen will have a salutary effect, and where they are trying to be helpful in calling attention to something amiss. Some of the policemen resented being called in to do the work of other people and sometimes, if a neighbour complained about loud music (a frequent occurrence in densely populated Amsterdam), they would maliciously inform the miscreant about the source of their information. At the same time the concern of neighbours could uncover serious situations which demanded some action:

Early on a Friday afternoon a patrol-car asked for the van to come to an address to fetch an old man and two dogs. On arrival we saw a small crowd around a door and two patrol-cars in the street. On the first floor we entered a flat which was indescribably filthy and which smelt like the foulest of sewers. Seated on a settee, in clothes which were matted to his body with filth, was an old man. Two spaniels snapped at the patrolmen who shouted at the old man to get up while they held handkerchiefs over their noses. There were piles of excrement from the dogs all over the carpet and the floor was covered with torn newspapers; the man was surrounded with charred paper where he had, either accidently or purposely, set fire to the settee and almost to himself. The smell of burning mingled with that of excrement. A neighbour had called the police when she smelt smoke and the story had come out about the man's condition. The neighbours had tried earlier to persuade him to go to the Social Services Department but he had replied by lightly wounding a woman in the chest with a knife. Tired of the almost overpowering smell, two patrolmen grabbed the old man, pulled him unwillingly down the stairs and shoved him, with his two yapping dogs, complaining into the back of the van. We drove with the windows wide open, with the sliding roof open, and with our heads out of the windows to escape the smell. The old man and his dogs were brought to the station where he faced an attempted murder charge.

(Field notes)

Often the policemen involved in such incidents were faced with the problem of deciding whether or not an offence had taken place (or, more crucially, if one of the parties would, when calmed down, be prepared to swear a statement); of ascertaining culpability in terms of the participants' accounts and visual evidence; of how much time to invest in the episode (many say 'Get out as quickly as possible'); of considering what sort of advice or warning to give and whether or not another service should be called in; and of weighing up the likely outcomes for themselves and the participants which might take into account some unspoken assumption such as the belief that neighbours had to learn to live with each other's peculiarities or that marital problems simply cannot be solved. These often unedifying private squabbles were rarely seen as social problems to be solved but more likely as inevitable frictions requiring a ritualised intervention, a few stereotyped phrases, and an avoidance of deep involvement. For example, early one evening we were called to a 'domestic dispute' in the Marninxstraat:

An elderly man opened the door and invited us into his archetypally furnished Dutch flat, overpopulated with staid furniture and menacing plants. The man who was in his pyjamas began agitatedly, 'We're at the end of our tether. My wife is completely destroyed with nerves and is under doctor's orders. She's taking five types of pills. It's the people upstairs – don't interrupt me dear [to his wife in hair-net and pyjamas], let me tell it. He is a ponce, excuse me for using the word, but they've turned this house into a brothel. They moved in and squatted in the flat and now that woman flaunts herself naked in front of an open window, ask the people on the other side of the road if you don't believe me, and she's just a foreign slut, a whore, that's all I can say. The police were here last week and took her to the station. The children are neglected and run wild around the house. I can't take any more. Look lads, if you can find me another flat you can have five thousand guilders in your hand, I mean it, five thousand guilders. Because I'm telling you that if something isn't done about them then I'll sink a knife in his back, believe me, I'll do him in.'

We went upstairs to investigate, expecting bedlam, and found a young couple with two children who appeared well looked after. The man himself had actually phoned the police to complain about the neighbour below whose card-games and parties were disturbing their peace. He was a quiet serious man himself, a bit of an intellectual in fact, who liked to read in peace. If his wife did occasionally appear in nightclothes near the window then it certainly was not consciously done and was quite normal. But if he met the old bloke again on the stairs abusing his wife then he would give him a thick ear. Herman issued a stern warning to both men not to resort to fists because he would be back to book them both for assault. In the car we discussed the problems that would have arisen if we had taken the older man's word; having talked to him first we were already prejudiced against the neighbours until we saw their well-ordered flat and had heard their side of the argument. Herman said it was really a housing problem but these old people paid very low rents and could not find anything in Amsterdam which they could afford and which suited them.

(Field notes)

Both accounts were convincingly portrayed. There was no attempt made to verify the counter-accusations and the incident was put down to 'housing' which, in Amsterdam, can be used to explain almost everything.

The avoidance of involvement in the social problems of people could easily be explained by saying that most policemen did not consider it part of their work. But two vital factors underpinned this feeling. On the one hand, the individual policeman knew that he was dealing with ambiguous cases which he was expected to pacify without resort to arrest because this would offend norms in the wider society surrounding domestic disputes, would present the station with 'limp' cases that might not result in a charge, and would show himself to be maladroit at coping with such disturbances. On the other hand, the police organisation generally resented the accumulation of ambivalent cases which were seen as devolving on to the police because of failures in the social services and their conspicuous absence outside of office hours. There was a tendency in the station to be disdainful of many cases which were unavoidably thrust upon the police by others and to attempt to get rid of them as quickly as possible. This could lead to a sort of 'tug of war' in reverse where the police and another agency endeavoured to rid themselves of an unwanted client. A doctor from the city health service explained:

The policemen should be able to understand something about the most important cases. But mostly they have an antipathy to junkies, do not take our work seriously, and feel that people are putting on an act. Sometimes I've had arguments in stations, usually about an overlapping of our responsibilities. For example, I have perhaps three or four places available in what are known as the cabins for serious cases but a duty-officer will try to get me to take a drunk whereas I want to keep the cabins free for really serious drunks or disturbed people. I remember once having an argument for a quarter of an hour about a drunken woman when the sergeant said, 'This is not a case for us either and if you don't take her she'll leave and I can't stop her', but eventually he gave in. Once at District 5 I was told, 'You take him or we'll put him outside on the street'. But usually you come to a compromise and negotiation is always possible.

For a station-sergeant also has his accommodation problems and preferred to keep the cells (or, following hotel parlance, 'rooms', as they were called in the Warmoesstraat) available for serious offenders. This sparring over responsibility for cases had a number of consequences. One was that policemen tried to rid themselves of drunks and people behaving 'strangely'. Given that norms concerning drunkenness were fairly tolerant in the city-centre, it meant that a drunk had to be either persistently difficult or else a danger to himself or others (like the Turk who stood in the middle of a one-way street urinating 'against the traffic flow'). Unless such a person was completely incapable he was placed on a bus, in a taxi or, in some cases, brought home. The difficulty of ridding the streets of a senseless drunk can be highlighted by an incident in which a German sailor lay absolutely flat out in the Oudezijds Achterburgwal. His face was a deathly colour and his trousers were half over his buttocks revealing excrement in his underpants. Two drunken compatriots were vainly trying to lift him. One constable remarked that he looked in a bad way and called an ambulance. The ambulancemen refused to take him. Eventually the friends staggered off with him. Twenty minutes later another patrol called the ambulance and again the drunk was refused. He was then carried to a taxi and taken back to his ship. If the man had not had friends to help him he would have had to be taken to the cells. In other cases people under the influence of alcohol or drugs behaved in such a way as to leave almost no alternative but to detain them:

At about four in the morning our car received a message to go to a street where someone was lying on the ground. A woman lay huddled in a sleeping position in one of the narrow, smelly passages in the 'warme buurt'. She appeared to be about 30 years old, was wearing jeans and a T-shirt, and had long red hair. Theo went over and said softly, 'What's the matter, mevrouw? Aren't you feeling well?' There was no answer. He began to remove the hair from her face when suddenly the slumbering figure exploded into a screaming creature which punched Theo hard on the nose. She was pulled to her feet whereupon she gave Theo a hefty kick in the shins with her clogs. He kicked back and Tom rushed up to grab her other arm but he too received a vicious kick. Both the men had her arms behind her back in arm-locks so she lashed out backwards like a wild horse and began to swear and spit. She received a punch in the back and was hauled off to the station some hundred and fifty yards away. Four men were necessary to get her arms together for the handcuffs; by going rigid she made it difficult for them to move her to a central-heating pipe in the corridor where she was handcuffed to the pipe. She lay there kicking, spitting and screaming, refusing all co-operation, and picking out each constable for some personal abuse. Eventually her feet were also handcuffed and she was carried to the van like a sack of potatoes. The driver had forgotten the keys so she was dumped on the road until he went back to get them. When the van was opened she was heaved on to the floor and when she swore too obscenely on the way to the hospital the driver stood on the brakes, making her roll around the floor. At the hospital she was transferred to a stretcher where the sister in charge strapped her with plastic handcuffs to the trolly. Screaming 'I'm not sick, I'm not sick', the woman was wheeled away to the crisis centre.

(Field notes)

Another side-effect of differences in responsibility was that the police would retaliate by dumping a serious case on the city health service. If the doctor on duty refused to attend because he felt it was a simple case of drunkenness or because the 'strange' behaviour did not seem serious enough to warrant his presence, then two men would take the 'patient' in an unmarked police-car to the nearest hospital, shove him out near the first-aid department, and then drive off at high speed. To a certain extent such practices have grown out of an incapacity to think in other than simple, straightforward and manageable categories and also out of a genuine aversion to being forced into making a medical diagnosis. This arises partly from an instinct of self-preservation, in that duty-officers always hope to end the day or night with a clean sheet and with nothing that rebounds. I heard of a bovine Marechaussee who dragged an unconscious drunk from an alleyway to the station only to discover that on arrival the man was dead. The body was quickly brought back to the alleyway and the city health service received an anonymous phone call that a man had been taken ill on the street. There was too a tendency in the city-centre to view people lying in the street as either drunks or junkies rather than as physically or mentally ill:

We received a call for 'man lying in the street' and arrived to find a small crowd gathered around a prostrate man. Herman had just lit a cigar and, without putting on his cap, got out of the car and strolled over to the man. With hands in his pockets and with the cigar in his mouth, he casually tapped the man in the ribs with his shoe and said, 'Come along, old boy, wake up'. A young woman was horrified and said, 'You don't have to kick him, he might be ill, or injured', but Herman replied, 'It wasn't really a kick, miss, and in ninety per cent of the cases they are just dead drunk, at least in this area anyway'. But the man was quite unconscious and had a bleeding wound on the back of the head so an ambulance was called; now that he had ceased to be a 'drunk' and had become 'injured' the two patrolmen became more solicitous, looked for further injuries, and assisted the ambulancemen to get the stretcher into the back of the ambulance.

(Field notes)

Occasionally this reductionism could have tragic consequences. For example, in another station a young man of eighteen was put in a cell to sober up when in fact he had been the victim of an assault by six youths. The account of the fight by his father was disbelieved, no medical advice was sought, and the boy was found dead in the cell in the morning, having died from serious brain damage (*De Telegraaf*, 12 Jan 1977). In the Warmoesstraat I saw a man enter two evenings running to complain that he was being followed. He came repeatedly and was treated with disbelieving good humour even when he threatened to fly. Eventually he went to Central Station, climbed on to the roof and jumped off. He fell half on to a rescue blanket held by firemen but died later of his injuries. But because the man could walk and talk there was no reason to detain him and no way of interesting the health service in his case. While gaps in services and mutual incomprehension can be used to explain such deficiencies, it was also the case that the policemen tended to have a somewhat brutalised and impersonal attitude to 'social' cases. Drunks were sometimes handled like objects to be transported and were heaved into the van like a parcel might be or even thrown over the shoulder of an extrovert constable who then swaggered into the station with his find. Because of the frequency of such cases, a man lying on the street in the city-centre was almost by definition a drunk and anyone acting strangely was 'flipped'. A rather bewildered Finnish girl entered the station one day to inquire about a friend but could find no language in which to communicate with the sergeant. She was taken to the cells, searched, and her identity was checked as if she was a suspect rather than someone merely seeking information (this episode was recorded for a television documentary). This incident was explained by the lack of time in the station whereby everything had to be done quickly, but more likely it portrays an inability to perceive people as other than potential suspects or as 'difficult'.

For a red-light district one very specific element in keeping the peace related to the relationship between prostitute and client. Men who came to the station to detail their complaints were generally told that the police could do nothing for them unless a crime had been committed. A girl who steals from a man's wallet can be charged with theft, but not so if the man has handed over money and later disagrees over the price or the amount of change. The police will, of course, intervene if the prostitute is attacked and calls for help (generally she has an older lady close by, who looks after the rooms and who has some form of alarm system for emergencies, or else has a ponce in close attendance). Although these cases are reported with humour and euphemism by the police, prostitutes have been violently assaulted and one was stabbed to death by a client during the research period. Indeed, in one month, January 1975, three attempted murders of prostitutes were recorded. This abrasive element has doubtless always been present in prostitution, but it has increased recently in Amsterdam with a number of criminally inclined prostitutes who are solely concerned with tricking or robbing their clients and with 'junkie' prostitutes who are desperate for money in order to buy heroin. Previously the red-light district was almost considered a wholesome part of Amsterdam's night-life and the prostitutes were often long-serving members of a deviant but well-ordered community. Norms about payment and performance were stable and accepted, the girls were well known to each other, and many were known throughout the area by their nicknames, e.g. Cor Cunt, Annie Head and Arse, Miep Shit and Marie Cross-eye (Groothuyse, 1970, p. 49). Now the girls complain that the old craft ways are in decline, that Black girls who rob are driving the good clients away, and that junkies catering for 'guest-workers' at cheap prices and without condoms (*Nieuwe Revu,* 4 Feb 1977) are undercutting the trade. Perhaps more than in the past, then, prostitution produces a proportion of aggrieved clients in the red-light district, some of whom ask for the police to arbitrate on their behalf.

If the police do intervene then the incident is usually recorded as 'assistance rendered'. This arises partly from the police definition of the situation, as not involving a clear-cut and provable offence, and also partly from the reluctance of one or both parties to press charges. For example, there was the case of a Spaniard who had 'made it with a prostitute in every conceivable manner' for 35 guilders but was still not satisfied and a scuffle broke out. As the woman had nothing on 'which the Spaniard could get hold of', he grabbed her by the hair and throat. The woman was a well-known junkie, who had turned to prostitution to pay for her habit, who welcomed the arrival of the police, but who preferred not to make a statement. Both were sent on their way. In another case, a girl had tried to earn the 30 guilders agreed price by 'hand-work' alone, and when the man complained she took another client. The dissatisfied client snatched her purse in order to get his money back and she began to scream for help. Generally, these cases are settled with a compromise, and with no police action, because the client had technically received something for his money. The prostitute agrees an initial price on the street but, once inside, she titillates the client and tries to make further services dependent on renegotiation of the price. If the client refuses, or because of drunkenness cannot perform adequately, he is pushed out in the street. He willingly parted with his money and received sexual favour in return so that there is no question of an offence, although the man may feel cheated. Sometimes the policemen can help to negotiate a settlement. An Irishman, whom the constables found difficult to understand because of his accent, had a difference of opinion with a Black prostitute, but when she agreed to return 10 guilders, both were satisfied with the deal.

With mutual accusations flying around it is sometimes difficult to ascertain what exactly has occurred. A man complained that, whilst he was in the toilet, the prostitute had stolen 110 guilders from his coat; she countered by declaring – with her 'madam' as eye-witness – that he was able to do whatever he wanted but that he later regretted spending so much on it. A Portuguese seaman was missing 100 marks after a visit to a prostitute and accused her of stealing it; she returned the money but protested bitterly that it had been earned by hard work (she was advised by the police to try a civil court). An Israeli agreed a price with a prostitute but, when he saw her naked, maintained that he had bidden too high and demanded a halving of the sum; the report continued: 'Actually the woman displayed understanding for the disillusionment she had caused him because she gave him 10 guilders back but not before the constables had intervened.' A twenty-eight-year-old American paid two prostitutes 100 guilders each to behave as lesbians for him; when he ordered them to perform cunnilingus they refused on the grounds that doctor's treatment had left them 'salt-less'. He called at the station to complain. On another occasion a man was taking down his trousers when the light went out and the prostitute he was visiting disappeared. A week later he saw her and called the police, claiming that she had taken his money. She explained that there had been an argument over how exactly the act was to be performed. He anticipated more for his money while she insisted that he could not achieve a state suitable for execution of his role in the affair. By these sorts of ploys some of the girls try to earn as much as possible while giving as little as possible. Furthermore, some victims often appear to ask for trouble. A sixty-two-year-old man was entertained by two girls; 'he was known as a pervert and wished to have his fun in a manner that was different from the usual. This special way contained, as part of the performance, a cushion being placed over his head. When he took the cushion away he was 1300 guilders lighter' (cases from Station Diary).

Although the policemen were intervening in disputes over implicit contracts based on illicit services, there was a tendency to adopt the norms of the area surrounding the prostitutes' trade. Predatory prostitutes, particularly if they were Black, were treated as suspects, but regular White prostitutes were normally supported in arguments with clients:

One evening a respectable, middle-aged man approached a foot-patrol in the Oudezijds Achterburgwal and said that he had been cheated out of 25 guilders by a prostitute. He was a Dutch American who listened to the girl's come-on chat to prospective clients in which 25 guilders was mentioned. He went up to her, spoke in English, and followed her into her room without discussing the price. Shortly afterwards he left not only dissatisfied but with only 50 guilders change from a 100 guilder note. He was claiming a further 25 guilders back, while complaining that he had received nothing for his money. We entered the premises of the young Black prostitute who was wearing the briefest of mini-skirts and a revealing blouse. In reply to the accusation she began a vehement tirade. In short she said, 'He followed me in and started talking English so I automatically doubled the price like I do for every foreigner. Then I got his prick out and he wanted to fuck me with my clothes off. Look, nobody fucks me with my clothes off for 25 guilders, nobody. Then the silly old fool couldn't get a proper hard-on and when he couldn't come after ten minutes I shoved him out. Then the bastard starts talking Dutch.' The policemen listened to this and then turned to the

man. Paul said, 'Did she hold your prick', and the man replied
sheepishly, 'Well, yes she did'. Paul went on, 'You didn't tell us that
did you? Anyway, you gave her the money, you didn't agree a price
but she did hold your prick, so you got something for your money,
and ten minutes is the rule around here. Then that business of
pretending not to understand Dutch, well, I think you tried to be a
bit of a smart Alec. But we can't do anything more for you.'

(Field notes)

More generally, the policemen in the Warmoesstraat were wary of
many social-welfare cases (cf. Reiss, 1971, p. 22) which were not
perceived as real police work and which placed the policeman in
awkward and even risky situations (cf. J. Wilson, 1968, p. 24, and for
policemen murdered while handling 'domestics', Snibbe and Snibbe,
1973, p. 410). The broader category of peace-keeping remained largely unarticulated although it played an important role both in policing
the inner city and in defining positively a policeman's ability to handle
his cases and cope with people. Perhaps developments in the structure
of police work and in the red-light district itself made peace-keeping
more difficult to accomplish for the younger constables. But the
evidence presented above hopefully aids in illuminating the arbitrari-
ness of the distinction between 'law-enforcement' and 'social work'.
Building on Bittner's concept of peace-keeping, which he in turn
initially derived from Banton (1964), it is possible to view the policeman as someone with unique access to the law as a means of maintaining order, including the use of legitimate physical force. A benign and
experienced constable, polished at handling 'domestics', still brings to
the situation a uniform, weaponry and a battery of resource charges
(Chatterton, 1973) which can be called upon if he fails to negotiate a
satisfactory outcome. Shearing and Leon (1976, p. 289) follow this
line of argument when they say:

In terms of this analysis of the police role, any suggestion, on the
basis of the fact that policemen seldom actually enforce the law or
use physical force, that the police in reality serve a 'social service'
rather than a 'law-enforcement' function is clearly unfounded.
Equally unfounded is any attempt to classify police activity into two
classes, 'social service' or 'law enforcement'. To suggest that a
policeman is a 'law officer' only when he is enforcing the law is as
misleading as to suggest that a surgeon is only a surgeon when he is
actually performing surgery.

Here I have endeavoured to move beyond that false dichotomy in order to investigate the reality of the help-control element in the peace-keeping continuum in concrete interactions and the complexities of the defining-labelling process.

Further, the policemen's encounters with civilians were shown to be largely routine and unproblematic. The handling of specific cases was rooted in a complex, unwritten code which was related to conceptions of sex, age, place, time and legitimacy and which was grounded in the social realities of inner-city life. A powerful latent notion of policing the area concerned order-maintenance practices which were particularly employed to deal with interpersonal tensions and conflicts where resort to legal measures was deemed inappropriate although it remained as a resource if a satisfactory outcome could not be achieved. Those who seriously threatened the order of the inner city and who engaged in behaviour that could more unambiguously be defined as 'criminal' will be dealt with in the following chapter.

6   Crime, Drugs and Blacks in the Inner City

(i) CRIME

The imagery of crime-fighting permeates the public stereotype of police work (Manning, 1977, pp. 13, 347 ff.) and Amsterdam is no exception. Press articles spoke of the 'sick' and the 'unsafe' city and the Mayor, Chief Constable and trade associations expressed their anxiety about the deleterious effect of crime and the shortcomings of the police ('Crime in Capital Disturbing', 'Shopkeepers Concerned about Crime', and 'Extra Police for the Capital', *De Telegraaf*, 7 Jan 1976, and 14 Apr 1977, and 21 May 1977, respectively). The normally staid daily, *De Volkskrant,* ran two major articles on crime in the city-centre and painted a bleak picture of people frightened to walk the streets and of business driven out to the safer suburbs (9 and 16 July 1977). A Trade Association for the City Centre stated, 'The street terror, muggings in dark alleys, molesting of foreigners, the aggressive drug trafficking, puking junkies, and ear-splitting noise at night in the Warmoesstraat police district all lead to racial hatred' ('Amsterdam Hoofstad?', 1977). To visit parts of the inner city at night was described as being as dangerous as an evening walk through Central Park or Harlem (*Elseviers Magazine,* 8 Oct 1977) while *De Telegraaf* (30 Apr 1977) ran an article under the headline 'Pickpockets, Knifings, Muggings, Homosexual Prostitution, Drug Dealing: Daily News in and around Central Station'. In effect, the media were making a clear relationship between crime and race and were depicting the inner city as a dangerous 'no-man's-land' (*De Telegraaf,* 16 Apr 1977). In a television documentary about the Warmoesstraat the head of the uniformed branch warned that if one of his men died 'all hell would break out', and the station chief foresaw the possibility of a 'minor war' developing. For the public, and the policemen who work there, the *leitmotiv* of the Warmoesstraat is combating dangerous crime

149

(*Elseviers Magazine,* 21 Feb 1976) and, in particular, the spotlight focuses on drugs and Surinamers.

Earlier we established that the Warmoesstraat area gave rise particularly to predatory or 'street' crime. There were many complaints of, and arrests for, 'muggings' (robbery on the street), drug possession and trafficking, carrying a weapon or firearm, breaking into and stealing from cars, pickpocketing on tram, bus and street, assaults and woundings, theft, for 'penniless' foreigners and for persons on the 'wanted' list. Many offences are committed within a few hundred yards of the station and a senior policeman who had visited many countries on police business told me that he had never encountered such a highly concentrated criminal area as in the inner city of Amsterdam. The Chief Constable admitted that the force could not cope with all the types of crime with which it was confronted and was being forced more and more to set priorities:

> You begin to set priorities with 'This and that we're prepared to tackle, but the rest we'll leave alone'. Stolen bikes, theft from a car, shoplifting, perhaps even pocket-picking, are things we cannot spend time on. It's sad, I know, but we don't have the organisation to cope with all these and if we did try to then we would lose our grip on the big cases. . . . It is a vicious circle and I don't know how we can break out of it. I know that the police have lost a lot of ground, quite a lot, but I don't know how they can win it back or even if it would be worthwhile to win back those areas (Punch, 1976b, p. 15).

This semi-official policy was, in effect, a recognition that the priorities were already being set by the reality on the streets, and by the neglect and failure of preventive measures. Detectives in the Warmoesstraat became adept at talking victims of minor offences out of making a statement, and the endemic stealing of bicycles led simply to a swift registration of the details with no attempt to trace the stolen property so that eventually insurance companies refused to provide cover for bikes (*Het Parool,* 16 June 1977; *De Telegraaf,* 19 Aug 1977). A detective complained:

> In fact it works out that you're almost always inside. Because you're always completing your cases. Everyone sits behind their typewriter. I can't say, 'I'll go and see what's happening in the district', because that's impossible in your normal duty hours. It is becoming pretty well impossible to stay in touch with the area and with your

informants. You just sit here like a sort of computer. You stick the
paper in at one end and it comes out the other end.

(Detective, 46 years)

This feeling of frustrating ineffectiveness also afflicted the uniformed policemen. They were conscious that their territory was repu-
ted to be one of the most dangerous and criminal areas in The
Netherlands if not in Europe, that much of the criminality occurred in a
small area that was relatively intensively patrolled, and that they were
largely incapable of combating that criminality. And crime for them
was not the spectacular case – the breakthrough, the photo in the
newspaper with the haul, and the public accolade – but street crime
which was petty, mean, unsophisticated and which concerned offences
involving small sums of money, crude burglaries, drunken destructive-
ness, aimless aggression, and with characters low in the criminal
hierarchy. An American policeman admitted this (Terkel, 1975,
p. 194) and one of my respondents lamented:

Let's face it, we only nick the shlemiels, the riff-raff, and never get
our hands on the big villains. If you go around 'de wallen' at three
o'clock in the afternoon and see the big cars parked outside certain
bars, and inside you see respectable-looking gentlemen in well-
tailored suits with ties, then they are the real villains who never get
their hands dirty. But you never get your hands on them.
Take —— for instance, you'll never catch him with anything on him
because he uses poor scum to do his dirty work for him on the
streets.

(Constable, 33 years)

Nevertheless, for many of them 'real' police work meant an arrest or a
search of a suspect. Rubinstein (1973, p. 362) notes, 'most policemen
enjoy nothing better than making a felony arrest. All of the ambiguities and contradictions that shroud so much of his work disappear
when the policeman is in pursuit of someone he believes has done
something criminal.'

This selective perception is understandable when one appreciates
that much of the routine activity of the patrolmen was mundane,
monotonous and devoid of crime-related activity and that some of
them felt they were actually being deflected from effectively tackling
crime. Local government policies, a liberally-minded judiciary, and
informal 'soft-line' attitudes to crash-pads, drug-treatment centres

and the Surinamers in the city-centre were alleged to hinder the policeman and to undermine his motivation:

> There are no priorities and there is no guidance for the young constables. They start as enthusiastic, good, willing lads and they end up with blinkers, walking around for two hours, not seeing things until they get back to the station, hand over to the next couple, and go upstairs and play cards. Within a week of coming here they are apathetic. Because the lads go out on the streets and they walk around seeing what is allowed–vice, pornography, gambling, and so on. But no one touches the big villains. So they end up picking up a Turk for pissing in an alley–for 'offending public decency', a great phrase!–and a Turk is a perfect prisoner because he can't speak the language, doesn't know what's going on, and doesn't resist. Or they go to the Zeedijk, throw a Black up against a wall, search him, and find something in his pocket so they take him to the station. Even if they know it's fake hash then they will still be inside for half an hour. On the way to the station they give the Surinamer a kick on his ankle and with a bit of luck they'll get a 'resisting arrest' charge as well.
>
> (Constable, 33 years)

Another policeman maintained that at one period the frustration among some men was so intense that they refused to write tickets for minor offences while, in their opinion, more serious incidents were being overlooked:

> I had a period when I said I'm not going to do anything any more. That was when we used to raid 'De Cotton Club' practically every week, or ''t Winkeltje'. But then the boss said, 'you're not allowed inside because it looks like discrimination against the Surinamers'. So we weren't allowed to carry out controls, also not in derelict houses, which is just in our opinion where the biggest scum is. All that was left over was the back light on a bike or someone driving through a red light on his way to work. Then we said to each other, 'An ordinary bloke who drives through a red light on his way to work won't get a ticket from us, as long as people can shoot heroin and handle stolen goods; so we will stop handing out tickets for ordinary people'. But that only lasted for a few days. We raided 'De Cotton Club' because we wanted to close it; it's a bad club with a lousy reputation. We had just come from the training school and we

knew the laws on closing times and on licences by heart. Then in practice, you see businesses that come nowhere near complying with the law, no licences, nothing. . . . We are also not allowed in the 'De Prinsenhof' any more. Heroin is illegal, so it's a simple business, you take away the heroin. They are shooting more or less legally and also with our money. They have to steal like magpies to get enough money to buy heroin. If I come across someone like that and he has heroin on him then he comes under the Drugs Act. There ought to be a much tougher line taken against these people.

(Constable, 26 years)

Occasionally there was a spectacular or peculiar case which brought the patrolmen satisfaction, but it is in the nature of street crime that it is easy to commit, easy to avoid detection, and that it reinforces the uniformed man's perception of his ineffectiveness and powerlessness. But in a sense, the large amount of undetected crime meant that the policemen took great pleasure in catching a thief actually at work or in uncovering drugs or stolen goods, for the prisoner represented all those who got away with it (Harris, 1973, p. 131). For example, 'Ad' recounted the best arrest he had ever made:

One evening an eighty-year-old woman and her daughter, aged about sixty, were robbed of around 1500 guilders and maltreated by several young men who drove off in a car with an Italian number plate. Later in the evening a car fitting the description was seen in the area. Two policemen were posted nearby. After a long wait, just when the men were thinking of giving up, a young man walked up to the car. They grabbed him and 'leaned' on him to find out where his mates were. His three friends, young Italians who needed the money for drugs, were staying at a hotel and, with reinforcements, the two patrolmen went to the hotel. There they rushed into the room with drawn pistols; one man was brushing his teeth, standing in his pyjamas at the sink, and swung around in panic. In short spurts he wet himself. Clearly the nature of the crime, the humiliation of the elderly ladies, the long wait, the successful outcome, and the panic-stricken reaction of the suspects, made it an unambiguous moral victory for the policemen.

(Field notes)

In practice, however, the uniformed man was often handicapped by his visibility in attaining arrests, unless he was lucky enough to catch someone red-handed, and a special group in plain clothes operated in the area in order to have more chance of apprehending suspects committing street crimes. Indeed, Chatterton (1976b, p. 110) shows that the public often provides the police with the prisoner. Picking up a shoplifter from the Bijenkorf department store was basically an escort task requiring no initiative on the part of the policemen. Spectacular and dramatic arrests were a rarity and there was often an anticlimactic element to 'crime-fighting' as in the following incident:

Late one evening in January we overheard a message to another car to attend to fighting in the Zeedijk. Immediately Hans headed the patrol-car towards the area but on the way the message was changed to 'Armed men have stolen a taxi and are heading in the direction of the IJ Tunnel'. Our car was close to the tunnel so we raced off, tearing around narrow corners and lurching over pavements, while Bert was holding on to the knob for the blue light which was not working properly and did not always make contact. Near Central Station the traffic lights were red and a car stood in the middle of the lane apparently impervious to the rapidly approaching patrol-car with its siren and intermittently functioning blue lamp. Hans grabbed the loud-hailer and shouted, 'Move over, you prick', while Bert swore and gesticulated furiously and I waved an angry fist through the rear window. On turning into the tunnel we were again confronted with red lights and waiting cars which were slow to react. Hans hit the brakes and the car juddered wildly across the carriageway, narrowly missing a saloon car and ending up on the central island. 'This car is a death-trap', Hans shouted as he tried to get it back in gear while messages came through continually that the suspects were not far in front of us. The men were complaining bitterly about the tardiness of the 'Beetle' which wouldn't go faster than 110 k.p.h. and Hans asserted that the conversion to gas had robbed it of its top speed. We reached the outskirts of Amsterdam-North and the limits of the city police jurisdiction but Headquarters ordered the car to keep up the pursuit. The taxi was still not in sight and we were on a cobbled, two-lane road with occasional traffic. Somewhat nervously Bert said, 'This is a highly dangerous road, you know', and Hans snapped back irritably, 'You think I don't know?'. The taxi was reported as passing through a village which we were approaching and both the men took out their pistols and cocked them. 'Maurice, you'd better stay in the car, this might be dangerous.' Hans tried to overtake a bus which did little to move to the side despite the flashing blue light (Bert was still fiddling with the knob), the siren, and the irate tooting of the horn. Because of oncoming traffic the first attempt failed and during the second attempt the bus-driver pulled over and slowed down just as Hans decided he was not going to make it and also braked, almost causing a collision, but we got past. Radio reception was getting poor and Bert cursed our equipment and asked why they did not use the State Police band to reach us. Approaching Hoorn [about 30 kilometres from Amsterdam] we heard that the suspects had turned off on to a side-road and that the State Police would continue the search. In disgust, we broke off the chase for a car we had never seen. On the way back we ran out of the reserve petrol. Hans called for the breakdown truck and indulged in a diatribe against the lousy equipment and poor communications with which the Amsterdam Police fought crime. A message came through that the suspects had been arrested by the State Police on a side-road near Alkmaar: 'Damn it, we should have had them. But they've been caught, and that's the main thing', the men agreed.

(Field notes)

The Warmoesstraat, then, was almost a by-word for involvement in criminal cases and its personnel were accused of being brutal, frightened, lax and corrupt in their 'fight' against crime. The policemen faced a background of constant publicity and a reality where certain deviant activities had been stabilised by informal agreement. This led indubitably to feelings of frustration and ineffectiveness in response to which some men adopted a rather surly ritualism. Another adaptation was to make the work interesting by generating prisoner-taking activity (Cain, 1973, p. 67) and, in the inner city, that meant the partly related areas of drugs and Surinamers.

(ii) DRUGS

In 1972 'hard' drugs (cf. Laurie, 1972) began to make an appearance in relatively large quantities in Amsterdam and did much to change the public image of the city, to alter styles of criminality in the inner city, and to influence daily police work in the Warmoesstraat. In the period January–March 1975 (which was really the 'close season') there were 123 recorded arrests in the Warmoesstraat district of whom the vast majority were young males under 25 years of age and of whom 71 per cent were either foreign nationals or Surinamers, in roughly equal proportions. But this was an underestimate of real activity because a large number of drug 'arrests' were not formally recorded, because the suspect was in possession of a trifling amount of 'soft' drugs or palpably fake hashish, and the suspect was simply released with a brief mention of his particulars in a 'temporary vistors' book. A glance through this book reveals that the majority of cases involved suspicion of drugs and concerned foreigners or Surinamers. The Warmoesstraat was foremost in countering the street drug trade because the drug subculture was centred in the inner city where the Chinese suppliers, the Surinamese dealers, the drug-treatment centres, the crash-pads, the houseboats, the cheap youth hotels and the busy clubs and discothèques all combined to support and supply a thriving industry. Dealers openly approached young foreigners in the main streets and junkies congregated impatiently around the Chinese restaurants of the Zeedijk. The patrolmen became knowledgeable about fake hashish, about 'brown sugar' (heroin which is smoked), about amphetamines, and about the rituals of dealing. They also became accustomed to 'flipped' people on a bad trip and to junkies who were scarcely responsible for their actions (cf. Smith, 1970, p. 82). The police attributed much of the burgeoning street crime directly to heroin; 'the heroin problem sometimes leads to weekends with 150–200 cases of pickpocketing and mugging' (*De Volkskrant,* 3 Oct 1977).

For the combination of liberal policies, open borders, a ready market in youth tourism, virtual refuges in crash-pads, light sentences, and a well-organised drugs syndicate in a hermetically sealed ethnic community meant that Amsterdam had acquired a resilient social problem which coloured a good deal of street life in the inner city (Cohen, 1969, 1975). The city attracted young people from Europe and America who became the victims of the drug industry and who became involved in a subculture where problems relating to drug use, health and disease, illegal residence and criminality were combined (Dahan, 1974).

At the time of the research, drugs were constantly in the headlines in Amsterdam – 'Long Chilly Summer of the "Horse" ', 'Death by Drugs End of Journey to Amsterdam', 'Police Losing Grip on Heroin Smugglers' and 'Heroin-Capital Battleground for Triads' (*De Volkskrant,* 3 Aug 1974; *De Telegraaf,* 2 Aug 1975, 1 May 1976) – and this clearly affected the police consciousness in the inner city. To a certain extent the initial critical publicity focused on the ineffectiveness of the police, but this was partly sponsored by certain senior policemen trying to attract resources to Amsterdam; one of them complained, 'What do you expect? These guys travel by jet and we have to chase them on push-bikes!' (*De Telegraaf,* 17 Aug 1974).

But for the man on the street the early ineffectiveness was daily apparent. For within a few minutes' walk of the Warmoesstraat was 'Chinatown', the heart of international syndicated crime on a massive scale (one uncovered shipment from Thailand of 138 kilos was alone estimated as being worth 30–40 million guilders on the European market: *De Telegraaf,* 1 Sep 1976). The constables could walk into Chinese gambling houses and be greeted deferentially or with smiles and the offer of an expensive cigar. In a way that friendliness only heightened their impotence because the intangible underworld behind the façade of restaurants and gambling was inaccessible to them. They felt that the big fish could operate with seeming impunity while the small fish were swiftly thrown back into the sea by the justice system. And this was against a background of recommendations to decriminal-ise much of the drug legislation (Commissie Hulsman, 1972), of discussions to provide free heroin for addicts in Amsterdam and of radio announcements declaring the market price of soft drugs (by the son of the Minister of Health!: *Elseviers Magazine,* 6 Mar 1975; *Haagse Post Extra,* 'Heroine', 1977). But the heroin 'fever' was all but rampant in the station and generally a 'pinch' for drugs had high status – especially one for hard drugs. If Amsterdam enjoyed the dubious distinction of being a world centre for drugs, then some of the 'Dutch Connection' mythology rubbed off on the policemen even though the uniformed branch mostly crossed swords with unfortunate users, caught in possession, or small-fry middlemen. Because the drug business is largely a 'victimless' crime, in the sense that it rarely produces complainants prepared to sign a statement implicating them-selves, action is produced by catching a deal in the moment of transaction or by anonymous tips (Manning, 1977, pp. 274–9). Often these tips were simply handed on to the specialised Drugs Squad; imprudent and independent initiative by the uniformed branch might seriously disturb months of patient investigation by dectives waiting for a decisive moment to move in. The uniformed men had to rely on luck or chance to be involved in a sizeable deal involving Chinese suspects, although they might be used to back up a raid by detectives.

This meant a subsidiary role for the policemen but they looked for drug arrests because they could initiate stop and search activity on 'suspicion' (rather than in response to a victim's statement or a call from the public). They were relatively easy arrests as street dealers and users were often visible and vulnerable (Young, 1971, p. 29), and they represented a degree of involvement in a nationally publicised problem. It is not surprising, therefore, that some patrolmen become almost obessed with drugs and kept an eye out for young White people hanging around a club for Surinamers, for dishevelled youngsters waiting outside a Chinese restaurant or gambling house, for possible transactions on the street, and for 'hippies' standing near parked cars in the area of drug centres and crash-pads. Many vehicle stops and searches of people on the street were motivated by the possibility of a drugs arrest.

[Are you allowed to search people on the street?]
No, not really, you're not supposed to. You can use the Drugs Act. You are supposed to find drugs before you can search but in practice the sequence is the other way around because you first have to search someone before you can find something. Legally it's a bit dicey, especially if you don't find anything, then a suspect can complain. With a car we're allowed to search under the Traffic Act. For instance, if it says on the log-book petrol and gas then you ask if you can look at the gas-tank in the boot. At the same time you have a good look around the whole boot but then using the Traffic Act and not the Drugs Act. It's all a bit unclear really.

(Constable, 26 years)

The once 'gezellig' (i.e. cosy) red-light district had been transformed as the Chinese, the Surinamers, the 'hippies', the guest-workers, the prostitutes and the underworld united around the supply and use of drugs. And, in particular, the involvement of Surinamers in dealing and street crime presented the patrolmen with an ideal opportunity to focus considerable attention on possibly the most visible and histrionic group in the inner city.

(iii) BLACKS

The Surinamers formed a convenient reservoir of symbolic assailants (Skolnick, 1975, pp. 45–8), of potential prisoners, and of members of a publicly stigmatised out-group for the policemen of the Warmoes-straat. Yet The Netherlands has traditionally enjoyed an enlightened image for race-relations and this was amplified by a sympathetic study in which Bagley (1973a) drew unfavourable comparisons between

British and Dutch attitudes to, and treatment of, mainly coloured
immigrants. But Bagley's field-work was conducted in 1969 before
mass migration from the Dutch West Indies. Since then anti-Black
feelings have been expressed by some elements of press and public
opinion which have developed stereotypes concerning criminality and
'sponging' on social security among immigrants, but especially
Surinamers (Bovenkerk and Bovenkerk-Teerink, 1972). Relationships with the police have also become a cause of controversy and the
police have been accused of brutal and racist methods ('Heldhaftig,
Vastberaden, Barmhartig', 1977), as witnessed by the following decla-
ration:

STATEMENT
On Friday, 8 September our compatriot Paul Heesbeen, aged 23
years, was shot dead in a most cowardly manner by an Amsterdam
policeman. As is always the case, the police have hidden behind the
claim of being 'threatened' in order to justify this senseless
murder. . . . [We demand]
1. That the constable concerned be prosecuted for murder with
   malice aforethought.
2. That the Amsterdam Police cease immediately with their racist
   enforcement against minority groups.
3. That the police organisation should be combed for the presence
   of notorious racists.
4. That the reports of the investigation be made open to the
   representatives of the demonstrative meeting, the composers of
   this statement, and representatives of all those Surinamese organisations that have signed below.
Should these demands not be met then we will step over to
conscious forms of self-defence, with all the attendant consequences. We call upon all Surinamers that, from this moment on,
they take the initiative into their own hands for the defence and
protection of their human rights.
            Amsterdam, 9 September 1972 – 8 September Movement

This emotional proclamation centres on the crucial relationship
between the police and minority groups which has clearly, as in Britain
and America, become a source of tension and grievance (Bayley and
Mendelsohn, 1969; Humphry, 1972; Banton, 1973; Brown, 1974;
Bovenkerk, 1976a). The Warmoesstraat has been singled out for
acrimonious accusations and we have seen how foreigners and

immigrants play an important role in the working life of the station. There are estimated to be about 40,000 Surinamers in Amsterdam, about 6000 of these in the inner city, and to be some 2000 Surinamese addicts in the city (*Haagse Post*, 21 Aug 1976). There can be also little doubt that some young male Surinamers in particular are more than caustic in their views on the host nation:

> Why have I come to Holland? Not to work! Who has got it into their stupid head that I'm going to work for the Dutch. They can drop dead. I've come to this lousy country to get back everything that the Dutch have stolen from my land over the past couple of hundred years. You must not think of me as a countryman. You should see me as an enemy. Because, whatever way you look at it, it is war between the Dutch and the Surinamers. We'll steal whatever there is to steal. And let Holland keep its hands off my dole, otherwise there'll be accidents. It is about time that the good Dutch citizens began to appreciate that the Black won't allow himself to be beaten anymore, and won't speak obediently to the White supermen. The Black is kicking back and is someone not to be sneered at. It is war between Black and White and let us forget all that twaddle about 'countryman' and 'friendship between peoples'. (Interview with 20-year-old Surinamer, allegedly one week after his arrival in The Netherlands, *Elseviers Magazine,* 27 Sep 1975)

In discussing this sensitive issue it is important to bear in mind that the Surinamers are but one of several groups in the city-centre with dark skins but that they tend to be singled out far more than Antillians or guest-workers. Suspects, for example, may describe an assailant as a 'Surinamer' when in fact there is no evidence of ethnic origin or nationality other than skin colour. For apart from occasional cultural friction, say over loud Arabic music or smoky attempts to barbecue a whole sheep, the guest-workers do not conspicuously draw attention to themselves. Their major contacts with the police come either because of illegal entry and false papers or else because of violence with knife or gun surrounding personal quarrels. In addition they are more vulnerable in relation to residence and work permits because of fear instilled by police methods in their home country. The guest-workers have brought some criminal elements with them but their role in street crime has largely been taken over by Surinamers in Amsterdam.

The arrival of the Surinamers and Antillians from the Dutch West

Indies (Surinam became independent in 1975) has brought to the surface hostile stereotypes based on colour (Bovenkerk, 1976b). Officially some 110,000 people have immigrated from Surinam since the war (plus around 10,000 from the Antilles), though the real figure may be closer to 150,000 (Van Amersfoort, 1974; *Beleid en Maatschappij*, 1975). Over the last few years the Surinamer 'problem' has become daily fare for the media with especial emphasis on housing, crime, unemployment, and the concentration of Surinamers in the concrete flats of the Bijlmermeer housing estate. The right-wing press rarely missed an opportunity to report cases of Surinamers who had been involved in muggings, drug cases, pickpocketing, fights and murders. Arriving at a time of recession, large numbers of Surinamers could not find work and accentuated the growing conservative swell that Dutch social security is too generous. (Banfield, 1974, p. 78, maintains that the Blacks arrived 'too late' in the northern cities of America.) An opinion poll among Surinamers claimed that 42 per cent of the respondents enjoyed some form of benefit, whereas officially the figure is put at around 25 per cent. There has been talk of repatriation (Bovenkerk, 1976b), but the relative affluence of The Netherlands in comparison with the native country makes this unlikely; indeed, some 90 per cent of Surinamers replied positively when asked to rate their feelings about The Netherlands (*Elseviers Magazine*, 27 Sep 1975).

Unlike the spreading of the Indonesian immigrants (Bagley, 1973a), there has been a tendency to allow freedom of movement to Surinamers, and this has meant a concentration in the 'randstad' cities of Amsterdam, Rotterdam, The Hague and Utrecht. The centre of Amsterdam in particular has attracted a criminalesque subculture of young Blacks (more than half the Surinamers under 24 are unemployed) who get involved in drugs and mugging and who are a constant headache to the police. The uniformed policeman bears the brunt of conflict situations with minority groups and it is against him that the most complaints are made. As a visible representative of authority the patrolman is called into volatile contact with sometimes embittered and aggressive young immigrants and with inter-racial disputes where he may easily get caught in a double-bind predicament by appearing to discriminate against one or other of the antagonistic groups. Furthermore, when initiating stop and search activities in relation to traffic or suspected criminal offences, the controlling of a member of a minority ethnic group – or indeed any group, such as homosexuals, who may feel discriminated against – may arouse negative reactions based on a feeling of selective enforcement (Rubinstein, 1973, p. 253). A number of studies have approached this dilemma for the policeman with a degree of sympathy for his predicament; for example, Skolnick (1975, p. 86) notes that policemen 'may appear to be discriminating against the Negro, when in fact the policeman is mainly implementing departmental goals by deciding against the poor, the unemployed, and residentially unstable (most of whom are Black)'.

In assessing and interpreting police conduct in this area it is important to keep this predicament in sight because in several societies there have been grave accusations of systematic abuse of minority groups by the police. There can be little doubt that police/minority group encounters are potentially tension-laden and, Sykes and Clark (1974, p. 6) draw attention to the possibility that both parties engage in mutual stereotyping so that they are *both* in a 'double-bind' predicament:

> Thus, it is in encounters between the formally subordinate and the symbolic representatives of the authority which subordinated them that both tend unintentionally to discredit each other. Even with the best intentions, an officer may become a 'racist pig' and the citizen a 'wise ass' if they misunderstand one another's indications. Each may impose on the other his definition of reality . . . but not just stereotyping is involved, for to each actor the indicators which express the asymmetrical status norm convey a double meaning. . . . The asymmetrical status norm, operative in most police–citizen encounters, is difficult to distinguish from the special asymmetrical status norm, operative when ethnic subordinates interact with superordinates.

In the centre of Amsterdam, along the Zeedijk and around the Nieuwmarkt, Surinamers have become a conspicuous element of the social order. In flamboyant clothes, walking jauntily, and talking loudly in 'dialect', groups of young Surinamers take part in a noisy and histrionic subculture centred on discos, clubs, drugs and street crime (Biervliet, 1975; Brana-Shute, 1977). They are frequently not compliant and respectful to bus-drivers, shop-assistants and policemen and have gained the reputation for being obstreperous and self-conscious about their colour. These observations are clearly related to the aggressive Black subculture of young males – suffering adjustment problems in education, employment and social acceptance – and are not generalisable to the Surinamese population as a whole, which has adjusted quite well to changing cultures (Bovenkerk, 1976c). Elements of this 'hustle culture', rooted in the presentation of self and the management of identity of Caribbean youth in a Northern European environment, have also been documented in an American urban ghetto where Suttles (1968, pp. 202–20) discusses the 'displays' of male Blacks, their street life and their encounters with the police. He notes, for instance, that Blacks are 'reduced to the most menial "hustles" that are left–pimping, casual prostitution, shoplifting, "policy" and "reefers" ' (ibid, p. 122).

The Warmoesstraat has been in the forefront of police confrontations with Surinamers and has, on occasion, been showered with complaints alleging discriminating behaviour (Coornhert Liga, 1974, p. 42). Bert said that he arrived in the Warmoesstraat and was immediately told, 'Look out for the Surinamers, you've always got problems with them', while Hans claimed, 'I've spent three years in Surinam and never thought much about it or ever had problems with Surinamers, but within a year of coming to the Warmoesstraat you are anti-Surinamer'. According to Hippler (1971, pp. 62–3), one element in police–Black antagonism is that Blacks sense that the police are both contemptuous and afraid of them and also that derogatory treatment by the police challenges their manliness; he writes of a San Francisco housing project: 'Many arrests and charges of "resisting arrest" or "assaulting an officer" originate from unbearable tongue-lashings by police which humiliate and emasculate young Negro males.' In Amsterdam one vocal Surinamer, Edgar Cairo, complained of the mistreatment by men from the Warmoesstraat and stated that 'it is rather a sad state of affairs that clearly every Surinamer is a suspect' (*De Volkskrant,* 1 Dec 1977). The view from the other side can be seen from an extract from the Station Diary (in which the place of birth is usually the clue to the ethnic origin of the suspect as in one entry I read: 'Born in Paramaribo–where else?'):

The reporters observed that——crossed the street against a red pedestrian light although about thirty people stood waiting. When approached he began immediately to conjure up the well-known catch-phrases such as 'This is racial discrimination' and 'It's because I've got a dark colour', etc. He categorically refused to give his name or other details for the ticket and was brought to the station. He was allowed to leave when he had made known his name and address. On departing, he complained that he had only been given back three rings instead of four, although he signed for three, and was told 'We can't make four out of three either'.

Although the general impression that is fostered in the Warmoes-straat is that the previous complaints were largely unfounded (and earlier we saw that there does seem to be a measure of truth in this viewpoint), one sergeant felt that there were tendencies present in enforcement which justified some of the criticism:

[The complaints of ill-treatment against the Warmoesstraat, were they justified?]
Perhaps that takes me on to slippery ice but I'm not worried about that. I've never been guilty myself of hammering a suspect. Also not during my time in the detectives. There they say now and again, 'If a suspect won't cough, then give him a clip around the ear and then he'll soon confess'. But, Jesus, I've never been around while some-one was being worked over. I did see three constables bring a Black in and he had a handcuff on each hand and these were set too tight so he was screaming. Obviously that's not necessary. But that it has never happened, well, I couldn't guarantee it one hundred per cent; I might rather say that it is probably sixty per cent truth. . . . But to get back to the police officers and especially the attitude of police-men here in the Warmoesstraat towards the Blacks, well, you've doubtless realised that for yourself during the last six months. It can get out of hand now and again. There are some lads who make it their hobby to chase Blacks, every Black in the street has done something wrong, he must be searched. That is not normal. You can tell them not to do it, but it keeps on happening. But, yet, let's hope the constable also becomes old enough to realise that a Black is a person and not an animal who you can say anything to and do anything with. And, once more, if a Black criminal is arrested then he must be treated the same as any normal suspect and be given every chance to make good.

(Sergeant, 36 years)

To a large extent, the patrolmen in the Warmoesstraat were brought into contact with Surinamers in relation to criminality; there was a tendency then to develop a negative stereotype of the Surinamers in the city-centre as parasitical layabouts, who 'sponged' off the dole and who threatened the well-being of mostly White passers-by. This hostility was perhaps magnified by the resilience of the Surinamese subculture and the impotence of the police in combating much of the street crime. Much of this crime occurred within walking distance of the station and yet frequently the suspect escaped detection and cases became entered in the records as crime committed by 'unknown coloureds'. There were even robberies in the Warmoesstraat itself, but the burden of proof was usually insurmountable:

> At about 3.40 a.m. a tall, thin, spotty young Turk in a sheepskin coat entered the station in an agitated state. Using a few words of English and mime – 'He's as mad as a hatter', remarked someone – he conveyed that he had been robbed in a café in the Warmoesstraat. It transpired that this was his first day in The Netherlands and he had gone into 'The Caribbean Nights' and asked a Surinamer to change some money for him. The Surinamer calmly took the wallet (which allegedly contained 800 marks, 300 guilders and 100 guilders worth of Turkish money) out of his hand and walked off. Four constables went the hundred metres to the club and accompanied the man inside. A large number of Surinamers were standing around and we threaded our way through the throng. He could not recognise anyone.
>
> (Field notes)

This may have been a drug deal which misfired so that the victim was also regarded with suspicion. But one night three men came to the station shortly after one another to complain of being 'rolled' in the same club within shouting distance of the station. Rarely is a suspect arrested for such offences, and one caught red-handed was considered a 'good pinch':

> At 10.30 a.m. a foot-patrol was asked to go to a bar in the Nieuwmarkt. There a small, sad-faced Colombian accused a Surinamer of picking his wallet while both were standing at the urinal. Four or five archetypal Latins supported him volubly in Spanish and broken English. They pointed to a corner where a thin, gangling Surinamer, dressed in drainpipe-tight jeans, a sheepskin coat and a white woollen cap, sat on a stool calmly drinking a beer. He denied having anything to do with the Colombian and when he was told that he was going to the station asked if he could finish his drink. He took his time and the patrolmen became impatient and told him he was being awkward and to pay up. Protesting his innocence volubly he was led away by the arm while one constable felt in his pockets. At this his protestations doubled and he began

struggling so both men took hand-locks on him. He tried to wriggle free and shouted at them that they were hurting him. They explained that this was entirely his own fault and that the more he resisted the more it hurt. Protesting he entered the station and protesting he was led into the search-room. The constable searching him emerged with the Colombian's wallet containing 475 guilders. When Henk saw it he roared with laughter and shouted, 'No, no, it can't be, I don't believe it', and jubilantly waved the wallet under the Surinamer's nose.

(Field notes)

In this case the suspect was unlucky and tried to bluff it out; he was working alone and had several people against him while a foot-patrol was conveniently at hand. Normally such an offence was carried out in a crowded tram, in the company of several accomplices, or in or near a Surinamese club. The booty was immediately dispersed and the wallet or purse thrown away. But the casual impudence of some Surinamers' activities led to an arrest on a sunny August morning in a busy street within two minutes' walk of the station:

We left the station on foot-patrol at around 9.30 a.m. and after a few minutes' walk suddenly came upon four Blacks mugging a German tourist. The patrolmen broke into a run and grabbed two of the Blacks while the other two assailants ran off. I found myself, alone, chasing the other two assailants down the street. They stopped for a second to look around and then disappeared into a club frequented by Surinamers. A prostitute came up to me and said, '— did it, but I daren't say anything openly because my man is a Surinamer'. It was a nice case for the patrolmen – two suspects caught in the act, a victim willing to make a statement, and enough information to trace the escaped suspects.

(Field notes)

The Surinamers spilled out on to the streets near their clubs on the Zeedijk or the Nieuwmarkt and sometimes 'molested' passers-by. But like the corner-boys of American cities it was difficult to disperse them because in a sense there was nowhere for them to go and they simply reassembled (Rubinstein, 1973, p. 170). A good deal of police patrol activity was focused here and the Surinamers' lowly street role in the drug hierarchy meant that they were frequently caught in possession of drugs. Their noisy street-corner subculture horrified some older residents who overlooked their clubs and there were many anonymous tips about dealing in the area:

Someone living in the Zeedijk phoned in a tip that dealing was going on outside a club frequented by Surinamers. Four constables hurried there and arrested two Surinamers who were standing outside and who had small pieces of hash in their pockets. On returning to the station the sergeant said that the same informant had phoned to say that the men had missed the dealers who had gone inside with a white plastic bag. We rushed back and when one Surinamer saw us he threw something under the table and made for the back. A constable grabbed him and opened up a plastic bag he was carrying; inside were five large oval pieces of hash [fake], wrapped in thin transparent paper, some packets of powder and some raw hash. The Surinamer was walked to the Warmoesstraat in handcuffs; when passing a group of Surinamers one of them called out sarcastically, 'Have you killed someone?' and a constable called back, 'yeah, he's wanted for murder'. The prisoner protested that he was only looking after it. Using the keys, two policemen searched the flat of the suspect but found nothing.

(Field notes)

But either acting on tips or their own initiative, the policemen made fairly frequent raids on the Surinamese clubs. Initially, these were often carried out by two patrolmen, but because of increasing tension a regulation had come into force whereby entry to these clubs could only be made with at least four men and with the permission of the duty-sergeant. Such raids were less likely to produce a dangerous reaction than when pairs of men entered clubs without backing:

I've never used my pistol but I've certainly drawn it. There was one occasion in 'De Cotton Club' when Paul and I were patrolling in the Nieuwmarkt; the door of 'De Cotton Club' was open, and we saw someone who was doing something, probably with heroin. The man had something in his hands and when he saw us he went to the back and left behind a folded 10 guilder note with heroin in it. O.K., the man had to come with us, and he resisted a bit but we had hold of him. We were on our way out and suddenly two beer bottles smashed against the wall above our heads. It was bursting with Surinamers so without saying anything we pulled out our pistols, but then the owner of 'De Cotton Club' jumped between us and she

calmed the Surinamers down. We took the man and locked him up.
(Constable, 26 years)

To a certain extent the raids became almost part of the routine for the
Surinamers, but there was invariably a hostile atmosphere of mutual
contempt:

> One afternoon a suspect was brought to the station for possession of
> heroin. He claimed that there was some more on the floor in "'t
> Winkeltje'. A raid was organised with a minibus carrying a
> brigadier, several men in uniform, and several men in plain clothes.
> Inside it was stifling hot and the place was packed with Surinamers,
> mostly young males, some with dark glasses and knitted caps, but
> with a couple of girls including one White girl. Everyone was
> searched. Some people were searched again on the way out because
> no one was sure exactly who had been searched. At this one Black
> got very upset and shouted, 'Do you want to look up my arse like
> you do in the Warmoesstraat?' and, uninvited, he took his pants
> down and bared his backside to the constables. One or two of the
> clients sat unperturbed on the bar stools, gazing into space as if
> stoned, others shouted to each other in dialect and one started to
> shadow-box with a constable on the door who viewed him with
> disdain. Several Surinamers were arrested. The barkeeper had
> hash, small packets of heroin, and scales hidden behind the bar and
> was already carrying a previous summons under the Drugs Act.
> Wearing rubber gloves, the policemen thoroughly searched the
> premises and then ordered the bar to be closed. After being checked
> at the station, several Surinamers were allowed to leave. On their
> way out one of the constables stood by the door, clapped them on
> the back, and said, 'Be seeing you', to which they reacted with
> sheepish smiles.
>
> (Field notes)

The policemen were sometimes angered by displays of almost
gratuitous violence by Surinamers against White victims. One
Surinamer spoke of 'revenge' against Whites (*De Volkskrant,* 16 July
1977) and, following the murder of a young student when getting off a
tram outside Central Station, a policeman entered a club for Blacks to
make inquiries about the suspect. When asked what the matter was, he
replied, 'A countryman of yours killed a countryman of mine' (F.
Bovenkerk, personal communication). One respondent, for instance,

was confronted with the, for him, almost unacceptable racial hatred of a Surinamese suspect:

[If you go into a Surinamese club isn't it sometimes a bit explosive?] Yes it is, but that depends a bit on your attitude and how you treat them. Personally I treat them simply as ordinary people. But you have colleagues who say, 'You're Black, you're a lousy nigger', or at least that's how they behave. I've arrested a lot of them for possessing hash or heroin but if they see me they always give me a friendly grin. I can understand the Surinamers quite well. They have been plundered for hundreds of years and now they've come to get their own back. Last week I was talking with one of them, that's a street-corner worker, and that man is so incredibly embittered about Dutch people, it's really unbelievable. He was arrested because he was selling hash. He started to talk about the colonialism of the Dutch and compared them with the Nazis in the Second World War. He said, 'The best Dutchman is a dead Dutchman'. The fellow was so bitter, I couldn't believe it. I couldn't talk to him. I tried but it didn't work. He is all for setting up a group of guerrillas here comprising Surinamers. He was so fanatical and full of hate. If someone can suddenly organise something with the Surinamers then a hell of a lot could happen here.

(Marechaussee, 27 years)

The criminalesque Surinamese subculture of the city-centre deserves study in its own right, with attention being focused on the inescapable cycle of drugs and crime into which some young, unemployed, home-less, family-less adolescents become confined (Breeveld, 1977a; *De Volkskrant,* 13 Nov 1976). There are very few facilities for these outcasts and they congregate for company around the clubs in the inner city. A leading figure on the Zeedijk is Emile and he told a reporter:

I've got here around four or five hundred men under my thumb. If I say, 'Lads, we're going to burn Amsterdam to the ground', then the town will be burned down within an hour. They've got respect for me – if I say 'sit down', they'll sit, and if I say 'walk' they'll walk. They listen to me. . . . Some lads are banned, that's true. But that's because they destroy everything, or steal or fight. And I'm not accepting that. . . . I never carry a gun and sort everything out with my fists. I'm quite handy with my fists and in '53 I was the first Black in the Karate school belonging to John Bluming. . . . Once I had to come to the police station and they said, 'There are too many pockets being picked around your place; it's got to an average of 12 a day and that's too many'. So I said, 'O.K., I'll do something about it', and I got two lads to keep a good eye open. One day they caught one and called me. I grabbed the kid by his neck and pants and threw him straight through the window. After that I've never had any more trouble from pickpockets and a few months after that Hartsuiker [the Public Prosecutor] came here and said, 'Emile, you sorted that out well'.

While this interview should be taken with a pinch of salt, because 'Emil's Place' is a continued source of criminality with many robberies taking place in or around it, what emerges is that some Surinamers are outlaws within their own community. Emile has his own bodyguard and decides who may or may not use his club. Surinamers who do not fit in, or who have no money to pay for rooms, drinks or drugs, are 'banned' and become, in a sense, doubly outlawed. Perhaps these hard cases are practically driven to rob and to steal in order to make their way back into the 'scene'. At closing time, the reporter quoted Emile,

'You see, the whole street is Black. When I close, there is nowhere else for them to go'. And Cameron stands with his hands on his hips. 'They can't go anywhere else. Look at these blokes. They're just waiting for me to let them back in again. Because that is what it is – letting them in.' (*Haagse Post*, 21 Aug 1976)

At one stage the Surinamers were particularly strident. They had begun to inhabit several new cafés and new haunts where they gathered in large groups and a number of complaints were made against them. Then in one night six men were 'rolled' in 'The Caribbean Nights'. There was a growing feeling in the station that things were going too far. The flash-point came one night when two inexperienced constables released a Surinamer, whom they had arrested, because of intimidation from a large crowd of Surinamers. The next evening some of the men were horrified by this and decided that the situation was getting out of hand. They arranged for one of their wives to phone in an anonymous tip that firearms were being sold in 'The Caribbean Nights' and a brigadier with ten men went along and raided the club. Fighting broke out in the street and the Surinamers were driven away with a baton charge. On respondent told me:

We chased them all the way to the Nieuwmarkt. The next morning a bouquet of flowers arrived as thanks from some old lady in the Zeedijk. The harder you hit them the bigger the flowers become. But some blokes lost their heads. ——, for example, rushed up to a Black in handcuffs from behind and hit him on the head with his truncheon. They can't control themselves. And it's just those ones who crap in their pants when there's trouble or thump a suspect in the station when there's no need to.

(Constable, 28 years)

The Surinamers went back to their old stamping grounds after two evenings of intimidation from the police. The build-up to these incidents confirms what others have written about policemen possessing a concern about control over the territory they police (Holdaway, 1977a, p. 131), about judging events in terms of being 'on top of the area' (Chatterton, 1976b, p. 115), and about their authority on the streets: 'For the patrolman the street is everything; if he loses that, he has surrendered his reason for being what he is' (Rubinstein, 1973, p. 167).

Many patrolmen make anti-Black remarks and jokes. Most of the men in the Warmoesstraat have developed a passable Surinamese accent and there were frequent mock confrontations played out between a 'Surinamer' and a policeman which were conducted in strident tones of protest, 'But, officer, you're only arresting me because I'm Black!' I doubt if the level and intensity of anti-Black verbal expression in the Warmoesstraat was more pronounced than in other male occupational groups in Dutch society (cf. Luning, 1976). It was extremely rare, for instance, to hear blind reactionary statements of the most prejudiced sort. In fact it was not uncommon to hear almost semi-liberal sympathetic views expressed on the plight of some Surinamers. A social scientist employed by the Amsterdam Police to discuss such issues with policemen found, contrary to his expectations, that the personnel from the Warmoesstraat expressed less crude stereotypes about Surinamers than some policemen from other districts who had almost no experience with them (I. de Wolf, personal communication). There appeared to be a cycle of attitudes to Surinamers. New men tended to be frightened and apprehensive about them; with experience they began to be socialised into the informal culture which defined Surinamers in the area as criminal and started to focus, perhaps excessively, on Surinamers; and then, as they became used to the language, style and reactions of Surinamers, the anxiety dropped away and they became either neutral or, in a curious way, almost compassionate as if they were dealing with wayward simpletons. After a while some Surinamers became well-known figures whose faces were regularly seen inside the station and if they were passed on the street a patrolman might say jocularly 'Want to buy some hash?' or just 'Hi, pickpocket'. Perhaps the general attitude of the patrolmen is summed up by the the saying, 'There are two things which I can't stand, discrimination and Surinamers'. In a way it crystallises a paradox which the police in a liberal society find difficult to face. The patrolmen knew that they were accused of discrimination and yet were not fully conscious of the role it played in their work; to recognise it would have meant accepting a negative definition in a society which ostensibly denigrates discrimination. The way out was to deny prejudice – and on occasion the men could become quite heated when denying discrimination – but to define the Surinamers as a difficult and delinquent group who were pursued because they were 'anti-social' but most definitely *not* because they were Black. Indeed, they perceived colour as a shield behind which Surinamers hid in order to use the imputation of discrimination as a tactic for generating sympathy and avoiding culpability.

In general, then, police work in the inner city generated a stereotype of Surinamers as criminal, loud-mouthed, aggressive, difficult to handle, and sometimes dangerous. A secondary stereotype, somewhat less negative yet in its way condescending, was that of the happy-go-lucky 'underdeveloped' Surinamer who is gregarious and spontaneous but without malice; if you treat him 'normally', i.e. laugh and joke with him, then he will laugh and joke back. At times, the Surinamers were treated in the station like yokels who have got lost in the big city; they were smiled at, patted on the back, joked with (and at), and given handshakes on the way out. At that level, relations could be congenial and the Surinamers were generally compliant and even respectful. But it was on the street that the confrontation was uncertain, laden with mutual antipathy, and charged with potentially escalating aggression. If we examine the encounters on the street more closely then it is possible to extract more detailed information about the relationship between the police and Surinamers. There were 57 cases involving Surinamers in the four-month period during which I kept details of encounters. In six other cases an alleged Surinamese suspect was not at the scene. This represents 13 per cent of the total number of police–citizen contacts. In the vast majority of cases the encounter concerned young males. There were four domestic disputes where

families were involved and three cases involving women (all prostitutes). Compared to the pattern in the overall total of cases, those
encounters involving Surinamers tended to exhibit more police initiative, more concern with criminality (especially drugs and
robbery/theft), a higher proportion of arrests, and more hostility on
the part of suspects. In ten of the cases an arrest was made and in five
cases the suspect was apprehended by someone else. There were six
cases where weapons were alleged to be involved, but in only three out
of 57 cases where a Surinamer was present at the encounter was a
weapon discovered on a suspect's person and in all three cases it was a
knife. Surinamers were also encountered in roles other than suspects –
twice as victim, twice as informant, and a couple of times as minor
offenders such as drunk or rowdy where the incident was handled with
a verbal caution. To a certain extent, 'police initiative' exaggerates the
positive role of the patrolman in tracking down Surinamers because
several offences were witnessed as they occurred. However, patrols
often operated in those areas where street crime was endemic and
where there was a good chance of catching someone in the act. The
Nieuwmarkt, the Zeedijk and occasionally the Nieuwendijk was where people were robbed and where drugs were sold
on the street. One could hardly expect the police not to pay special
attention to those areas.

Where police initiative could assume a dubious dimension in terms
of discrimination was that in the city-centre Surinamers were much
more likely to be questioned than White people. For example, there
were 13 cases involving potential traffic offences where it was excep-
tionally difficult to separate the police interest in the offence with the
fact that the driver was Black. This was because the patrolmen saw a
minor traffic infringement on the part of a Black as a licence to carry
out a stop and search operation in the hope of uncovering a more
serious offence. In other words, a Black was more likely to be an object
of suspicion in other roles apart from potential predatory criminal than
was a White person. One evening, for instance, a patrol controlled a
white Alfa-Romeo sports car driven by a man with an 'Afro' hairstyle.
When the car was stopped, however, it transpired that the man was
White but his silhouette made him look *like* a Surinamer. And he was
driving an *expensive* sports car. A Surinamer driving an expensive car
around 'de wallen' is considered to be either a pimp or a dealer and is
'worth' a control (cf. Rubinstein, 1973, p. 257). The difficulty of
interpreting police behaviour in this area is to filter out the likelihood
of racial discrimination, specifically against Surinamers, from the

perceptual framework with which policemen generally recognise symbolic assailants. Is it simply that race presented the men with one specific visible characteristic that overrode secondary characteristics, or were the patrolmen guilty of, or indeed victims of, a perspective which generated a self-fulfilling prophecy? (Bovenkerk, 1976a). One entry in the Station Diary read:

> —— passed reporters running hard, *presumably in relation to a previously committed offence.* He was brought to the station for further inquiries and, while being searched, put something in his mouth which he later admitted was heroin. Nothing on records so allowed to leave. On leaving the station he claimed that he had been mistreated and was informed of his rights. [My emphasis]

In short, Surinamers running in the city-centre were automatically suspect (Rubinstein, 1973, p. 235).

On neutral territory, police enforcement against Blacks in general was motivated largely by the same symbolic signals given off by other categories of potential suspects. In marginal cases the colour of an individual could swing the balance as to whether or not to move from suspicion to action. Where race became a primary characteristic for fulfilling the role of symbolic suspect was with regard to street crime in the city-centre. Anyone with a dark skin in the inner city was virtually by definition a suspect. This aggravating position for dark-skinned people was arrived at in the following way. Street crime was concentrated in the inner city. Surinamers were frequently complained against by people who had been robbed, assaulted or 'rolled'. The police began to focus more attention on Surinamers. In stop and search operations a proportion of Surinamers were found to be in possession of drugs and/or weapons. The stereotype developed that Surinamers were dangerous and deal in drugs. Police vigilance increased. Because of the higher rate of stop and search activity aimed at Surinamers more and more cases were uncovered of possession of drugs and weapons which confirmed the stereotype. In resentment against police harassment the Surinamers became more homogeneous and organised, and more efficient at escaping detection. Perhaps partly for 'self-defence' in a rough area they began to arm themselves. Imperceptibly over time the scene became set for mutual reaffirmation of hate and hostility between police and Surinamers. As more and more Black suspects were processed by the station, the stronger was the conviction that the Surinamers formed a primary criminal culture in the area. Any Surinamer who entered the area was now a suspect. If he was with a group or in an expensive car then that was further evidence that he might be involved in crime (cf. Young, 1971a, b; Laurie, 1971). The vicious circle of the self-fulfilling prophecy was activated and the actors became almost locked into the predicament with little chance of altering their scripts. However, it would be naïve to suggest that the Surinamers are guiltless citizens whose alleged 'crimes' have been concocted by the hostile stereotypes of White policemen. That some Surinamers in the inner city are criminal is not at issue; rather we are concerned with the importance that the police reaction has in confirming that criminal identity and in imputing guilt to totally innocent Surinamers. It requires merely a good pair of eyes in Amsterdam to see Surinamers working as dealers and pickpockets. And all the people who complain about being robbed by 'unknown coloureds' cannot have been mistaken about the pigmentation of their assailant's skin. What is crucial, however, is that two consequences flow from this. In the first place, press coverage of Black crime fosters a stereotype that *every* Surinamer is a mugger or pickpocket. That effect is part of a more general question of the generating of negative stereotypes about specific cultural or racial groups. But more importantly for our purposes is the effect that Black crime had on police mentality and behaviour.

The inner city is a criminal no-man's-land where respectable citizens tread at their own risk and where predatory crime flourishes. Some of that crime is reported to the police but an unknown proportion, possibly the majority, is not reported. Who precisely is responsible for that crime is impossible to say. The police base their enforcement on current information, tips, informants, complainants and accumulated experience. The consensus was that the Surinamers formed an important element in street crime, and police behaviour became focused on them. That was not difficult because the Surinamers fulfilled their role in all the details. They congregated in clubs which were frequently named by complainants; they gathered in menacing groups on the streets; and they dressed extravagantly and behaved histrionically. Because they represented the lower echelons of the criminal hierarchy they engaged in high-risk street crimes which increased the likelihood of apprehension. Because drugs played a vital role in their subculture, either as a commodity or for their own use, they were more likely to be found in possession of incriminating substances. In short, individually and collectively, tne Surinamers provided the police with a reservoir of archetypal symbolic assailants – instantly visible and readily available (Spradley, 1970, p. 179, argues similarly for drunks on skid-row). One evening I went out in a patrol-car with two men who were looking for action. After a couple of lousy calls from the radio-operator one of them said, 'Why don't we go and pick up a Black on the Dam?'

I would sketch the scenario for the policeman in Amsterdam as follows. The policeman steps on to the street and is perceptually surrounded by chaos in the form of an insoluble traffic problem and a triumphantly concealed and flourishing criminality. Where shall he begin? Who is guilty? The simple answer is Surinamers. Theoretically the patrolman could start selecting people at random to ask for identification and to demand explanations. But that is crude, unrewarding, and likely to provoke unwelcome hostility. What is important, however, is crime related to drugs, weapons and violence against the person. These are areas where the policeman feels the moral consensus of the wider society breathing encouragingly down his neck. And, after all, is not 'real' police work concerned with stop, search and arrest operations? In brief, he can perform the symbolic rights of police work by focusing on Surinamers. They are a morally outcast group who palpably do not work, because they hang around the streets in the day-time, and who prey on the gullible and the weak, because they operate in gangs after dark when honest citizens are between the sheets. Much police work is defined for the patrolman by citizens and superiors, but here is an area of autonomy which legitimates his occupational ideology (Holdaway, 1977b). What is difficult to calculate, however, is how much street crime goes undetected because the police have become 'colour-blind'. Is it easier for White or non-Surinamer criminals to commit theft and robbery because they have better chances of escaping apprehension and because the Surinamers will be blamed for crimes with 'unknown suspects'? And to what extent does police enforcement help to create and reinforce a militant Black subculture which defines itself by 'anti-social' behaviour and which asks of its members that they steal, deal and rob?

The complex factors involved in the interaction between Surinamers and police in the city-centre make it difficult to decide on the extent to which police work there is racially prejudiced. The difficulty is that the sociological explanation in terms of police work as a collective enterprise where colour may be an incidental, but important, factor among many others, leaves open the question of individual prejudice. An officer may pursue Surinamers either because he is an enthusiastic crime-fighter or because he dislikes Blacks (or both). In terms of selective enforcement, for instance, it is as clear as daylight that the men of the Warmoesstraat 'discriminate' against Surinamers, but it is difficult to ascertain the extent of colour or racial prejudice in that behaviour. But whatever the motivation of individual patrolmen, it is almost inescapable that collective police behaviour will foster racial antagonism. In the first place it is not pleasant to be raided, to be searched, and to be carted off in handcuffs to the police station. In the second place, crude raids and sweeping stop and search operations will doubtless include Surinamers who are innocent of any offence and who will stand a much higher chance of being stopped than a White person in the area. Because black skin is a primary identification characteristic, a Surinamer near the scene of a crime may be apprehended simply because he is a Surinamer. With a White person some secondary characteristic – green trousers or a black leather jacket – would probably have to be signified by a complainant or eye-witness before a patrolman would effect an inquiry. The implication is that a Surinamer – innocent or guilty, respectable or disreputable – will feel that he is being stopped simply because he is Black. A guiltless White citizen who has been stopped riding a large car slowly around the red-light district looking for a parking place might be given an apology and accorded deference once his plausible explanation has been accepted. A guiltless Black citizen, on the other hand, when faced with an identical situation might sense or perceive hostility or disagreeable suspicion, might be offered no explanation or apology, and might generate antagonism by *demanding* an explanation. In other words, enforcement against Surinamers – or any minority group – may generate consequences that are less likely to emerge from contacts with fellow members of the dominant ethnic group. And it was certainly the case that Surinamers were often searched on the street on the merest pretext of suspicion, and that their premises were sometimes searched illegally. They were not perceived as enjoying the privacy of an 'ordinary' citizen with a stable job and a fixed residence (Rubinstein, 1973, p. 194; Bittner, 1967a, p. 709). One of the policemen recognised this but saw no way out of the dilemma:

It used to be that everyone with long hair was scum but now it's Blacks. I know its a form of discrimination but you can't avoid it. For example, most searches are actually illegal. You shove a Black up against a wall and search him. It's wrong but it's the only way you get anywhere, otherwise you might as well give up and go home. What it comes down to is that there are two law books – the written one and the unwritten one. It's simply impossible to work with the written one here in the city-centre.

(Constable, 33 years)

Having etched a portrait of discriminatory law-enforcement in the centre of Amsterdam, it is perhaps worth documenting that gross prejudice was rarely encountered during the research. While in no way wishing to minimise the issue, which is potentially explosive and latently damaging to race relations elsewhere in the country, I did not see incidents which were patently racist. On the street the Surinamer is vulnerable to police attention. Because of the crimes of which he is mostly accused or suspected, the Surinamer is probably more likely to be arrested, handcuffed and taken to the station than a White person. At that level – as a suspect – he is perhaps more likely to be treated in a disagreeable manner. If he resists it may be that he is more quickly assaulted by the police than a White person (I cannot judge this and it is a knotty issue open to conflicting interpretations). But generally my observations were that Surinamers were not ill-treated, were not subject to racist remarks, and were not treated any differently as suspects once they had reached the station (cf. Holdaway, 1977b). Generally the tension was at its most volatile during the confrontation stage – the raid, the search, the arrest – and had mostly subsided at the processing phase in the station. Surinamers in a group in opposition to young policemen on the streets could be explosive. But individual Surinamers in the station, faced with sergeants who had experience with Surinamers, were rarely an issue. In addition, Surinamers who appeared in non-suspect roles – as victims, informants, complainants, etc. – were generally treated with the formality accorded to a Dutch person. This was also true of Surinamers encountered outside of the inner city or who exhibited secondary characteristics indicating respectability and moral worth (well-dressed businessmen or concerned mothers looking for runaway daughters). If non-suspects were treated in a derisory or a prejudiced fashion then that would be strong evidence of discriminatory distinctions, but that was not the case in my experience.

In conclusion, I would argue that it is extremely difficult to distinguish between racial, and especially colour, discrimination and the intrinsic craft orientation of the policeman to categorise and differentiate the indistinguishable mass of the public into a moral hierarchy of socially approved types among whom the Black may be a visible and instantly recognisable potential deviant. It could be argued, indeed, that it is the policeman's job to 'discriminate' and that police work would founder on random enforcement. That is not to deny that his perceptual shorthand, which zones in on what seems to be out of place and on the deviant actor, may combine with racial prejudice to form an abrasive and potentially explosive mix with important consequences for race relations and the nature of the social order in the inner city.

7 Conclusion: Police and the Inner City

(i) THE NETHERLANDS: THE LIMITS OF TOLERANCE

In this book I have sketched a sociological portrait of law-enforcement in the inner city of Amsterdam. The analysis attempts to extend and go beyond the work of earlier investigations, which are now somewhat dated, in order to explore the ambivalences and dilemmas facing the police in a 'tolerant', cosmopolitan community. The major perspective which guided the investigation and which was largely instrumental in defining the limits of my inquiry was an interactionist and interpretative approach to the occupational culture of uniformed policemen. The methods employed have been qualitative and impressionistic but these were considered appropriate to a one-man, explorative study of limited scope. For, while this work hopefully extends our sociological knowledge of the police by presenting a cross-cultural element which is missing in most studies of the police and which can be of interest to researchers in other countries, it must be stressed that the field-work was confined to one group of policemen in one police station in one city in The Netherlands. This cannot be viewed, then, as a study of 'the Dutch Police', although it may reflect themes present in Dutch policing. The relevance of this case study is that it sets out to examine the role that patrolmen play in the social life of the inner city with the intention of illuminating some of the micro-processes which contribute to a more general analysis of the nature and quality of social order in such an environment.

The utility of this perspective is that inner cities can be viewed as testing-grounds for the consequences of social change in that they often contain elements of ethnic and cultural diversity, of tolerance for conspicuous displays of deviancy, and of certain deleterious by-products of socio-economic change (Banfield, 1974). In the sense that the spread of values and behaviour associated with advanced urbanism seems almost invincible (Wilsher and Righter, 1976), the inner city provides a glimpse of a prospective future that awaits many urbanites. Paradoxically, The Netherlands provides almost a laboratory situation of a society where such developments have only recently taken place, compared to Anglo-American society, and actually affords a glance backwards. Heine's contention that everything happens fifty years later in The Netherlands (Goudsblom, 1967, p. 21) is somewhat overdrawn, but it is clear that the country does not exhibit the massive urban problems and deprivation of say some American cities, where even firemen face harassment and sniping (Smith, 1973). The interest of The Netherlands, then, is that we can observe the process of acclimatising to the criminal practices associated with advanced industrial societies in general and inner-city communities in particular as it occurs. Almost imperceptibly over the last five years Amsterdammers have become accustomed to news of armed robbery, muggings, pickpocketing, purse-snatching, knifings, Chinese underworld assassinations, foreign youths dying in hotel rooms of overdoses, to television surveillance and private police in shops, and to routine warnings about thieves over the public address systems of railway stations and in buses and trams. This is particularly painful for a somewhat complacent society which enjoys one of the highest standards of living in the world and which, with a combination of a Calvinist sense of responsibility and a Catholic sense of conscience, has endeavoured to build a social democracy of enviable facilities, and with prescient long-term planning (Blanken, 1976). The obscenity of crime in The Netherlands is that nobody needs to commit it. At least that is what I sometimes discern in the reactions to crime, as if they represent pained bewilderment that it should be necessary to rob and steal when no one need go unprovided for in a generous and comprehensive welfare state system.

The central dilemma for the police in such a society becomes how to cope with rising crime when there is an increasing level of tolerance for unorthodox, and even technically illegal, behaviour and a heightened consciousness of individual group rights (Schuyt, 1972). Manning (1977, p. 99) argues that, in effect, the American police have presented themselves predominantly as embattled crime-fighters and that attempts to 'liberalise' the police have been either failures or shams; in brief, 'American police rarely seek to prevent crime, characteristically utilise excessive violence, mobilise systematic organisational effort to increase the schism between police and public, and seize hungrily upon evidence of police action or intervention as a verification of their effectiveness.' Some American police forces are equipped like standing armies and have used 'improvement' grants which were dispensed in the wake of the President's Commission to strengthen their 'hard-ware' (ibid., pp. 89, 360ff.).

Although certain of these tendencies may be present, and may even be increasing, in The Netherlands I do not believe them to be valid for the Dutch Police in general. It is true that the Dutch Police is moving towards a substantial reorganisation along familiar lines – more technology, larger units, more specialised and centralised groups, and so on – with the primary purpose of increasing 'efficiency' (112 of the smaller forces have fewer than 100 men) and that this reflects developments elsewhere where preoccupation with means has obscured the classification of ends. Alongside these largely technical developments, however, there is emerging a diffuse and uncoordinated debate about the wider role of the police in a modern society. While opinions are deeply divided, there does seem to be room for what might be considered elsewhere 'liberal' arguments and there does appear to be a preoccupation with achieving a good image, with being well informed, and with listening to enlightened opinion (Anema, 1973). Without drawing too optimistic a picture, I do think that elements in the Dutch Police have a measure of tolerance and are concerned with their role in a democratic society (*Politie in Verandering*, 1977; Broer, 1977). Others, in contrast, employ the occasional skirmish with international terrorists (such as recent incidents with 'R.A.F.' members) and the much-publicised activities of 'domestic' terrorists (particularly the South Moluccans, with their train sieges in 1975 and 1977) to demand improved weaponry, better training in counter-terrorism, and more sweeping powers. Behind this dualism lies a real uncertainty about the role of the police in a changing society (cf. Lewis, 1976, and Mark, 1977, for the situation in Britain).

This takes us into a complex area, which cannot be developed here, but which relates the police organisation and police work to the state apparatus (Cain, 1977; Bunyan, 1977) and to changing societal values. But my overriding impression in studying the Dutch Police has been of uncertainty and insecurity at all levels. This is common to other countries – in Britain, for example, a senior police officer spoke of 'the Police Service and the Police College groping in the dark' (*Police Journal*, XLVI (4), 1973) for a philosophy to inform their role – but I feel that it is acute at this moment in The Netherlands. This is because Dutch society displays the paradox of an outward appearance of tolerant liberalism and even anti-authoritarianism while many conventional facets of social life are still cemented in traditionalism and ambivalence (*De Telegraaf*, 27 Aug 1977). There does seem to be a pervasive challenging of legitimate authority (which Schaar, 1970, p. 278, argues to be true of all modern states) which often exposes the internal strains and weaknesses of the police. Indeed, in a modern industrial society, where a dissemination and diffusion of authority takes place over a multitude of bureaucratic ministries and other impersonal institutions (ibid., p. 303), the police remain visible and approachable representatives of government and handy scapegoats for 'authority' in general. As such, the police represent a crucial institution of normative conflict, reflecting axial dilemmas in society. For example, The Netherlands has espoused a humanitarian judicial and penal system of which the police are the 'front-line' troops. Strains in operating such a system during a period of rapid change are first likely to appear among the police. The civility and deference which were traditionally fostered by elite manners and habits begin to founder in a pluralist, culturally divergent society espousing 'tolerance'. The cost of an ostensibly socially responsible police at the institutional level may be a degree of frustration, lack of motivation and inffectiveness at lower levels where the 'infantry' feel isolated and aggrieved in a system where there is a growing schism between higher and lower ranks (Punch, 1976d, pp. 144–5).

As such, the inner city represents a microcosm where the ambivalences and tensions at the societal and institutional level are most likely to surface. For it is there that, following a complex series of developments, the tolerance begins to wear thin. In my opinion the Amsterdam situation represents the unintended and unforeseen consequences of a decade of change in many areas. The formation of a deviant area has back-fired in a manner that was not foreseen, and the unhappy mix of tolerance and burgeoning crime has saddled the police with an almost impossible set of contradictions, where their efforts can do little more than exert a restraining influence on excesses. Its criminal subculture is a challenge to enlightened social and judicial policies and the debate surrounding its functioning reveals some of the anbivalences at the macro-level. For example, there are politicians at the local and national level who ideologically support progressive solutions and who find it difficult to accept fully the racial and criminal problems of the inner city. On the other hand, more conservative elements seem to operate with an outmoded belief in the efficacy of stability and orderliness while not recognising the implications of rapid change (Punch, 1977a). Of course, the rhetoric of the debate is often inflated by the media (Cohen and Young, 1973; Chibnall, 1977) and this can distort the day-to-day reality of social life. For example, after three unsolved murders within six months one of the more 'law and order'-oriented newspapers carried the headline 'Murder Maniac in Capital' while a senior police officer said, 'This could happen to any one of us' (*De Telegraaf*, 22 Feb 1977). Yet I spent a good deal of time in the city-centre over a period of years and did not perceive it as a seething cauldron of aggressive and motiveless crime, although, once I had perceived it from the police point of view, I began to be wary and suspicious, particularly if I was on my own. Indeed, the average working-day experience from a police point of view was mostly humdrum and even uneventful. To a certain extent, events there are manipulated and interpreted to provide fodder for the socio-political rhetoric at higher levels. Nevertheless, the inner city of Amsterdam is capable of generating heated and contrasting views regarding toler- ance, crime, immigration, drugs and 'safety on the streets' even when actual levels of reported crime and violence are low compared to cities in other countries (yet in a study of the inner city of Dordrecht, Olila and Hulsman, 1977, pp. 17–18 speak of people using three to four locks on their doors and of a pervasive anxiety about 'crime').

This places the police organisation in a vulnerable and exposed position between conflicting parties. Bittner (1975, p. 19) contends that the American Police have never effectively indulged in critical self-scrutiny compared to other occupations dealing with people:

All the other occupations – physicians, clergymen, teachers, lawyers, nurses, social workers, sales people, even the military – have, at some time in this century, once or repeatedly, to a greater or lesser extent, taken a hard look at themselves, asked fundamental questions, purged their ranks and practices, updated their role in society, and generally sought to reason things out among them- selves.

This is equally if not more true of the Dutch Police, and one respon- dent saw this lack of vision as endemic to the police organisation in Amsterdam:

People just don't have any vision about what might happen in five minutes' time. Problems in the future are not faced up to. They let it happen to see what it looks like. That really is the greatest mistake. Actually they see the crisis coming along but they let it first grow to extremes before they react and do something about it. And you find that attitude from top to bottom in the police. I'm not pointing the guilty finger at anyone in particular. It's simply locked up in the whole system.

(Adjutant, 52 years)

My contention, then, is that there exists a degree of confusion about the role of the police in Dutch society and that this is symptomatic of unresolved structural and ideological differences, that the police organisation has not shown itself to be conspicuously capable of employing vision and foresight in analysing its own ambivalences (Punch, 1977c), and that police work in the inner city of Amsterdam represents some of the strains and cross-pressures of policing in a liberal legal system in particular and an inner-urban area in general. This background has directed my attention to the men who endeavour to maintain order at the nerve-edge of Dutch society, where tolerance limits are pushed to extremes and where social tensions are abrasively exposed, namely the uniformed patrolmen of the Warmoesstraat.

(ii) AMSTERDAM: POLICE CULTURE IN THE FRONT-LINE

The occupational world of the Warmoesstraat, observed and analysed as a case study, is of value in unravelling an occupational culture on the defensive, a traditional craft in decline, and a work-force whose frustrations and uncertainties reflect both pregnant issues in the wider society and the increasingly ineffective and repressive role of law-enforcement in the inner city. The normlessness and insecurity of the young uniformed personnel in the Warmoesstraat appeared to me to be symptomatic of irresoluteness and lack of guidance from senior officers which, in turn, was a reaction to political and social pressures from the city leaders and influential groups. The normative confusion of the policemen was partly a response to a sort of authority vacuum from above as well as to rapid structural changes in police work. This ambivalent and endangered culture is taken as an amplification of previous work on the police which tended to emphasise the solidarism of the occupational culture. In Amsterdam, on the other hand, there was a dilution of informal police networks outside of work, while the identification of patrolmen with a particular territory was absent and the men were used indiscriminately within the entire district. Westley (1970, p. 310), however, was one of the first sociologists to specify the isolation of the police in urban society, and Alex (1976) has recently looked at White New York policemen in terms of a 'beleaguered

minority'. The bitter tirades against 'soft' legislation by Alex's policemen show the police to be caught between the militancy of minority
groups and the crime problem with the result that they feel afraid to do
their job properly for fear of disciplinary action, become ritualistic
about the futility of arrests, and turn to right-wing militancy (with
'White power' buttons and off-duty protests about Black militancy; cf.
Alex, 1976; pp. 63, 85, 168, 200). Here the 'front-line' analogy has
been used to typify the ideology of policemen in the Warmoesstraat.
Not only does this mirror accurately their organisational status, as
relatively solitary workers with considerable autonomy on the street to
make decisions which can implicate the rest of the organisation (Sykes
and Clark, 1974, p. 473), but also conveys something of a garrison
mentality in alien territory (see the military analogies about police
work in Manning, 1977, *passim*). At times the policeman in the
Warmoesstraat feels like a mercenary in an army of occupation
engaged in a lonely, unpopular and losing struggle against two opposed
terrorist factions while politicians and press criticise him from a safe
distance (Bordua, 1967, p. 98).

This mentality is one of the consequences of a vicious circle which
leads to diminishing returns in law-enforcement. Nowadays the demands of specialised units and a high turnover mean that few men stay
for more than a few years in the patrol function on the street (J. Wilson,
1968, p. 52). The police in Amsterdam, and other large cities, recruits
from other areas of the country with perhaps more conventional social
values. The recruit has to adjust to the mentality of the new urban
environment while also learning its physical layout and its social-
criminal life *as a stranger*. He spends but a few years on the streets
before he is moved to other duties or moves voluntarily to another
force where there are better promotion and housing prospects. This
means that the traditional concept of policing with men who knew the
district and its characters inside-out has broken down. Today the
young recruit in Amsterdam is sent out on to the city streets with a
'mentor', not much older than himself, and may be led by a sergeant in
his late twenties. In adapting to the easy-going manner of the Amsterdammers, the lack of close supervision, and the sometimes casual
attitudes of his colleagues, he can easily become somewhat off-hand
and cynical, and may quickly become impudent and sarcastic. The
attitudes can perhaps be reinforced by a frustration at the seemingly
insoluble problems of traffic and crime in the city-centre. And when
there is widespread deviance, then many police interventions, say in
trivial areas such as parking offences, are made to appear arbitrary and

can easily generate antagonism in the citizen. It could well be that, semi-consciously, he applies to a smaller city force because there he hopes to receive the respect from the public (and can more clearly see the results of his work) that attracted him to police work in the first place. The structural and ideological changes in police work appear to have contributed to a decline in the police craft which was traditionally learned over a period of years through accumulating experiences and developing the ability to handle people and situations while receiving an informal apprenticeship from senior colleagues. This facet of the police culture has not been adequately dealt with elsewhere, although it is implicit in Bittner (1967a), Chatterton (1975a) and Holdaway (1977a). The police in the Warmoesstraat seemed caught in a vacuum between the decline of traditional practices and the swing to autonomous professional norms and a reliance on technology (Cain, 1973, p. 245).

This fragmentation of the police craft, with its consequences for encounters and relationships with the policemen's publics, has been reinforced by the development of the red-light district, from being a stable and distinctly Dutch deviant community (Hoenderdos, 1976) into a plural cultural and ethnic melting-pot with a predatory criminal element. Initially informal policies led to the creation of a normative ghetto where deviance could flourish and where accommodation was reached between police and underworld in the interests of regulating social life in the area. This segregation, which was somewhat hypocritically sold to the outside world as an indication of 'tolerance' (when, for instance, all the original legislation on prostitution was retained on the statute book as a resource to keep 'respectable' areas free from vice), began to break down when a combination of factors – including youth tourism, the hard-drug trade, the concentration of immigrants and the rise of the sex industry – fundamentally altered the character of the area. Previously 'de wallen' was part of Amsterdam night-life and the underworld element was recognised, recognisable and accepted. Now, however, there is a constant flow of naïve tourists, attracted to the 'wickedness' of the area (cf. Becker and Horowitz, 1971, p. 10, for San Francisco), who provide a ready supply of affluent victims and who do not see the potential mugger or pickpocket. To a certain extent this is explainable by the democratisation of dress – practically everyone in the inner city is casually dressed (how many times have I heard over the radio 'The suspect is a young man in jeans and leather jacket?') – so that criminals do not present themselves in stereotypical fashion. The visible demarcation between 'rough' and 'respectable' styles of dress has diminished while the foreigner/native dichotomy scarcely exists in a multiracial society where, as the police put it, the borders with Belgium and Germany have been moved to Amsterdam. In addition, the criminal subculture of 'de wallen' did not confine itself to the red-light district but foraged out for lucrative pickings in the shopping streets, on the trams and buses, and along the inner ring of canals where only businesses and wealthy individuals can normally afford houses (Davis, 1971, p. 161, comments on the mix of rich people alongside people on welfare in San Francisco). It was as much the growing publicity about the aggressiveness of street crime *outside* of 'de wallen' which alarmed public opinion, rather than the scale of the activities inside the notorious area. At the same time, Amsterdam was in financial difficulties (*Elseviers Magazine*, 8 Oct 1977) and the city-centre businesses, threatened by falling profits and poor accessibility, blamed their plight on rising crime as a stick with which to beat the town council in retribution for its policies in other areas (Sherman, 1974, p. 34, notes how the perception that New York was falling apart magnified the reactions to the police corruption scandal there).

This transformation of 'de wallen' from a benign, accepted deviant area to a sort of threatening no-man's-land, where allegedly citizens are at jeopardy on the streets, has also led to new practices in the area. For example, as the moral panic about criminality increases and people begin to feel unsafe in the inner city, the barkeepers, bouncers and shopkeepers begin to arm themselves for self-protection. The impudence and openness of the criminality can also blossom because the people of the area either do not want, or are frightened, to make statements to the police. Overwhelmed with work, the detective is largely confined to the station, typing out statements from victims and interviewing suspects, and rarely gets out to see the scene of a crime, to keep his finger on the pulse of the area, or to work his informants. This means that the major burden of law-enforcement in the inner city falls upon the patrolman who perceives the area as increasingly hostile and dangerous because he can rely less and less on active citizen co-operation. He finds that rather than being an upholder of law and order, respected by the community, he is more of a first-aid man picking up the pieces after the event, much to the contempt and amusement of the local deviants.

One consequence of this is that frustration is apparent among the policemen of the Warmoesstraat as they feel their identity and autonomy threatened by prohibitions on enforcement and as they half-consciously perceive the vicious cycle of which their own behaviour is part cause and part response. There were many adaptations to the feelings of powerlessness, normative confusion and hopelessness which were said to be characteristic of the Warmoesstraat (*De Volks-krant*, 3 Oct 1977). Some men engaged in aggressive and dubious practices which earned them the reputation of 'asphalt cowboys', others became 'uniform-carriers' who survived by clock-watching ritualism, while others developed personal specialisms and hobbies which they pursued to the detriment of general police tasks. But perhaps the most powerful plank in the informal culture fostered norms of 'real' police work which emphasised speed, excitement and prisoners (or the 'bring in a body' mentality; cf. Manning, 1977, p. 170) and which contrasted with the tedious, pedestrian and often unsought-for odd-jobs of routine policing. I do not think that there was the mistrust and disillusionment with law-enforcement which led to cynicism and right-wing sympathies among New York policemen (Maas, 1973, p. 59; Alex, 1976, p. 35), but there was often a sour litany of complaints about being left in the lurch by superiors, about feeble judicial decisions, and about ungrateful public (Sykes, 1973, p. 190). This could lead to slipshod and surly behaviour and conspicuous displays of role-distance. Some policemen, moreover, began to wear blinkers and to filter out incidents and suspects unconnected with the promise of drugs and firearms. Apart from fitting the 'front-line' ideology, this also had practical advantages in terms of the formal and informal reward systems. The arrest on grounds of possessing drugs, for example, was a question of returning to the station (perhaps a welcome relief on a cold, wet night), locking the suspects up (to be interviewed later by a detective) and typing out a short charge-sheet. Arrests of suspects for drug offences were normally accompanied by the drawing of pistols and the use of handcuffs. Of the various groups in the city-centre the Surinamers were one of the most conspicuous and, given their involvement in street crime, formed a ready pool of potential prisoners (as do drunks on 'skid-row': Spradley, 1970, p. 179).

The importance of the Surinamers in the life of the inner city was, apart from being ideal scapegoats for the 'decline' of the area, that they were the group which most consistently and most aggressively challenged the policemen's control of the streets, and relationships between the two were often characterised by fear, uncertainty and volatile hostility. The territorial segregation of the inner city meant that they had established stamping-grounds and this led to 'stigma by location' (Suttles, 1968, p. 15) whereby the presence of a Black in a certain area automatically incurred suspicion. Encounters between police and Blacks were laced with mutual contempt and latent aggression (cf. Brown, 1977, on Black militant groups in Birmingham and the 'blitz mentality' of the policemen, and Evans, 1974, p. 50, on Blacks who state 'We must kill policemen'), and the Warmoesstraat had attracted a good deal of negative publicity related to discrimination and violence towards Blacks. The men experienced almost a deviancy amplification process in reverse caused by critical public scrutiny. It was argued that racial discrimination may well have been present in the practices of the station but that the emphasis on 'real' police work and the availability of Surinamers as a reservoir of suspects could mean that a disproportionate amount of attention was directed at them; moreover, that the policemen's perceptions of place, intention, posture and suspicion were rooted in the social reality of inner-city life (Rubinstein, 1973, p. 263) and were shared by many inhabitants of the area. Rather, the policemen's attitudes and behaviour to Surinamers were grounded in taken-for-granted knowledge about the area and embedded in shared background expectancies about police work and how it should be done. One aspect of this largely unexplicated code which helped the policemen to categorise, define and negotiate their daily reality was a feeling for the balance of social order in the area which could lead to the fabrication of incidents to justify punitive raids on clubs for Surinamers if their belligerent activities appeared to be 'getting out of hand'. The abrasive and resilient element of racial tension between police and Surinamers was one of the most potentially explosive issues in the area and yet both sides seemed irresistibly attracted to each other. Black identity was reinforced by police hostility (Brana–Shute, 1977) while a number of factors conspired to make the Surinamers 'good' prisoners. The bewildered policemen could always subjugate his frustrations by performing the symbolic rites of stop, search and arrest with a Surinamer as suspect. The vicious circle of police–Black hostility was locked into this symbiotic relationship between street criminal and legally legitimated hunter, and there was almost a ritual quality about it (Manning, 1977, pp. 8–19, 319 ff.).

While I have concentrated on occupationally induced frustration and prisoner-generating activity, it is also true to say that neither were typical of the daily round. On the one hand much activity was carried out in a laconic, matter-of-fact, routine manner without any obvious soul-searching (an imposingly built sergeant growled, 'If it scares you then you might as well stay at home and become a milkman'). There was often a fatalistic attitude to the futilities of the disorganised world about them and to the seeming inability of the police apparatus to cope with them. On the other hand, the patrolmen rarely dealt with 'crime' and 'criminals' (cf. Manning, 1977, p. 325) but with a wide range of service requests and/or order-maintaining functions. Given the importance of these activities and the evident lack of preparation of the policemen for handling these largely interpersonal disputes, I can only echo Bittner (1975, p. 22) when he states that policemen receive practically no instruction, guidance or recognition for 'peace-keeping' tasks, while Manning (1977, p. 289) writes, 'The striking thing about order maintenance methods is how little they are taught, how cynically they are viewed, and how irrelevant they are thought to be in most police departments.' Yet the press and public opinion, together with the police organisation itself, judges police work on the effectiveness of its crime-fighting activities. Even in the Warmoesstraat, with its heavy emphasis, by Dutch standards, on crime work, there was a wide range of general police tasks performed and these were almost exclusively carried out by the uniformed men. A crucial problem there, and elsewhere, appears to be that the indispensable cutting edge of the police enjoys low status and rewards and is employed on a rag-bag of miscellaneous tasks so that the patrolmen felt they were being used as unrewarded 'messenger boys'. They were cut off from the sources of social order in the area, were scarcely able to perform a preventive role, and were thrown back on reactive work at the bidding of citizen calls or repressive activities against conspicuous deviant groups in the district. The absence of suitable reference groups in the area threw them back on themselves and the group or shift was often a comforting and cohesive unit.

There was at times, an almost normless or anomic quality about police work in the Warmoesstraat with many policemen glumly asking 'What am I working for?' (the radical criminologists invite us to demoralise control agents: Young, 1974; this is virtually unnecessary in Amsterdam). The policeman has become a stranger policing strangers, a significant proportion of whom are foreigners, and this accentuates his isolation and reinforces his reactive role. To understand what it was like to work in this criminalesque limbo, divorced from respectable society as if by invisible walls, I have focused on the cross-pressured predicament of the patrolman in a mixed, cosmopolitan inner city. The meaning of his work for the uniformed policeman was taken as central. As such, the material presented reflects strongly the rather sombre police definition of the situation, when clearly other interpretations are also possible (imagine the views that would emerge from, say, a study of Surinamers in the Zeedijk), and also a degree of empathy with their predicament. One advantage of this approach is that we can view the police as a strategic elite, who are observers of a wide and often submerged range of activity, and who can provide oral evidence of how society is changing.

In entering the social world of the policemen in the red-light district of Amsterdam, I have attempted to construct an ethnographic portrait of the complex factors that generate a vicious cycle leading to dilution of the police culture and the undermining of the police craft, to increasingly ineffective law-enforcement, and to repressive norms of policing. These developments are likely to be true of police work and street life in the inner city of large, international cities which have to cope with mass tourism, mobile foreign criminals and immigration at a time of economic recession. These areas become repositories for the 'poor, the unsuccessful, and the disreputable' (Suttles, 1968, p. 7) who endeavour to survive alongside bustling stores, expensive restaurants, affluent tourists and well-off inner-city dwellers. Rather like parts of San Francisco in the sixties, Amsterdam's red-light district developed into a natural experiment in the consequences of tolerating deviance. The unintended effects of this conspired to make Amsterdam in the middle seventies a test-case for contemporary inner-city police work.

APPENDIX

The Structure of the Dutch Police

There are three distinct types of police force in The Netherlands. Firstly, there is a national force ('Korps Rijkspolitie' – at c. 8000 men the largest single force) which is subordinate to the Minister of Justice and which operates in the countryside, in municipalities with fewer than 10,000 inhabitants and in some of the municipalities between 10,000 and 25,000. All the remaining municipalities, and there are in excess of 130 of them, have their own City Police Force ('Gemeente Politie'). Control over the police resides in a dual structure of responsibility whereby a city police force is responsible to the mayor, who is a Crown appointment, regarding 'preservation of public order' and ultimately to the Minister of Internal Affairs. But with regard to criminal investigation the police are also under the authority of the Public Prosecutor ('Officier van Justitie') and the Minister of Justice. A third style of police force is the 'Marechaussee' which is a more militaristic organisation concerned with guarding the royal palaces, controlling border areas and, since 1967, with supplementing the Amsterdam City Police. It can be used to strengthen city forces in times of need, as can the State Police, and, because of its training and equipment, is employed in counter-terrorist actions and riots.

The rank structure of the city police forces is as follows:

Lower ranks	Constable and Constable First Class
	Sergeant
	Adjutant
Higher ranks	Inspector (grades 1 and 2)
	Chief-Inspector (grades 1 and 2)
	Commissioner (grades 1 and 2)
	Chief Commissioner

The most striking difference between the British police and the Dutch police structure is that the latter operates a rigid caste division between lower ranks and higher ranks (rather like 'officers' and 'men' in the British Army). A recruit to the lower ranks must be between 17 and 28 and must have a secondary school diploma roughly equivalent to G.C.E. 'O' Level (though candidates over 21 can have these educational requirements waived). He will receive approximately eighteen months' training consisting of twelve months' full-time instruction at a Training School, three months on attachment with the riot-squad, and three months at a training station under the supervision of an experienced 'mentor', before being sent to a district station. It is possible for him to be promoted to 'hoofdagent' after five years' service and after another five years, with an examination plus further full-time training, he can try for the rank of sergeant. With a minimum of four years in the rank of sergeant, plus higher training of about 50 weeks including attachments to various divisions and departments, he may attempt promotion to adjutant, although very few reach this rank. But he can go no further. Adjutant is the highest rank that a constable can aspire to, for promotions from adjutant to inspector, while not unknown, are extremely rare.

For higher ranks their career begins at the Dutch Police Academy ('Nederlandse Politie Academie' or N.P.A.) in Apeldoorn which runs a four-year course leading to officer status. Recruits are aged between 18 and 24 and must possess a high school diploma (equivalent to 'A' Level G.C.E.). At the N.P.A. the trainee officers receive three years' formal training, including three foreign languages, followed by a one-year training period with a larger police force comprising six months as constable, two months at sergeant level, and four months' staff work at the level of inspector. A graduate from the Academy enters a force directly as an inspector. In contrast to the more achievement-oriented structure of the lower ranks, the officers require no further formal training or diplomas in order to progress to the top of the ladder. For example, promotion to Chief Inspector II can take place after twelve years of service and to Chief Inspector I after another three years' service, but no examinations are required. Commissioners and Chief Commissioners are appointed by the Queen (in effect the Ministry of the Interior). All ranks serve until they are 60.

In Britain there is a powerful ideology against the formation of an officer class which finds expression in the necessity for every recruit to work his way up from constable. In contrast, the Dutch police structure appears highly ascriptive and elitist. In practice, the caste division is almost complete as officers do not work with a shift and rarely go out on duty with lower ranks. The social world of the shift is confined largely to constables and sergeants, and officers appear occasionally on the periphery in a supervisory or managerial capacity. In Amsterdam during the evenings and weekends a young officer usually has responsibility for the whole city to back up the men on the beat but he is assisted by an experienced brigadier and adjutant. So one gets the situation of a young inspector in his late twenties, with say two years' service, being responsible for the city while accompanied by a brigadier in his late forties with over twenty years' experience who is technically subordinate to the officer but who, in practice, may give indispensable advice to his young superior. Again in contrast to Britain, The Netherlands appears to be a patchwork quilt of police forces, with over 130 city forces plus the 'Rijkspolitie' and the 'Marechaussee', displaying high local autonomy, small size of units and little regional co-operation. In fact the Metropolitan Police in London is nearly as large as all the Dutch city police forces put together. The basic training is impressively long in The Netherlands compared to the short basic training for constable in England while there is no English equivalent of the N.P.A. (the Police College at Bramshill is for in-service training only, *not* direct entry). However, there does seem to be a certain amount of criticism that the formal training in The Netherlands is too bookish and overly concerned with learning the law. A visiting inspector from England commented on the emphasis on legal knowledge in the longer Dutch training as opposed to the emphasis on practical ability to deal with everyday occurrences in Britain (Rainton, 1974).

For a long time there has been a recognition that the existing structure is archaic and inefficient and that the forces should be reorganised into twenty-six larger regional forces while the State Police should merge with the City Police. Concrete proposals have been made to amalgamate existing forces into regional forces based on new administrative boundaries under the direction of the Ministry of Internal Affairs, but the two losers in the reorganisation, the Ministry of Justice and the mayors, have been dragging their heels and effectively postponing the implementation of the new structural changes. The purpose of the exercise is to increase efficiency and to lead to the disappearance of the State Police together with many small city forces (112 of which have fewer than 100 men). It is impossible to say what will be lost in this reorganisation, but presumably some of the toy-town atmosphere of small communities with tiny localised forces will disappear, and we can expect more technology, larger units, more specialised and centralised units, and so on.

Finally, it is worth mentioning that in The Netherlands civil rights and watchdog agencies have not achieved the influence and acumen of their counterparts elsewhere so that there are areas of considerable ambiguity surrounding police powers and suspects' rights. Only recently have radical lawyers begun to inform people about rights of arrest in detention and with regard to search, powers about complaints procedures, and about legal aid. Basically a citizen can only be arrested on the basis of suspicion of having committed a criminal offence (although he or she may be detained for his or her own good, e.g. for sobering up, after which the person is frequently released without being charged). Suspects can be detained for up to six hours without being formally charged or cautioned (the period 12 midnight to 9 a.m. is *not* included so the actual period may be longer). But after six hours the suspect must be brought before an 'assistant district attorney' (which invariably means a police officer) and be informed that he is formally detained. At this stage he can ask for a lawyer but at no stage is he obliged to co-operate with the police. In effect, then, the detention on the street is not accompanied by a caution and the police have a breathing-space in which to decide whether or not to press charges. While there is pressure from lawyers to be allowed earlier access to their clients, in effect to be present during that initial six hours when the police have the initiative to obtain information and even a confession from a suspect who is alone and without support, there is little sustained effort to improve suspects' rights and little of the commotion surrounding Supreme Court decisions on police powers of search and arrest in the United States. But increasingly police forces are using an official handout, 'You have been arrested . . .', which details suspects' rights in several languages, and interest groups have produced their own advice (Hagoort et al., 1976). In effect, the structure and equipment of the Dutch Police can appear somewhat old-fashioned and inefficient compared to foreign police forces, such as those in America or West Germany, while the powers of arrest and detention seem relatively wide compared to legal restrictions in Anglo-American police practice.

Bibliography

ENGLISH SOURCES

Agar, M. (1973): *Ripping and Running: A Formal Ethnography of Urban Heroin Addicts* (New York and London: Seminar Press).

Akers, R. L. and Hawkins, R. (1975): *Law and Control in Society* (Englewood Cliffs, N. J.: Prentice-Hall).

Alderson, J. C. and Stead, P. J. (eds.) (1972): *The Police We Deserve* (London: Wolfe).

Alex, N. (1976): *New York Cops Talk Back: A Study of a Beleaguered Minority* (New York: Wiley).

Anderson, N. (1923): *The Hobo* (Chicago: Chicago University Press).

Baena, Duke de (1967): *The Dutch Puzzle* (The Hague: Boucher).

Bagley, C. (1973a): *The Dutch Plural Society: A Comparative Study in Race Relations* (London: Oxford University Press).

Bagley, C. (1973b): 'Holland's Red Niggers', *Race Today*, Mar, pp. 6–7.

Baldwin, J. (1962): *Nobody Knows My Name* (New York: Dell).

Baldwin, J. and Bottoms, A. E. (1976): *The Urban Criminal* (London: Tavistock).

Banfield, E. C. (1974): *The Unheavenly City Revisited* (Boston: Little, Brown).

Banton, M. (1964): *The Policeman in the Community* (London: Tavistock).

Banton, M. (1970): 'Social Order and the Police', *Advancement of Science*, Sep, pp. 48–56.

Banton, M. (1973): *Police Community Relations* (London: Collins).

Banton, M. (1974): 'Policing a Divided Society', *Police Journal*, Winter, pp. 1–18.

Bard, M. (1970): *Neighbourhood Police Teams* (Washington, D.C.: U.S. Government Printing Office).

Bard, M. (1973): *Family Crisis Intervention* (Washington, D.C.: U.S. Government Printing Office).

Barnes, H. E. and Teeters, N. K. (1959): *New Horizons in Criminology* (Englewood Cliffs, N. J.: Prentice-Hall).

Bayley, D. (1976): *Forces of Order: Police Behaviour in Japan and the United States* (Berkeley: University of California Press).

Bayley, D. H. and Mendelsohn, H. (1969): *Minorities and the Police* (New York: Free Press).

Becker, H. S. (ed.) (1963): *The Other Side* (Glencoe, Ill.: Free Press).

Becker, H. S. (1967): 'Whose Side Are We On?', *Social Problems*, XIV, 239–47.

Becker, H. S. (1970): *Sociological Work* (London: Allen Lane).

Becker, H. S. (ed.) (1971): *Culture and Civility in San Francisco* (Chicago: Aldine Transaction Books).

Becker, H. S. and Greer, B. (1958): 'The Fate of Idealism in Medical School', *American Sociological Review*, XXIII, 50–6.

Becker, H. S. and Greer, G. (1968): *Institutions and the Person* (Chicago: Aldine).

Becker, H. S. and Horowitz, I. L. (1971): 'The Culture of Civility', in Becker (ed.) (1971).

Becker, H. S. and Strauss, A. L. (1956): 'Careers, Personality and Adult Socialisation', *American Journal of Sociology*, LXII, 253–63.

Becker, H. S., Greer, B. and Hughes, E. (1961): *Boys in White* (Chicago: University of Chicago Press).

Becker, H. S., Greer, B. and Hughes, E. C. (1968): *Making the Grade* (New York: Wiley).

Bell, D. (1960): *The End of Ideology* (New York: Free Press).

Belson, W. A. (1975): *The Public and the Police* (London: Harper & Row).

Bent, A. E. (1974): *The Politics of Law Enforcement* (Lexington, Mass.: Heath).

Berger, P. L. and Luckman, T. (1967): *The Social Construction of Reality* (Harmondsworth: Penguin).

Berreman, G. D. (1964): *Behind Many Masks: Ethnography and Impression Management in a Himalayan Village*, Monograph No. 4 (Ithaca, N.Y.: Society for Applied Anthropology).

Bianchi, H., Simondi, M. and Taylor, I. (eds.) (1975): *Deviance and Control in Europe* (London: Wiley).

Biervliet, W. E. (1975): 'The Hustle Culture of Young Unemployed Surinamers', unpublished paper, delivered at Applied Anthropology Congress, Amsterdam.

Bittner, E. (1967a): 'The Police on Skid Row: A Study of Peace-Keeping', *American Sociological Review*, XXXII (5), 699–715.

Bittner, E. (1967b): 'Police Discretion in the Emergency Apprehension of Mentally Ill Persons', *Social Problems*, XIV, 278–92.

Bittner, E. (1970): *The Functions of the Police in Modern Society* (Washington, D.C.: U.S. Government Printing Office).

Bittner, E. (1974): 'A Theory of the Police', in Jacobs (ed.) (1974).

Bittner, E. (1975): 'Police Research and Police Work', in Viano (ed.) (1975).

Black, D. J. (1968): 'Police Encounters and Social Organisation', unpublished Ph.D. thesis, University of Michigan.

Black, D. J. (1970): 'The Production of Crime Rates', *American Sociological Review*, XXXV, 733–47.

Black, D. J. (1971): 'The Social Organisation of Arrest', *Stanford Law Review*, 23 (June), 1087–111.

Black, D. J. and Reiss, A. J., Jr (1967): *Patterns of Behaviour in Police and Citizen Transactions*, Studies in Law Enforcement in Major Metropolitan Areas, Field Survey 3, 2 vols. (Washington, D.C.: U.S. Government Printing Office).

Black, D. J. and Reiss, A. J. (1970): 'Police Control of Juveniles', *American Sociological Review*, XXXV, 63–77.

Blanken, M. (1976): *Force of Order and Methods: An American View into the Dutch Directed Society* (The Hague: Martinus Nijhoff).

Blau, P. M. (1955): *The Dynamics of Bureaucracy* (Chicago: Chicago University Press).

Block, R. (1975): 'Homicide in Chicago: A Nine Year Study', *Journal of Criminal Law and Criminology*, LXVI (4), 496–510.

Block, R. (1977): *Violent Crime: Environment, Interaction, and Death* (Lexington, Mass.: Heath).

Blumberg, A. S. (ed.) (1970): *The Scales of Justice* (Chicago: Aldine Transaction Books).

Blumberg, L. V., Shipley, T. E. and Shandler, I. W. (eds.) (1973): *Skid-Row and its Alternatives* (Philadelphia: Temple University Press).

Blumer, H. (1969): *Symbolic Interactionism* (Englewood Cliffs, N. J.: Prentice-Hall).

Bopp, W. J. (ed.) (1971): *The Police Rebellion: A Quest for Blue Power* (Springfield, Ill.: Thomas).

Bopp, W. J. (ed.) (1972): *Police–Community Relations* (Springfield, Ill.: Thomas).

Bordua, D. J. (ed.) (1967): *The Police: Six Sociological Essays* (New York: Wiley).

Borland, M. (ed.) (1976): *Violence in the Family* (Manchester: Manchester University Press).

Bowes, S. (1968): *Police and Civil Liberties* (London: Lawrence & Wishart).

Brana-Shute, G. (1977): ' "Hosselen" Reconsidered: A Polemic on Afro-Surinamer Identity Management in a Neo-Colonial Situation', unpublished paper, University of Utrecht.

Brittan, A. (1973): *Meanings and Situations* (London: Routledge & Kegan Paul).

Brown, J. (1970): *The Unmelting Pot* (London: Macmillan).

Brown, J. (1974): *Police–Immigrant Relations* (Cranfield Insititute of Technology).

Brown, J. (1977): *Shades of Grey: Police–West Indian Relations in Handsworth* (Cranfield Institute of Technology).

Brown, J. and Howes, G. (eds.) (1975): *The Police and the Community* (Farnborough: Saxon House).

Brunt, L. (1975): 'Anthropological Fieldwork in The Netherlands', in Kloos and Claessen (eds.) (1975).

Buckner, H. T. (1967): 'The Police: The Culture of a Social Control Agency', unpublished Ph.D. thesis, University of California at Berkeley.

Buikhuisen, W and Timmerman, H. (1972): 'The Development of Drug-Taking among Secondary School Children in The Netherlands', *Bulletin on Narcotics*, XXV (3), 7–16.

Buikhuisen, W., Dijksterhuis, F. P. H., Hemmel, J. J., Jongman, R. W., Smale, G. J. A. and Timmerman, H. (1971): 'Hash Users: Characteristics and Policy. An Empirical Investigation', *Sociologia Neerlandica*, VII (2), 73–87.

Bunyan, T. (1976): *The Political Police in Britain* (London: Quartet).

Burgess, E. W. and Bogue, D. J. (eds.) (1964): *Contributions to Urban Sociology* (Chicago: Chicago University Press).

Burnham, D. (1968a): 'Police Misconduct', *New York Times*, 5 July 1968.

Burnham, D. (1968b): 'Police Violence', *New York Times*, 7 July 1968.

Cain, M. (1973): *Society and the Policeman's Role* (London: Routledge & Kegan Paul).

Cain, M. (1977): 'An Ironical Departure: The Dilemma of Contemporary Policing', in *Yearbook of Social Policy in Britain* (London: Routledge & Kegan Paul).

Caplan, G. (1976): 'Studying the Police', Address to the Executive Forum on Upgrading the Police, Washington D.C., 13 Apr.

Carey, J. T. (1975): *Sociology and Public Affairs: The Chicago School* (Beverly Hills, Calif.: Sage).

Carte, G. (1973): 'Changes in Public Attitudes to the Police: A Comparison of 1938 and 1971 Surveys', *Journal of Police Science and Administration*, I (2), 182–200.

Carte, G. E. and Carte, E. H. (1975): *Police Reform in the United States: The Era of August Vollmer, 1905–32* (Berkeley: University of California Press).

Chambliss, W. J. (ed.) (1969): *Crime and the Legal Process* (New York: McGraw-Hill).

Chambliss, W. J. and Seidman, R. B. (1971): *Law, Order and Power* (Reading, Mass.: Addison-Wesley).

Chatterton, M. R. (1973): 'Working Paper on the Use of Resource-Charges and Practical Decision-Making in Peace-Keeping', unpublished paper, Police Seminar, University of Bristol.

Chatterton, M. R. (1974): 'Fixed Point System of Patrol Work', unpublished paper, University of Manchester.

Chatterton, M. R. (1975a): 'Organisational Relationships and Processes in Police Work: A Case Study of Urban Policing', unpublished Ph.D. thesis, University of Manchester.

Chatterton, M. R. (1975b): 'Images of Police Work and the Uses of Rules: Supervision and Patrol Work under the Fixed Point System', unpublished paper, Police Seminar, University of Bristol.

Chatterton, M. R. (1976a): 'The Social Contexts of Violence', in Borland (ed.) (1976).

Chatterton, M. R. (1976b): 'The Police in Social Control', *Cropwood Conference: Control Without Custody* (Institute of Criminology, University of Cambridge).

Chevigny, P. (1968): *Police Power: Police Abuses in New York City* (New York: Pantheon).

Chevigny, P. (1972): *Cops and Rebels* (New York: Pantheon).

Chibnall, S. (1975): 'The Crime Reporter', *Sociology*, IX (1), 49–66.

Chibnall, S. (1977): *Law and Order News* (London: Tavistock).

Christie, N. (1973): *The Police* (Oslo: Institute of Criminology and Criminal Law).

Cicourel, A. V. (1968): *The Social Organisation of Juvenile Justice* (New York: Wiley).

Clark, J. P. (1965): 'The Isolation of the Police', *Journal of Criminal Law*,

Criminology and Police Science, LVI, 307–19.

Clark, J. P. and Sykes, R. (1974): 'Some Determinants of Police Organisation and Practice in a Modern Industrial Democracy', in Glaser (ed.) (1974).

Clarke, M. (1975): 'Survival in the Field: Implications of Personal Experience in Field-Work', *Theory and Society* II (1), 95–123.

Coates, R. B. and Miller, A. D. (1974): 'Patrolmen and Addicts: A Study of Police Perception and Police–Citizen Interaction', *Journal of Police Science and Administration*, II, 308–21.

Cohen, B. and Chaiken, J. M. (1973): *Police Background, Characteristics, and Performances* (Lexington, Mass.: Heath).

Cohen, H. (1976): 'Drugs, Drug-Users and Drug-Scenes', *Sociologia Neerlandica*, XII (1), 3–18.

Cohen, S. (ed.) (1971): *Images of Deviance* (Harmondsworth: Penguin).

Cohen, S. (1972): *Folk Devils and Moral Panics* (London: Macgibbon & Kee).

Cohen, S. (1974): 'Criminology and the Sociology of Deviance in Britain', in Rock and McIntosh (eds.) (1974).

Cohen, S. and Young, J. (eds.) (1973): *The Manufacture of News: Deviance, Social Problems and the Mass Media* (London: Constable).

Crawford, T. J. (1973): 'Police Overperception of Ghetto Hostility', *Journal of Police Science and Administration*, I (2), 168–74.

Critchley, T. A. (1967): *A History of Police in England and Wales: 900–1966* (London: Constable).

Critchley, T. A. (1969): *The Conquest of Violence : A History of Law Enforcement in Britain* (London: Constable).

Cruse, D. and Rubin, J. (1973): *Determinants of Police Behaviour: A Summary* (Washington, D.C.: U.S. Government Printing Office).

Cumming, M. (1971): 'Police and Service Work', in Hahn (ed.) (1971).

Cumming, E., Cumming, I. and Edel, L. (1965): 'Policeman as Philosopher, Guide and Friend', *Social Problems*, XVII, 276–86.

Davis, F. (1959): 'The Cab Driver and his Fare: Facets of a Fleeting Relationship', *American Journal of Sociology*, LXV, 158–65.

Davis, F. (1971): 'The San Francisco Mystique', in Becker (ed.) (1971).

Davis, F. J. and Stivers, R. (1975): *Collective Definition of Deviance* (New York: Free Press).

Dawe, A. (1973): 'The Underworld View of Erving Goffman', *British Journal of Sociology*, XXIV, 246–53.

Denfield, D. (ed.) (1974): *Street-Wise Criminology* (Cambridge, Mass.: Schenkman).

Dodd, D. J. (1967): 'Police Mentality and Behaviour', *Issues in Crinimology*, III 47–67.

Douglas, J. D. (ed.) (1970a): *Observations of Deviance* (New York: Random House).

Douglas, J. D. (1970b): *Deviance and Respectability* (New York: Basic Books).

Douglas, J. D. (ed.) (1971a): *Crime and Justice in American Society* (Indianapolis: Bobbs-Merrill).

Douglas, J. D. (ed.) (1971b): *Understanding Everyday Life* (London: Routledge & Kegan Paul).

Douglas, J. D. (ed.) (1972): *Research on Deviance* (New York: Random House).

Driscoll, J. M., Meyer, R. G. and Schanie, C. F. (1973): 'Training Police in Family Crisis Intervention', *Journal of Applied Behavioural Science*, IX (1), 62–82.

Edmond-Smith, J . (1974): 'Police Forces in France', *New Community*, III (3), 227–33.

Evans, P. (1974): *The Police Revolution* (London: Allen & Unwin).

Faris, R. E. L. (1970): *Chicago Sociology* (Chicago: University of Chicago Press).

Ferdinand, T. and Lucterhand, E. (1970): 'Inner City Youths: The Police and Justice', *Social Problems*, XVII, 510–27.

Ferracuti, F. (1967): *European Migration and Crime* (Strasbourg: Council of Europe).

Fichter, J. H. (1973): *One Man Research* (New York: Wiley).

Filstead, W. J. (ed.) (1971): *Qualititive Methodology* (Chicago: Rand-McNally).

Fox, J. C. and Lundman, R. J. (1974): 'Problems and Strategies in Gaining Research Access in Police Organisations', *Criminology*, XII (1), 52–69.

Freeling, N. (1973): *Over the High Side* (Harmondsworth: Penguin).

Freilich, M. (ed.) (1970): *Marginal Natives: Anthropologists at Work* (New York: Evanston).

Furstenburg, R. and Wellford, C. (1973): 'Calling the Police', *Law and Society Review*, VII, 343–406.

Galanter, M. (1973): 'Notes on the Future of Social Research on Law', mimeographed paper presented to Conference on Developments in Law and Social Science Research.

Gardiner, J. (1969): *Traffic and the Police* (Cambridge, Mass.: Harvard University Press).

Garrett, M. and Short, J. F. (1974): 'Delinquent Stereotypes: Police in the Labelling Process', unpublished paper, American Sociological Association, Annual Meeting.

Glaser, B. G. and Strauss, A. L. (1971): *Status Passage* (Chicago: Aldine).

Glaser, D. (ed.) (1974): *Handbook of Criminology* (Chicago: Rand-McNally).

Goffman, E. (1959): *The Presentation of Self in Everyday Life* (Harmondsworth: Penguin).

Goffman, E. (1961): *Encounters* (Harmondsworth: Penguin).

Goffman, E. (1971): *Relations in Public* (Harmondsworth: Penguin).

Goffman, E. (1972): *Interaction Ritual* (Harmondsworth: Penguin).

Goldstein, H. (1977): *Policing a Free Society* (Cambridge, Mass.: Ballinger).

Goldstein, J. (1960): 'Police Discretion Not to Invoke the Criminal Process', *Yale Law Journal*, LXIX, 543–94.

Goudsblom, J. (1967): *Dutch Society* (New York: Random House).

Gould, L. (1971): 'Crime and its Impact on an Affluent Society', in Douglas (ed.) (1971a).

Grahm, H. D. and Gurr, T. R. (eds.) (1969): *Violence in America: Historical and Comparative Perspectives* (New York: Signet Books).

Green, P. and Levinson, S. (eds.) (1970): *Power and Community: Dissenting Essays in Political Science* (New York: Vintage Books).

Grimminger, H. (1970): 'Sociology for the Police', *Forward*, no. 4, Autumn, pp. 9–10.

Gross, N., Mason, W. S. and McEachern, A. W. (1958): *Explorations in Role Analysis* (New York: Wiley).

Gurr, T. R. (1969): 'A Comparative Study of Civil Strife', in Grahm and Gurr (eds.) (1969).

Hacker, A. (1977): Review Article on the Police, *New York Review of Books*, XXIV, (14), 1–4.

Hahn, H. (ed.) (1971): *The Police in Urban Society* (Beverly Hills, Calif.: Sage).

Hannertz, V. (1969): *Soulside* (New York: Columbia University Press).

Harris, R. N. (1973): *The Police Academy* (New York: Wiley).

Hartjen, C. A. (1972): 'Police–Citizen Encounters: Social Order in Interpersonal Interaction', *Criminology*, X (1), 61–84.

Harvey, D. (1973): *Social Justice and the City* (London: Arnold).

Have, P. ten (1970): 'Emancipation and Culture', *Mens en Maatschappij*, XLV, 246–57.

Have, P. ten (1972): 'The Counter Culture on the Move', unpublished paper read at American Sociological Association, Annual Meeting.

Hayes, M. and Pearce, F. (1976): *Crime, Law, and the State* (London: Routledge & Kegan Paul).

Heijder, A. (1974): 'The Recent Trend Towards Reducing the Prison Population in The Netherlands', *International Journal of Offender Therapy and Comparative Criminology*, XVIII (3), 233–40.

Henslin, J. M. (1974): 'The Underlife of Cab-driving: A Study in Exploitation and Punishment', in Stewart and Cantor (eds.) (1974).

Hippler, A. E. (1971): 'The Game of Black and White at Hunter's Point', in Becker (ed.) (1971).

Holdaway, S. (1977a): 'Changes in Urban Policing', *British Journal of Sociology*, XXVIII, (2), 119–137.

Holdaway, S. (1977b): 'Police–Black Relations: The Professional Solution', in Holdaway (ed.) (1978).

Holdaway, S. (ed.) (1978): *The British Police*, forthcoming (London: Arnold).

Hood, R. (1975): *Crime, Criminology, and Public Policy* (New York: Free Press).

Hopper, M. (1977): 'Becoming a Policeman: Socialisation of Cadets in a Police Academy', *Urban Life*, VI (2), 149–58.

Horowitz, I. L. and Liebowitz, M. (1971): 'Social Deviance and Political Marginality: Toward a Redefinition of the Relation Between Sociology and Politics', *Social Problems* XV, 280–96.

Hughes, E. C. (1953): *Men and their Work* (New York: Free Press).

Hughes, E. C. (1963): 'Good People and Dirty Work', in Becker (ed.) (1963).

Hughes, E. C. (1971): *The Sociological Eye*, vol. II: *Work, Self and the Study of Society* (Chicago: Aldine).

Humphreys, L. (1970): *Tearoom Trade: Impersonal Sex in Public Places* (Chicago: Aldine).

Humphreys, L. (1972): *Out of the Closet* (Englewood-Cliffs, N. J.: Prentice-Hall).

Humphry, D. (1972): *Police Power and Black People* (London: Panther).

Jackson, R. M. (1967): *The Machinery of Justice in England* (Cambridge: Cambridge University Press).

Jacobs, H. (ed.) (1974): *The Potential for Reform of the Criminal Justice System* (Beverly Hills, Calif.: Sage).

Jacobs, J. (1965): *The Death and Life of Great American Cities* (Harmondsworth: Penguin).

Jacobs, J. (1969): 'Symbolic Bureaucracy', *Social Forces*, XLVII, 413–22.

Johnson, J. M. (1975): *Doing Field Research* (New York: Free Press).

Jones, C. (1977): *Immigration and Social Policy in Britain* (London: Tavistock).

Joseph, N. and Alex, N. (1972): 'The Uniform: A Sociological Perspective', *American Journal of Sociology*, LXXVII, 719–30.

Judge, A. (1972): *A Man Apart* (London: Barker).

Juris, H. A. and Feuille, P. (1973): *Police Unionism* (Lexington, Mass.: Heath).

Katz, E. and Danet, B. (eds.) (1973): *Bureaucracy and the Public: A Reader in Official–Client Relations* (New York: Basic Books).

Kilby, R. and Constable, T. (1975): 'The Police and Social Workers', in Brown and Howes (eds.) (1975).

Kirkham, G. L. (1974): 'From Professor to Patrolman', *Journal of Police Science and Administration*, II (2), 127–37.

Kirkham, G. L. (1976): *Signal Zero* (Philadelphia: Lippincott).

Kloos, P. and Claessen, H. T. M. (eds.) (1975): *Current Anthropology in The Netherlands* (The Hague, Government Publishing Office).

Knapp, W. (1972): *The Knapp Report on Police Corruption* (New York: Braziller).

Krisberg, B. (1975): *Crime and Privilege: Toward a New Criminology* (Englewood Cliffs, N. J.: Prentice-Hall).

La Fave, W. R. (1965a): *Arrest: The Decision to Take a Suspect into Custody* (Boston: Little, Brown).

La Fave, W. R. (1965b): *The Decision to Charge a Suspect with a Crime* (Boston: Little, Brown).

Larsen, R. (1972): *Urban Police Patrol Analysis* (Cambridge, Mass.: M.I.T. Press).

Lasswell, H. D. and McKenna, J. B. (1972): *The Impact of Organised Crime on an Inner City Community* (New York: The Policy Sciences Center).

Laurie, P. (1971): *Drugs* (2nd ed.) (Harmondsworth: Penguin).

Laurie, P. (1972): *Scotland Yard* (Harmondsworth: Penguin).

Lefkowitz, J. (1973): 'Attitudes of Police Toward their Job', included in Snibbe and Snibbe (eds.) (1973).

Lemert, E. (1972): *Human Deviance* (Englewood Cliffs, N.J.: Prentice-Hall).

Lewis, R. (1976): *A Force for the Future* (London: Temple Smith).

Liebow, E. (1967): *Tally's Corner* (Boston: Little Brown).

Lijphart, A. (1968): *The Politics of Accommodation* (Berkeley: University of California Press).

Lipset, S. M. (1969): 'The Politics of the Police', *New Society*, XIII (336), 355–8.

Lipset, S. M., Trow, M. A. and Coleman, J. S. (1956): *Union Democracy* (Glencoe, Ill.: Free Press).

Lipsky, M. (ed.) 1971): *Police Encounters* (Chicago: Aldine Transaction Books).

Lofland, J. (1969): *Deviance and Identity* (Englewood Cliffs, N.J.: Prentice-Hall).

Lundman, R. J. (1974): 'Domestic Police–Citizen Encounters', *Journal of Police Science and Administration*, II (1), 22–7.

Lyman, S. M. (1971): 'Red Guard on Grant Avenue', in Becker (ed.) (1971).

Maanen, J. van (1973): 'Observations on the Making of a Policeman'. *Human Organisation*, XXXII, 407–18.

Maanen, J. van (1974): 'Working the Street', in Jacobs (ed.) (1974).

Maanen, J. van (1975): 'Police Socialisation', *Administrative Science Quarterly*, XX, 207–28.

Maas, P. (1973): *Serpico* (London: Collins).

McCall, G. and Simmons, J. L. (eds.) (1969): *Issues in Participant Observation* (Reading, Mass.: Addison-Wesley).

MacDonald, K. (1976): 'A Police State in Britain?', *New Society*, 8 Jan, pp. 50–1.

MacDonald, K. M. (1977): 'The Forces of Social Control: Community Liaison by the Police', unpublished paper, British Sociological Association, Annual Conference.

McDonald, L. (1976): *Sociology of Law and Order* (London: Faber & Faber).

MacInnes, C. (1969a): *The London Novels* (New York: Farrar, Straus & Giroux).

MacInnes, C. (1969b): 'Mr Love and Justice', in MacInnes (1969a).

McIntosh, M. (1976): *The Organisation of Crime* (London: Macmillan).

McNaughton-Smith, P. (1976): 'What People Think the Police are For', in van Outrive and S. Rizkalla (eds.) (1976).

Manning, P. K. (1971):'The Police: Mandate, Strategies, and Appearances', in Douglas (ed.) (1971a).

Manning, P. K. (1972): 'Observing the Police', in Douglas (ed.) (1972).

Manning, P. K. (1973a): 'Dramatic Aspects of Policing', mimeo, Michigan State University.

Manning, P. K. (1973b): 'Organisations as Situationally Justified Action', mimeo, Michigan State University.

Manning, P. K. (1974a): 'Police Lying', *Urban Life and Culture*, III (3), 283–305.

Manning, P. K. (1974b): 'Dramatic Aspects of Policing: Selected Propositions', *Sociology and Social Research*, LIX (1), 21–9.

Manning, P. K. (1976): 'The Decline of Civility: A Comment on Erving Goffman's Sociology', *Canadian Review of Sociology and Anthropology*, XIII, 13–25.

Manning, P. K. (1977): *Police Work* (Cambridge, Mass.: M.I.T. Press).

Mark, R. (1977): *Policing a Perplexed Society* (London: Allen & Unwin).

Marshall, P. (1974a): 'Juvenile Crime: A Vicious Perplexity', Community Relations Branch, Metropolitan Police.

Marshall, P. (1974b): 'The Community Relations Aspect of Policing', *New Community*, III (3), 193–8.

Marshall, P. (1975): 'Urban Stress and Policing', in Brown and Howes (eds.) (1975).

Martin, J. P. and Wilson, G. (1969): *The Police: A Study in Manpower* (London: Heinemann).

Matarazzo, J. D., Saslow, B. V. and Wiens, A. N. (1964): 'Characteristics of Successful Policeman and Fireman Applicants', *Journal of Applied Psychology*, XLVIII (2), 123–33.

Matza, D. (1969): *Becoming Deviant* (Englewood Cliffs, N. J.: Prentice-Hall).

Meltzer, B. N. Petras, J. W. and Reynolds, L. T. (1975) *Symbolic Interactionism* (London: Routledge & Kegan Paul).

Merricks, F. R. (n.d.): 'The Development of Community Relations in the Metropolitan Police', mimeo, Community Relations Branch, Metropolitan Police.

Merton, R. K., Reader, G. G. and Kendall, P. L. (1957): *The Student Physician* (Cambridge, Mass.: Harvard University Press).

Meyer, J. C. Jr (1972): 'Methodological Issues in Comparative Criminal Justice Research', *Criminology*, X (3), 295–313.

Middendorp, C. P. (1976): 'Progressiveness and Conservatism', unpublished Ph.D. thesis, University of Amsterdam.

Miller, F. W. (1970): *Prosecution: The Decision to Charge a Suspect with a Crime* (Boston: Little, Brown).

Mosse, G. L. (1975): *Police Forces in History* (Beverly Hills, Calif.: Sage).

Moynihan, D. P. (1969): *Violent Crime: The Challenge to our Cities* (New York: Brazillier).

Newman, D. (1966): *Conviction: Determination of Guilt or Innocence without Trial* (Boston: Little, Brown).

Newman, O. (1973): *Defensible Space: People and Design in the Violent City* (London: Architectural Press).

Niederhoffer, A. (1967): *Behind the Shield: The Police in Urban Society* (New York: Anchor).

Niederhoffer, A. (1975): *The Police Family* (Farnborough: Saxon House).

Niederhoffer, A. and Blumberg, A. S. (1970): *The Ambivalent Force* (Boston: Ginn/Blaisdell).

Norris, D. F. (1973): *Police–Community Relations: A Program that Failed* (Lexington, Mass.: Heath).

Olila, J. H. and Hulsman, L. H. C. (1977): 'What do Urbanites Mean by "Crime"? An Exploratory Research into the Problems of Criminal Definition in a Dutch Urban Area', unpublished paper, Dutch Sociological–Anthropological conference.

Oliver, J. (1974): 'Police and the Community', *Residential Care*, III (7), 1–2.

Outrive, L. van and Rizkalla, S. (eds.) (1976): 'Final Report: International Seminar on Police Research', Catholic University of Leuven and University of Montreal.

Park, R. E., Burgess, E. W. and McKenzie, R. D. (1925): *The City* (Chicago: Chicago University Press).

Parsons, T. (1951): *The Social System* (Glencoe, Ill.: Free Press).

Patrick, C. H. (ed.) (1972): *The Police, Crime and Society* (Springfield, Ill.: Thomas).

Pepinsky, H. E. (1976): *Crime and Conflict* (London: Martin Robertson).

Phillips, D. (1973): *Abandoning Method* (London: Jossey-Bass).

Piliavin, I. and Briar, S. (1964): 'Police Encounters with Juveniles', *American Journal of Sociology*, LXX, 206–14.

Plant, M. A. (1975): *Drugtakers in an English Town* (London: Tavistock).

Platt, A. and Cooper, L. (eds.) (1974): *Policing America* (Englewood Cliffs, N. J.: Prentice-Hall).

Polsky, N. (1971): *Hustlers, Beats, and Others* (Harmondsworth: Penguin).

Potholm, C. P. and Morgan, R. E. (1977): *Focus on Police* (Chichester: Wiley).

Preiss, J. J. and Ehrlich, H. J. (1966): *An Examination of Role Theory: The Case of the State Police* (Lincoln: University of Nebraska Press).

Pulling, C. (1964): *Mr. Punch and the Police* (London: Butterworths).

Punch, M. (1974a): 'Amsterdam Gone Sour' *New Society*, 21 Nov, 217–19.

Punch, M. (1974b): 'The Policeman's Role in the Community: A Field Note', *Nederlands Tijdschrift voor Criminologie*, XVI, 59–70.

Punch, M. (1974c): 'Area Bobbies, Rotterdam Style', *Police*, VI (8), 14–15.

Punch, M. (1975a): 'Research and the Police', in Brown and Howes (eds.) (1975).

Punch, M. (1975b): 'Rayonagent: Politieman als Maatschappelijk Werker', *Algemeen Politieblad*, CXXIV (3), 51–4.

Punch, M. (1975c): 'Warmoesstraat: Een Sociologisch Rapport', *Tijdschrift van de Amsterdamse Politie*, XXIX (11/12), 2–5.

Punch, M. (1975d): 'Policing a Cosmopolitan City-Centre', *Gardai Review*, III (4), 7–11.

Punch, M. (1976a), 'Report on Workshop: Police Action and the Public', in van Outrive and Rizkalla (eds.) (1976).

Punch, M. (1976b): 'Front-line Amsterdam: Policework in the Inner city', *British Journal of Law and Society*, III (2), 218–32.

Punch, M. (1976c): 'Participant Observation and Police in Amsterdam: A Working Paper', in van Outrive and Rizkalla (eds.) (1976).

Punch, M. (1976d): *Fout is Fout: Gesprekken met de Politie in de Binnenstad van Amsterdam* (Meppel: Boom).

Punch, M. (1976e): 'De Politieagent als Welzijnswerker', *Maandblad Geestelijke Volksgezondheid*, XXXI (4), 203–14.

Punch, M. (1976f): 'Politie en Publiek in de Binnenstad van Amsterdam', *Nederlands Tijdschrift voor Criminologie*, XVIII, 3–14.

Punch, M. (1976g): 'The Commissioner of Amsterdam', *Gardai Review*, IV (5), 13–19.

Punch, M. (1976h): 'Anatomy of a Riot', *Police*, VIII (6), 16–18.

Punch, M. (1976i): 'Gevraagd: Een Sociologie van de Politie', *Intermediair*, XII (44), 33–9.

Punch, M. (1976j): 'Sociologie uit het Leven', *Sociodrome*, III, 14–15.

Punch, M. (1977a): 'Warmoesstraat: Einde Afschuifsysteem', *Vrij Nederland*, 25 June.

Punch, M. (1977b): 'Frontline Amsterdam: politiewerk in de Binnenstad', *Het*

Tijdschrift voor de Politie, XXXIX (7/8), 307–18.

Punch, M. (1977c): 'Politie en Beleid: Leren Leven met een Gespleten Persoonlijkheid', *Beleid en Maatschappij*, IV (10), 280–91.

Punch, M. (1977d): 'Participerende Observatie bij de Politie', in Brunt (ed.) (1977).

Punch, M. (1978a): 'The Secret Social Service', forthcoming in Holdaway (ed.) (1978).

Punch, M. (1978b): 'Backstage: Observing Police Work in Amsterdam', forthcoming in *Urban Life*.

Punch, M. (1978c): 'Participant Observation and the Police', forthcoming in *Police Journal* (translation of Punch, 1977d).

Punch, M. and Naylor, T. (1973): 'The Police: A Social Service', *New Society*, XXIV (554), 358–61.

Purcell, W. (1973): *British Police in a Changing Society* (London: Mowbray).

Quinney, R. (1970): *The Social Reality of Crime* (Boston: Little, Brown).

Quinney, R. (1973): *Criminal Behaviour Systems* (New York: Holt).

Quinney, R. (ed.) (1974): *Criminal Justice in America* (Boston: Little, Brown).

Quinney, R. (1975): *Criminology* (Boston: Little, Brown).

Radzinowicz, L. and King, J. (1977): *The Growth of Crime* (London: Hamish Hamilton).

Rainton, D. (1974): 'Police–Community Relations in The Netherlands', unpublished report (Strasbourg: Council of Europe).

Rainwater, L. (ed.) (1970): *Black Experience: Soul* (Chicago: Aldine Transaction Books).

Rainwater, L. (ed.) (1974): *Inequality and Justice* (Chicago: Aldine).

Ray, G. (1977): 'Police Militancy', *Crime and Social Justice*, VII, 40–8.

Reiner, R. (1976): 'The Blue-coated Worker: A Sociological Study of Police Unionism', unpublished Ph.D. thesis, University of Bristol.

Reiss, A. J., Jr (ed.) (1964): *Louis Wirth on Cities and Social Life* (Chicago: Chicago University Press).

Reiss, A. J. Jr (1967): 'Career Orientations, Job Satisfaction, and the Assessment of Law Enforcement Problems by Police Officers', *Studies of Crime and Law Enforcement in Major Metropolitan Areas*, vol. II, section, II (Washington, D.C.: U.S. Government Printing Office).

Reiss, A. J. Jr (1968): 'Police Brutality: Answers to Key Questions', *Transaction*, V (8), 10–19.

Reiss, A. J. Jr (1971): *The Police and the Public* (New Haven: Yale University Press).

Reiss, A. J. Jr and Bordua, D. J. (1967): 'Environment and Organisation: A Perspective on the Police', in Bordua (ed.) (1967).

Rhead, C. (1968): 'The Psychological Assessment of Police Candidates', *American Journal of Psychiatry*, CXXIV (11), 1575–80.

Robertson, R. and Taylor, L. (1973): *Deviance, Crime and Socio-Legal Control* (London: Martin Robertson).

Rock, P. (1973): *Deviant Behaviour* (London: Hutchinson).

Rock, P. and McIntosh, M. (eds.) (1974): *Deviance and Social Control*

(London: Tavistock).

Rubington, E. and Weinberg, M. S. (eds.) (1968): *Deviance: The Interactionist Perspective* (New York: Macmillan).

Rubinstein, J. (1973): *City Police* (New York: Ballantine).

Ruchelman, L. (1974): *Police Politics* (Cambridge, Mass.: Ballinger).

Sacks, H. (1972): 'Notes on the Police Assessment of Moral Character' in Sudnow (ed.) (1972).

Schaar, J. H. (1970): 'Legitimacy in the Modern State', in Green and Levinson (eds.) (1970).

Schuyt, C. J. M. (1975): 'Law, Social Order and Civil Disobedience', unpublished typescript, University of Nijmegen.

Schwendinger, H. and Schwendinger, J. (1970): 'Defenders of Order or Guardians of Human Rights?', *Issues in Criminology*, V (2), 123–58.

Selosse, J. and Lenke, L. (1972): *Crime in Five Countries* (Strasbourg: Council of Europe).

Shearing, C. D. and Leon, J. S. (1976): 'Reconsidering the Police Role: A Challenge to a Challenge of a Popular Conception', in van Outrive and Rizkalla (eds.) (1976).

Sherman, L. W. (1974): *Police Corruption* (New York: Anchor).

Shoham, S. G. (1976): *Social Deviance* (New York: Gardner Press).

Short, J. F. Jr (ed.) (1970): *Modern Criminals* (Chicago: Aldine Transaction Books).

Short, J. F. Jr (ed.) (1971): *The Social Fabric of the Metropolis* (Chicago: Chicago University Press).

Sikes, M. P. (1973): 'Police–Community Relations: The Houston Experiment', in Snibbe and Snibbe (eds.) (1973).

Silver, A. (1967): 'The Demand for Order in Civil Society', in Bordua (ed.) (1967).

Skogan, W. (1974a): 'Citizen Reporting of Crime: Some National Panel Data', unpublished paper.

Skogan, W. (1974b): 'The Validity of Official Crime Statistics', *Social Science Quarterly*, LV, 25–38.

Skogan, W. (1976): 'Citizen Reporting of Crime: Some National Crime Panel Data', *Criminology*, XIII (4), 535–49.

Skolnick, J. H. (1975): *Justice Without Trial*, 2nd ed. (New York: Wiley).

Smit, N. W. de (1972a): 'Psychiatry and Criminal Law as Conflicting Systems: The Challenge of a Stalemate', *Annals of System Research*, II, 87–92.

Smit, N. W. de (1972b): 'Crisis Intervention and Crisis Centers: Their Possible Relevance for Community Psychiatry and Mental Health Care', *Psychiatra, Neurologia, Neurochirurgia*, LXXV, 299–301.

Smith, D. (1970): 'The Death of Haight-Ashbury', *New Society*, XVI (407), 98–101.

Smith, D. (1973): *Report from Engine Co. 82* (New York: Pocket Books).

Smith, D. E. (1965): 'Front-line Organisation of the State Mental Hospital', *Administrative Science Quarterly*, X (3), 381–99.

Snibbe, J. R. and Snibbe, H. M. (eds.) (1973): *The Urban Policeman in Transition* (Springfield, Ill.: Thomas).

Spradley, J. P. (1970): *You Owe Yourself a Drunk: An Ethnography of Urban*

Nomads (Boston: Little, Brown).
Spradley, J. P. and McCurdy, D. W. (eds.) (1972): *Anthropology: The Cultural Perspective* (New York: Wiley).
Stark, R. (1971): *Police Riots* (San Francisco: Wadsworth).
Steer, D. (1970): *Police Cautions: A Study in the Exercise of Police Discretion* (Oxford: Blackwell).
Steinmetz, S. K. and Straus, M. A. (eds.) (1974): *Violence in the Family* (New York: Dodd Mead).
Stewart, P. L. and Cantor, M. (eds.) (1974): *Varieties of Work Experience: The Social Control of Occupational Groups and Roles* (New York: Halsted Press).
Stinchcombe, A. L. (1963): 'Institutions of Privacy in the Determination of Police Administrative Practices', *American Journal of Sociology*, LXIX, 150–60.
Stoddard, E. (1968): 'The Informal Code of Police Deviancy: A Group Approach to Blue Collar Crime', *Journal of Criminal Law, Criminology and Police Science*, LIX, 201–13.
Strauss, A. (ed.) (1968): *The American City: A Sourcebook of Imagery* (Chicago: Chicago University Press).
Sudnow, D. (ed.) (1972): *Studies in Social Interaction* (New York: Free Press).
Suttles, G. (1968): *The Social Order of the Slum* (Chicago: Chicago University Press).
Suttles, G. (1976): 'Urban Ethnography: Situational and Normative Accounts', *Annual Review of Sociology*, II, 1–18.
Sykes, R. E. and Clark, J. P. (1974): 'A Theory of Deference Exchange in Police–Citizen Encounters', unpublished paper, American Sociological Association, Annual Meeting.

Tauber, R. K. (1967): 'Danger and the Police: A Theoretical Analysis', *Issues in Criminology*, III (1), 69–81.
Taylor, I., Walton, P. and Young, J. (1973): *The New Criminology: For a Social Theory of Deviance* (London: Routledge & Kegan Paul).
Taylor, L. (1971): *Deviance and Society* (London: Nelson).
Terkel, S. (1975): *Working* (New York: Avon).
Thompson, H. (1967): *Hell's Angels* (Harmondsworth: Penguin).
Thrasher, F. M. (1960): *The Gang* (Chicago: Chicago University Press).
Toch, H. J., Grant, D. and Galvin, R. T. (1975): *Agents of Change: A Study in Police Reform* (New York: Halsted Press).
Treger, H. (1975): *The Police–Social Work Team* (Springfield, Ill.: Thomas).

Viano, E. (ed.) (1975): *Criminal Justice Research* (Farnborough: Heath).
Vidich, A. J., Bensman, J. and Stein, M. R. (1964): *Reflections on Community Studies* (New York: Wiley).

Walther, R. H., McCune, S. D. and Trojanowicz, R. C. (1973): 'The Contrasting Occupational Cultures of Policemen and Social Workers', in Snibbe and Snibbe (eds.) (1973).
Wambaugh, J. (1970): *The New Centurions* (Boston: Little, Brown).
Wambaugh, J. (1972): *The Blue Knight* (Boston: Little, Brown).

Wambaugh, J. (1974): *The Onion Field* (New York: Dell).

Wambaugh, J. (1975): *The Choirboys* (New York: Delacorte Press).

Westley, W. A. (1953): 'Violence and the Police', *American Journal of Sociology*, LIX, 34–41.

Westley, W. A. (1956): 'Secrecy and the Police', *Social Forces*, XXXIV, 254–7.

Westley, W. A. (1970): *Violence and the Police: A Sociological Study of Law, Custom, and Morality* (Cambridge, Mass.: M.I.T. Press).

Westley, W. A. (1974): Review of Rubinstein's *City Police*, *Contemporary Sociology*, III (2), 309–11.

Weppner, R. S. (1977): *Street Ethnography* (Beverly Hills, Calif.: Sage).

Whitaker, B. (1964): *The Police* (Harmondsworth: Penguin).

Whittemore, L. H. (1973): *Super Cops* (New York: Bantam).

Whyte, W. F. (1955): *Street Corner Society*, 2nd ed. (Chicago: Chicago University Press).

Williams, D. (1967): *Keeping the Peace: The Police and Public Order* (London: Hutchinson).

Wilsher, P. and Righter, R. (eds.) (1976): *The Exploding Cities* (London: Deutsch).

Wilson, C. H. (1968): *The Dutch Republic* (New York: McGraw-Hill).

Wilson, J. Q. (1968): *Varieties of Police Behaviour* (Cambridge, Mass.: Harvard University Press).

Wirth, L. (1928): *The Ghetto* (Chicago: Chicago University Press).

Wittman, C. (1970): 'Refugees from Amerika: A Gay Manifesto', *San Francisco Free Press*, 22 Dec–7 Jan.

Wolfe, T. (1973): *The New Journalism* (New York: Harper & Row).

Yablonsky, L. (1973): *Hippy Trip* (Harmondsworth: Penguin).

Young, J. (1971a): *The Drugtakers* (London: MacGibbon & Kee).

Young, J. (1971b): 'The Role of the Police as Amplifiers of Deviancy', in Cohen (ed.) (1971).

Young, J. (1974): 'Abuses of Criminological Knowledge', session paper, European Group for the Study of Deviance and Social Control, Second Conference, University of Essex.

DOCUMENTS AND REPORTS

Attica: New York State Special Commission (1972) (New York: Bantam Books).

Council of Europe (1972): 'Violence in Society', 10th Congress of Directors, Criminal Justice Institutes, Strasbourg.

Crime in Eight American Cities (1974): U.S. Department of Justice (Washington, D.C.: U.S. Government Printing Office).

Memorandum on Police – Immigrant Relations (1972): Haringey Community Relations Committee.

'Police and Community' (1967): *Issues in Criminology*, III (1).

Police-Immigrant Relations in England and Wales (1973): Cmnd. 5438 (London: H.M.S.O.).

'Police in a Democratic Society: a Symposium' (1968): *Public Administration Review,* XXVIII (5).

President's Crime Commission (1967): *Task Force Report: The Police* (Washington, D.C.: U.S. Government Printing Office).

President's Crime Commission (1967): *The Challenge of Crime in a Free Society* (Washington, D.C.: U.S. Government Printing Office).

'Race and Police' (1968): *Issues in Criminology,* IV (1).

Report of the Commissioner of Police of the Metropolis for the Year 1975, Cmnd. 6496 (Lindon: H.M.S.O.).

Royal Commission on the Police (1962): Cmnd. 1728 (London: H.M.S.O.).

'Sociology of the Police–1' (1971): *Police Journal,* XLIV (3), 227–43.

'Sociology of the Police–2' (1973): *Police Journal,* XLVI (4), 341–62.

'Sociology of the Police–3' (1975): *Police Journal,* XLVIII (4), 379–92.

Walker Report (1968): *Rights in Conflict* (New York: Bantam).

United Nations (1975): 'Fifth Conference on Prevention of Crime and Treatment of Offenders', Geneva.

DUTCH SOURCES

Accent:
    4 Aug 1976, 'Demonstreren, maar dan Zonder Uniform'. 4 Sep 1976, 'De Zaak Kalma'. 16, 23 and 30 Apr, 7, 14 and 21 May 1977, 'Hoe Fout was Oom Agent in '40–' 45?', series. 8 Oct 1977, 'Politie Machteloos tegen Diefstal op Bestelling'.

Amersfoort, J. J. M. van (1968): *Surinamers in de Lage Landen* (Den Haag: Staatsuitgeverij).

Amersfoort, J. J. M. van (1971): *De Sociale Positie van de Molukkers in Nederland* (Den Haag: Staatsuitgeverij).

Amersfoort, J. J. M. van (1974): *Immigratie en Minderheidsvorming* (Alphen a/d Rijn: Samson).

Amersfoort, J. J. M. van and Biervliet, W. E. (1975): 'Criminaliteit van Minderheden', *Intermediair,* XI (36), 1–7.

Andriessen, M. F. (1976): *Kijken bij de Kinderpolitie* (IJmuiden; Vermande).

Anema, B. L. (1973): 'Politiecontrole en Maatschappij', *Algemeen Politieblad,* CXXII (19), 453–7.

Anema, B. L. (1977): 'Politietoezicht', in van der Wolk (ed.) (1977).

Angenent, H. L. W. and Steensma, H. O. (1977): *Onveilig Nederland?* (Nijkerk: Callenbach).

Arts, J., Bruijn, G. de, Boomen, G. van den and Soest, M. van (1973): *Van Provo tot Groenevelt* (Amsterdam; De Nieuwe Linie, van Gennep).

Bavel, G. J. van and Haaren, L. van (1971): 'Algemene Informatie over N.P.A.–Opleiding', *Algemeen Politieblad,* CXX (26), 622–9.

Beek, G. A. van (1975): 'Krisisinterventie' (Apeldoorn; Nederlandse Politie Academie).

Bergeijk, G. A. van and Ovaa, W. (1975): 'Roofovervallen in Nederland, 1968–1973', *Intermediair,* XI (23), 13 – 19.

Bergsma, R. L. (1970): 'Verdachten onder Stress' (Criminologisch Instituut, Vrije Universiteit Amsterdam).

Bergsma, R. L. (1977): *In Verzekerde Bewaring* (Meppel: Boom).

Blaey, J. M. de and Muller, A. (1976): 'De Hulpverlening als Onderdeel van de Politietaak en de Voorbereiding Hierop', *Het Tijdschrift van de Politie,* XXXVIII (10), 325 – 30.

Boer-Laschuyt, T. de (1959): 'Eurasian Repatriates in Holland', *R.E.M.P. Bulletin,* VIII, 23 – 45.

Bos, B., Jong, A. de, Jungschleger, I. and Vroemen, j. (1971): *Praten met Politie* (Utrecht: Bruna).

Bovenkerk, F. (1976a): *'Wie Gaat er Terug naar Suriname? Een Onderzoek naar de Retourmigratie van Surinamers uit Nederland 1972 – 73'* (Anthropologisch-Sociologisch Centrum, Universiteit van Amsterdam).

Bovenkerk, F. (1976b): 'Gaan de Surinamers nog terug?', *Intermediair,* XII (17), 1 – 11.

Bovenkerk, F. (1976c): 'De Nederlandse Politie in Botsing met Etnische Minderheden', *Algemeen Politieblad,* CXXV (1), 3 – 5.

Bovenkerk, F. (1977): 'Een Onderzoek naar Rasdiscriminatie in Nederland', *Haagse Post,* 5 Mar 1977.

Bovenkerk, F. and Bovenkerk-Teerink, L.M. (1972: 'Surinamers en Antillianen in de Nederlandse Pers' (Anthropologisch-Sociologisch Centrum, Universiteit van Amsterdam).

Bovenkerk, R. (1975): 'Hulpverlening aan Krisis-Jongeren in het Slop' (Amsterdam: Gemeentelijke Sociale Dienst).

Braam, A. van (1971); 'Onzekerheid in het Politieambt', *De Politie,* IV, 1 – 6.

Brandes, M. (1977): 'Verstrekking van Heroine en Methadon, een Literatuuronderzoek' (Amsterdam; Stichting voor Wetenschappelijk Onderzoek van Alcohol – en Druggebruik).

Breeveld, W. (1977a): 'Het Problematies Druggebruik bij Surinameese Migranten', nota Commissie Baars (Den Haag: Ministerie van Culturele, Recreatie, en Maatschappelijke Werk).

Breeveld, W. (1977b): 'Protestdelikten van Surinamers', *Kri,* VII (2), 7.

Broer, W. (1975): 'De Funktie van de Rayonagent' (Rotterdam: Erasmus Universiteit).

Broer, W. (1977): Politie in Schoksgewijze Verandering (Rotterdam; Erasmus Universitieit).

Brongersma, E. (1977): 'De Hervorming van de Zedelijkheidswetgeving', in van de Wolk (ed.) (1977).

Brugmans, I. J. (1969): *Paardenkracht en Mensenmacht: Sociaal-economische geschiedenis van Nederland 1795 – 1940* (Den Haag; Martinus Nijhoff).

Brunt, L. (ed.) (1977): *Anders Bekeken* (Meppel: Boom).

Buikhuisen, W. (1964): *Achtergronden van Nozemgedrag* (Assen: van Gorcum).

Buikhuisen, W. and Timmerman, H. (1970a); 'Druggebruik onder 'Middelbare' Scholieren', *Nederlands Tijdschrift voor Criminologie,* XII, (Sep), 176 – 181.

Buikhuisen, W. and Timmerman, H. (1970b): 'De Ontwikkeling van het

Druggebruik onder Middelbare Scholieren', *Nederlands Tijdschrift voor Criminologie,* XIII (Dec), 193–210.

Buikhuisen, W., Jongman, R. W. and Oving, W. (1969): 'Ongeregistreerde Criminaliteit onder Studenten', *Nederlands Tijdschrift voor Criminologie,* XI (June), 69–89.

Buitelaar, W. and Sierksma, R. (1972): *Gevangen in de Gevangenis* (Meppel; Boom).

Coenen, A. W. M. and Dijk, J. J. M. van (1976): 'De Ontwikkeling van de Misdaadverslaggeving in de Nederlandse Dagbladen Tussen 1965–1974', W.O.D.C. (Den Haag: Ministerie van Justitie).

Cohen, H. (1969): 'Psychologie, Sociale Psychologie en Sociologie van het Deviante Druggebruik' (Amsterdam: Instituut voor Sociale Geneeskunde).

Cohen, H. (1975): 'Drugs, Druggebruikers, en Drug-Scene' (Universiteit van Groningen).

Cohen, H. (1976): 'Het Drugbeleid in Nederland: Een Pijnlijke Bevalling', *Delikt en Delinkwent,* I (Jan), 12–17.

Cozijn, C. and Dijk, J. J. M. (1976): 'Onrustgevoelens in Nederland', W.O.D.C. (Den Haag; Ministerie van Justitie).

Dahan, G. (1974): 'Nota: Hulpverlening aan Buitenlanders in Nederland' (Amsterdam: Stichting voor Hulp aan Jongeren, De Laurier).

Denkers, F. A. C. M. (1976a): 'De Presentatie van de Politie' (Amsterdam: Gemeente Politie).

Denkers, F. A. C. M. (1976b): 'Discussie Nota over Klachten van Burgers Tegen de Politie' (Amsterdam: Gemeente Politie).

Denkers, F. A. C. M. (1976c): *Criminologie en Beleid* (Nijmegen: Dekker en van de Vegt).

Dijk, J. J. M. van (1977): 'De Geweldsgolf: Schijn of Harde Werkelijkheid?', in van der Wolk (ed.) (1977).

Dikkers, J. (1975): 'De Opleiding, Opvang en Begeleiding van de Jonge Agent van Politie', *Algemeen Politieblad,* CXXIV (9), 218–25.

Doorn, J. A. A. van (1973): *Met Man en Macht* (meppel: Boom).

Duinter-Kleijn, M. R. (1976): 'Hulpverlening door de Politie' *Justitiële Verkenningen,* VI, 418–33.

Duyn, R. van (1967): *Het Witte Gevaar: een Vademecum voor Provos* (Amsterdam: Meulenhoff).

Duyn, R. van (1969): *De Boodschap van een Wijze Kabouter* (Amsterdam: Kritiese Bibliotheek).

Elseviers Magazine:
1 March 1975, 'Afgang van een Stads-Bestuur'.
1 March 1975, 'Ontsnappen uit de Genangenis'.
5 July 1975, 'Wij Moeten toe naar één Groot Landelijk Politiekorps: Oud-Hoofdcommissaris van der Molen'.
27 Sep 1975, 'Heeft hij Toekomst in Dit Land?'
21 Feb 1976, 'Warmoesstraat Rapport – Gevecht tegen de Misdaad op een Vierkante Kilometer'.
21 Feb 1976, 'Duitsland (Luilekkerland voor Vuurwapens) Doet Grenzen bijna Dicht'.

6 Mar 1976, 'Opiumwet 1976 Gaat op Kruiken'.

17 Apr 1976, 'Bob Mitric Doodde in Amsterdam Drie Joegoslaven'.

20 Nov 1976, 'Een Patholgisch Pacifist in Politie-Uniform'.

19 Feb 1977, 'Amsterdam: Het Chicago van Europa?'

4 June 1977, 'De Gijzelingen'.

20 June 1977, 'Rescue'.

8 Oct 1977, 'Het Verloederende Wijf Amsterdam'.

Elseviers Weekblad, 28 July 1973, 'Criminaliteit Vereist thans Internationale Aanpak'.

Entzinger, H. B. (1975): 'Nederland Immigratieland?' *Beleid en Matschappij,* II (12), 326–36.

Frenkel, F. E. (ed.) (1966): *Provo, Kanttekeningen bij een Deelverschijnsel* (Amsterdam: Polak – van Gennep).

Fris, T. (1972): *Gelegenheidsaggressie* (Meppel: Boom).

Fris, T., Wolf, I. M. de and Dijk, R. A. van (1974): 'Oordelen en Vooroordelen ten Opzichte van het Werken bij de Politie' (Amsterdam: Gemeente Politie).

Fynaut, C. (1971): 'De Selectiviteit van het Justitiële en Politiële Optreden' (Katholieke Universiteit van Leuven).

Fynaut, C. (1976a): 'De Opbouw van het Nederlandse Politiewezen – 1', *Nederlands Tijdschrift voor Criminologie,* XVIII (June), 119–30.

Fynaut, C. (1976b): 'De Opbouw van het Nederlandse Politiewezen – 2', *Nederlands Tijdschrift voor Criminologie,* XVIII (Oct), 248–57.

Groothuyse, J. W. (1970): *De Arbeidsstructuur van de Prostitutie* (Deventer: van Loghum Slaterus).

Haagse post:

9 July 1966, 'Redactioneel'.

21 Aug 1976, 'De SOSA van de Surinamers'.

28 may 1977, 'De Gijzelingen'.

4 June 1977, 'De Stripper'.

29 Oct 1977, 'De Potenrammers'.

Haagse Post Extra, 1977, 'Heroine'.

Haaren, L. van (1975): 'De Reorganisatie van de Nederlandse Politie', *Algemeen Politieblad,* CXXIV (26), 635–6.

Haarlems Dagblad, 15 June 1973, 'Amsterdam Raakt Steeds Meer in de Greep van de Misdaad en de Heroine'.

Haas, G. C. de (1977): 'Afwijkend Jeugdgedrag', in van der Wolk (ed.) (1977).

Hagoort, G., Wabeke, J. W. and Withagen, J. (1976): *Strafrecht Moeilijkheden?* (Odijk: Sjaloom).

Hall, G. van (1976): *Ervaringen van een Amsterdammer* (Amsterdam: Agon Elsevier).

Hartsuiker, J. F. (1965): *De Souteneur in het Nederlandse Recht* (Den Haag: Bakker/Daamen).

Have, P. ten (1971): 'Jeugdtoerisme 1971' (Sociologisch Instituut, Universiteit van Amsterdam).

Have, P. ten (1973a): 'Notities over de Opkomst van de Jeugdige Tegen-

Kultuur', Nederlandse Sociologische-Anthropologische Vereniging, Voorjaarsconferentie.

Have, P. ten (1973b): 'Jeugdtoerisme in Amsterdam 1972' (Sociologisch Instituut, Universiteit van Amsterdam).

Heek, N. V. J. van (1934): *De Chineesche Immigranten in Nederland* (Amsterdam: Emmerings).

Heinemeyer, W. F., van Hulten, M. en De Vries-Reilingh, H. D. (1968): *Het Centrum van Amsterdam* (Amsterdam: Polak en van Gennep).

Heyder, A. (1966): *Resocialisatie, een Ideaal in de Gevangenis* (Deventer: Kluwer).

Hoekema, A. J. (1977): 'Politie' (Faculteit der Rechtsgeleerdheid, Vrije Universiteit van Amsterdam).

Hoenderdos, N. (1976): *Kind Onder Hoeren* (Utrecht/Antwerp: Bruna).

Hollander, A. N. J. den and Hofstee, E. W. (1962): *Drift en Koers: Een Halve Eeuw Sociale Verandering in Nederland* (uitg. 25e Jaar Jubileum van N.S.A.V., 1961: 2e druk 1962).

Hollander, A. N. J. den and Muyzenberg, O. D. van den (1966): *De Plurale Samenleving: Bergrip Zonder Toekomst* (Meppel: Boom).

Hopmans, J. P. M. and Scheur, A. van de (1975): 'De Beroepscultuur van de Nederlandse Politie' (Apeldoorn: Nederlandse Politie Academie).

Hulsman, L. H. C. (1970): 'De Maatshappelijke Funktie van de Politie in de Komende Decennia', *Jubileumuitgave Korps Rijkspolitie: 1945–1970,* pp. 95–105.

Jansma, L. and Veenman, J. (1977): 'De Schiedamse Rel', *Mens en Maatschappij,* LII (2), 127–63.

Jongman, R. W. and Buikhuisen, W. (1970): 'Druggebruik en de Relatie Leeftijd–Criminaliteit bij Studenten', *Nederlands Tijdscrift voor Criminologie,* XII (Mar), (1–9.

Jongman, R. W. and Cats, P. F. (1974): 'De Ontwikkeling van de Jeugdcriminaliteit in Nederland, 1950–70', *Nederlands Tijdschrift voor Criminologie,* XVI (sep), 154–65.

Junger-Tas, J. (1972): 'Schooljeugd en Drugs', publicatie Nr. 29 (Brussel: Studiecentrum voor Jeugdmisdadigheid, V.Z.W.O.).

Junger-Tas, J. (1977): 'De Relatie tussen de Primaire Politieopleiding en de Politiepraktijk', W.O.D.C. (Den Haag: Ministerie van Justitie).

Knibbeler, J. M. H. (1966): *De Verhouding Burgers – Politieambtenaren in Nederland in een Criminologisch Perspectief,* Katholieke Universiteit te Leuven (Sittard: Albert's Drukkerijen).

Krantz, D. E. and Vercruijsse, E. V. W. (1959): *De Jeugd in het Geding* (Amsterdam: De Bezige Bij).

Kruijer, G. F. (1973); *Suriname: Neo-Kolonie in Rijksverband* (Meppel: Boom).

Kuitenbrouwer, F. (1977): 'De Strijd om het Politiebestel', in van der Wolk (ed.) (1977).

Lijphart, A. (1968): *Verzuiling, Pacificatie en Kentering in de Nederlandse Politiek* (Amsterdam: De Bussy).

Luning, M. (1976): 'Politie en Surinamers' (Anthropologisch-Sociologisch Centrum, Universiteit van Amsterdam).

Meinesz, A. (1976): *Mijn Nachten met de Thermische Lans* (Amsterdam; De Geïllustreerde Pers).
Middendorp, C. P. (1974): 'Culturele Veranderingen in Nederland 1965–70', *Intermediair*, X (11), 1–9.
Middendorp, C. P. (1975): 'Verdere Culturele Veranderingen in Nederland, 1970–74', *Intermediair*, XI (19), 1–5.
Mulisch, H. (1966): *Bericht aan de Rattenkoning* (Amsterdam: Kwadraat).
Myjer, E. (1975): 'Beheersing van de Politie', *Delikt en Delinkwent*, IV (Apr), 208–19.

De Nieuwe Linie, 29 May 1974, 'Politieman: "Oom Agent" of Scherpschutter?'
Nieuwe Revu:
28 Jan 1977, 'Politie Bezwijkt voor Geld'.
4 Feb 1977, 'Hoeren en Heroine'.
Nieuws van de Dag:
2 June 1966, 'Openbare Orde'.
17 Aug 1977, 'Zomeragent Weg'.
Nijboer, J. A. (1975): *Voorspellen van Recidive,* Rijksuniversiteit van Groningen (Assen: Van Gorcum).
Nordholt, E. E. and Valkenburgh, P. (1970): *Enige Aspecten van de Verhouding Burgerij – Politie* (Alpen a/d Rijn: Samson).
N. R. C. Handelsblad, 5 May 1977, 'Klacht over Mishandeling Politie A'dam'.
Nuis, A. (1966): *Wat is er Gebeurd in Amsterdam?* (Amsterdam: Meulenhof).

Ooijen, D. van (1971): 'De Opleiding van de Politieambtenaar', *Algemeen Politieblad,* CXX (3), 51–6.
Oomens, G. J. J. and Tromp, G. J. W. (1975): 'Hulpverlening Hoofdtaak', (Apeldoorn: Nederlandse Politie Academie).

Panorama:
11 Apr 1975, 'Klompen, Tulpen, en Heroïne'.
8 Aug 1975, 'De Revolutie is Voorbij'.
4 Mar 1977, 'Van Pinda-Reep tot Heroïne-Roes'.
Het Parool:
21 Mar 1966, 'Onrust in Hoofdstad'
24 Aug 1974, ' "Misdaad Wordt Agressiever": Interview met Hoofdcommissaris P. A. de Jong'.
9 Aug 1976, 'Rassenrel in Schiedam'.
16 June 1977, 'Fiestendiefstal "Miljoenenzaak" '.
Perrick, F. (1968): *Naar een Nieuwe Politiebestel: Een Pleitnota* (Arnhem: Brouwer en Zoon).
Praag, C. S. van (1975): 'Molukse Jongeren in Botsing met de Nederlandse Maatschappij: de Gevolgen van een Beleid', *Beleid en Maatschappij,* II (12), 342–8.

Reenen, P. van and Verton, P. C. (1974): 'Over de Legitimiteit van het Hedendaags Politieoptreden', *Mens en Maatschappij,* XLIX (1), 74–87.

Riessen, J. C. van and Graeve, P. P. J. (1977): 'Riskant Druggebruik in Amsterdam', *Algemeen Politieblad,* CXXVI (24), 583–6.

Rinsampessy, E. (1976): 'De Mogelijke Gronden van Agressie onder Molukse Jongeren' (Utrecht: Gerakan Pattimura).

Romein-Verschoor, A. H. M. and Romein, J. M. (1973): *De lage Landen bij de Zee: Een Geschiedenis van het Nederlandse Volk,* 5e herzieningen (Amsterdam: Queriodo).

Ruller, S. van (1973): 'Literatuuroverzicht Penologie', *Nederlands Tijdschrift voor Criminologie,* XV (Apr), 91–3.

Schuyt, C. J. M. (1972): *Recht, Orde, en Burgelijke Ogehoorzaamheid* (Rotterdam: Rotterdam University Press).

Sinner, L. (1966): *Provos en Justitie* (Amsterdam: De Bezige Bij).

Smits, H. (1973a): *Crimineel? Meedenken over Misdaad en Straf* (Utrecht: Het Spectrum).

Smits, H. (1973b): 'De Verontrusting over Onveiligheid Wordt ons Aangepraat', *Vrij Nederland,* 27 Oct 1973.

Smits, H. (1973c): 'Een Amsterdamse Agent Komt Zelden voor de Rechter', *Vrij Nederland,* 3 Nov 1973.

Smits, H. (1974a): 'Het Grimmige Sprookje van Nederland als Gangsterland', *Vrij Nederland,* 29 June 1974.

Smits, H. (1974b): 'Ook Agenten Hebben Recht op Behoorlijke Werkomstandigheden', *Vrij Nederland,* 13 July 1974.

Smits, H. (1974c): 'De Politie Loste 31 Gericht Schoten', *Vrij Nederland,* bijlage 21 Dec 1974.

Soetenhorst-de Savornin Lohman, J. (1975), *Kwaad Dat Mag? Strafrechtspleging tussen Traditie en Vernieuwing* (Rotterdam: Rotterdam University Press).

Stachhouwer, J. F. F. (1945): *Criminaliteit, Prostitutie en Zelfmoord bij Immigranten in Amsterdam* (Utrecht/Nijmegen: van de Vegt).

Stadsblad (Utrecht), 14 April 1976, 'Toename Diefstallen Verontrust Politie'.

Suyver, J. J. H. (1976): *De Zeggenschap over het Politieorgaan* (Arhem: Gouda Quint).

De Telegraaf:
  19 Dec 1974, 'Overval Zonder Wapen Wordt Uitzondering'.
  10 Aug 1974, 'Dagelijks Gaan er Duizenden Guldens in Bodemloze Put'.
  17 Aug 1974, 'In Amsterdam Woedt Strijd tegen Wreedste Drugs'.
  26 Aug 1974, 'Krachtiger Aanpak van de Misdaad'.
  28 June 1975, 'Wijnhaven Wordt Prostitutiegebied' and 'Overvaller Gedood bij Gijzeling'.
  28 July 1975, 'Woonwagenbewoners Halen Arrestant uit Handen van Politie'.
  2 Aug 1975, 'Dood door Drugs Einde van Reis naar Amsterdam'.
  11 Aug 1975, 'Taxichauffeur Werd in Zijn Eigen Wagen Doodgestoken'.
  2 Oct 1975, 'Politie Woedend over Oproep tot 2 Minuten-Actie'.
  7 Jan 1976, 'Criminaliteit in Hoofdstad Zorgwekkend'.

10 Jan 1976,' Campagne tegen Wapen-Stroom uit West-Duitsland'.

17 Jan 1976, 'Frankfortse Heroinhandel Drijft op Amsterdam'.

13 Feb 1976, 'Het Mes Moet in de Wapenhandel'.

8 Mar 1976, 'Dubbele Moord Begon met Ruzie om f 2,50'.

13 Mar 1976, 'Politie Brengt Café-Bezoek naar Bureau'.

23 Mar 1976, 'Politie Kan Bonnen Ellende Niet Aan'.

23 Mar 1976, 'Onderzoek naar Stress bij Surveillance-Agent'.

24 Mar 1976, 'Hagenaars Niet Tevreden over Politie'.

25 Mar 1976, 'Collegialiteit van Taxi-Chauffeurs Ging te Ver'.

27 Mar 1976, 'Veertien Jaar Cel voor Treinkapers'.

10 Apr 1976, 'Roofovervallers Breken Alle Records'.

1 May 1976, 'Ontbreken van Controle Gaf Aage Vrij Spel'.

1 May 1976, 'Politie Verliest Greep op Heroine-Smokkel'.

1 May 1976, 'Heroine-Hoofdstad Amsterdam Slagveld der Triades'.

15 May 1976, 'Rotterdam Wil het Illegaal Gokken Helemaal Uitroeien'.

10 June 1976, 'Hasan Betaald Zijn Schuld met Kogels'.

10 June 1976, 'Ministers Zijn het Niet Eens over de Politie'.

31 July 1976, 'De Burgerij Krijgt het Gevoel dat de Politie Heel Ver Weg Is'.

31 July 1976, 'Charmante Chinezen Maakten Meisjes tot Heroïnekoeriers-ters'.

21 Aug 1976, 'Verscherpte Bewaking bij Wapendepots'.

21 Aug 1976, 'Ho Liet het Leven in een Opiumkit'.

31 Aug 1976, 'Heroinevangst van 15 Miljoen'.

1 Sep 1976, 'Uniformenmanie Werd Wilderbras uit Sneek Fataal'.

2 Sep 1976, 'Onstrafbare Misdaad is Nachtmerrie voor Politie'.

11 Sep 1976, 'Heroine Smokkelen of Vermoord Worden'.

30 Sep 1976, 'Gevaarlijke Gangsters Ontsnapt'.

9 Oct 1976, 'Sleutelfiguur Heroinezaak Nog Spoorloos'.

22 Oct 1976, 'Noodsituatie onder de Surinameese Jongeren'.

30 Oct 1976, 'Een Nacht in het Hol van de Hell's Angels'.

24 Nov 1976, 'Blijf van Mijn Lijf Succes in Groter Huis'.

4 Dec 1976, 'De Moordzaak Akersloot: Verbijsterend tot het Eind'.

5 Jan 1977, 'Invalide Vrouw al Vijf Keer Beroofd'.

12 Jan 1977, 'Onderzoek van Justitie naar Dood van Ferry'.

22 Jan 1977, 'Roofovervallers Zoeken Steeds Meer Buit op het Platteland'.

29 Jan 1977, 'Politie Mag Vluchthaven van Textiel-Bende niet Uit-kammen'.

17 Feb 1977, 'Jonge Fransman Doodgestoken'.

22 Feb 1977, 'Moord Nog Niet Opgelost'.

25 Feb 1977, 'Noord-Brabant Zucht onder de Criminaliteit'.

28 Feb 1977, 'Moorden, Steek-en Schietpartijen: Weekend vol Misdrijven'.

3 Mar 1977, 'Chinees Moord is een Groot Raadsel'.

21 Mar 1977, 'Moordmaniak in Hoofdstad'.

25 Mar 1977, 'Agenten Bezweken bij Zien van Geld'.

22 Mar 1977, 'Politie Vertwijfeld na Straatmoorden'.

6 Apr 1977, 'Politie Boos op Minister'.

16 Apr 1977, 'De Warme Buurt, één Vierkante Kilometer Ellende'.

14 Apr 1977, 'Winkeliers in Zorgen over Criminaliteit'.

Policing the Inner City

30 Apr 1977, 'De Verloedering van het Centraal Station'.

7 May 1977, 'Rotterdamse Politie Heeft Genoeg van Chef Kalma'.

9 May 1977, 'Van Agt Bezorgd over Criminaliteit'.

21 May 1977, 'De Nederlandse Politieman Loopt over van Vriendelijkheid'.

21 May 1977, 'Extra Bijstand voor Hoofdstad'.

7 June 1977, 'Voor Heroïne-Moord Vijf jaar Cel Geeist'.

8 June 1977, 'Arrestanten Maakten Kennis met Vuisten van Agent Tonny'.

11 June 1977, 'Tuchtschool Lijkt Inderdaad Wel op Luilekkerland'.

25 June 1977, 'Nederlands-Duits Politie-Team Zoekt Moordenaar van Collega'.

28 June 1977, 'Hasj Kost Nederlander 7 Jaar Cel'.

19 Aug 1977, 'Fiets Niet Meer in Verzekering'.

27 Aug 1977, 'Teleurgestelde Onderofficieren Verlaten het Leger'.

1 Oct 1977, 'Chinees Gok-Geld Bracht de Politie Geen Geluk'.

Thurlings, J. M. G. (1971): *De Wankele Zuil* (Nijmegen: Dekker en van de Vegt).

De Tijd, 28 Nov 1973, 'Kortsluiting in Contact Burgerij en Politie'.

Toebosch, J. (1975): 'Politie en Wetenschap', *Rijks Politie Magazine,* XVI (9), 5–7.

Tuynman, H. (1966): *Full-time Provo* (Amsterdam: Kwadraat).

Veendrick, L. and Jongman, R. (1976): *Met de Politie op Pad* (Groningen: Kriminologisch Instituut).

Veer, H. Y. van der (1974): 'De Politie en Haar Hulpverlenende Taak' (Apeldoorn; Nederlandse Politie Academie).

Vellinga, M. L. and Wolters, W. G. (1971): *De Chinezen van Amsterdam* (Anthropologisch–Sociologisch Centrum, Universiteit van Amsterdam).

De Volkskrant:

3 Aug 1974, 'De Lange Kille Zomer van de Horse'.

3 Apr 1975, 'Gemiddelde Vrijheidsstraf Duurt Langer dan Vroeger'.

3 July 1975, 'Meisje in de Ban van Children of God'.

24 July 1975, 'Plaatsgebrek Groter in Gevangenissen'.

3 Oct 1975, 'Provinciale Politie in Voorbereiding'.

20 Jan 1976, 'Onderzoek naar Gedrag Agenten bij Arrestatie'.

20 Jan 1976, 'Haagse Prostitutie Krijgt Eigen Wijk'.

27 Jan 1976, 'Jeugdwerkloosheid Steeg Sterk in '75'.

12 May 1976, 'Buitenlandse Werknemers zijn Nieuwe Prolereriaat'.

12 May 1976, 'Politiebond Vraagt om Betere Wapens'.

13 July 1976, '"Rookcafé" Heeft Sociale Functie'.

17 July 1976, 'Al 14,000 Gerugulariseerd'.

4 Aug 1976, 'Bond Achter Vrije Mening Politieman'.

8 Sep 1976, 'Rapport: Toenemen Misdaad Onbewezen'.

22 Sep 1976, 'Trekken Dienstpistool Fel Veroordeeld'.

27 Oct 1976, 'Twee Broers Bekennen Dubbele Moord'.

13 Nov 1976, 'Opvang Verslaafden is Bedroevend'.

24 Dec 1976, 'Justitie Gaat Vertoning Porno-Films Aanpakken'.

4 Feb 1977, '"Vluchthaven" Gaat Mogelijk Weer Open'.

6 May 1976, 'Advocatuur Wenst Opheldering Politie'.

7 May 1977, 'Statenlid Vraagt Snel meer Politie in Amsterdam'.

7 May 1977, Weer Klacht Tegen de Politie'.

28 May 1977, 'Politie op Zoek naar Zichzelf'.

9 and 16 July 1977, 'Amsterdam: De Verziekte Stad'.

7 July 1977, 'Uitbreiding Politie Tienduizend Man'.

26 July 1977, 'Politie-Agenten Geschorst na Klacht Vrouw'.

3 Oct 1977, 'Beelden van Bureau'.

5 Oct 1977, 'Bestemming Hasj voor Recherche Nog Raadsel'.

1 Dec 1977, 'Klacht tegen Politie'.

Vos, H. M. (1971): 'De Democraterising en het Functioneren van Het Politieapparaat'. *Algemeen Politieblad*, LXX (21), 512–16.

Vos, H. M. (1975): 'De Politie als Middel van Sociale Beheersing', *Algemeen Politieblad*, CXXIV (5), 99–103.

Vries J. de (1973): *De Nederlandse Economie Tijdens de Twintigste Eeuw: Een Verkenning van het Meest Kenmerkende* (Antwerpen/Utrecht: Het Spectrum).

Vries, R. de (1973): 'Verslag: Vondelpark Project' (Bureau Jeugdzaken, Gemeente Amsterdam).

Vrij Nederland:
27 July 1974, 'Een Monsterverbond tussen Bouwkapitaal en Drughandel'.
3 May 1975, 'Taxi!'.
27 Aug 1977, 'De Machteloosheid van de Gewone Burger'.

Vuure, J. van and Dijke, H. (eds.) (1968): *Protest en Beweging* (Rotterdam: Rotterdam University Press).

Weerlee, D. van (1966): *Wat de Provo's Willen* (Amsterdam: De Bezige Bij).

Wolk, E. van der (1977): *De Bedreigde Burger* (Antwerpen/Utrecht: Intermediair/Het Spectrum).

Zee-Nefkens, A. A. van der (1975): 'Onderzoek Assistentieverlening; Gemeentepolitie Den Haag', W.O.D.C. (Den Haag: Ministerie van Justitie).

Zwezerijnen, J. J. A. (1972): *Dwang en Vertrouwen* (Alpen a/d Rijn: Samson).

DOCUMENTS AND REPORTS

'Aangiftenboek Nieuwmarkt' (1975): Juridische Groep Nieuwmarkt, Amsterdam.

Algemeen Handelsblad, 10 Mar, 21 Mar, 22 Mar, 9 Apr, 12 Apr, 13 Apr, 14 June, 15 June, 16 June, 17 June 1966.

Algemeen Politieblad (1970): 'Het Politie-Onderwijs', CXIX (24), 559–64.

Algemeen Politieblad (1975): 'Nauwere Samenwerking Rijks- en Gemeentepolitie in Afwachting van Gewestvorming', CXXIV (9), 207–8.

'Amsterdam: De Zorg voor de Veiligheid' (1974): Begroting Debaat 1974, Gemeenteraad, Amsterdam.

'Amsterdam Hoofdstad?' (1977): Junior Kamer, Amsterdam.
'Analyse van de Berichtgeving over Criminaliteit in de Nederlanse Dagblad-pers, 1965–1974' (1975): W.O.D.C. (Den Haag: Ministerie van Justitie).

Beleid en Maatschappij (1975): 'Allochtone Minderheden in Nederland', II (12).
Bevrijding, 25 June 1966.
'Bloemlezing uit de Klachten en een Overzicht der Werkzaamheden' (1977): Stichting Klachten en Adviesburo Politieoptreden, Amsterdam.

Commissie Enschedé (Rapport van de Commissie van Onderzoek Amster-dam) (1967): *Eerste Interim-Rapport; Tweede Interim-Rapport; Slotrapport* (Den Haag: Staatsuitgeverrij).
Commissie Hulsman (1971): *Ruimte in Drugbeleid*, Rapport van de Stichting Algemeen Centraal Bureau van de Geestelijke Volksgezondheid (Meppel: Boom).
Coornhert Liga (1972, 1973, 1974): 'Alternatieve Justitiebegroting', (De-venter: Kluwer).
Coornhert Liga (1973): 'Alternative Beantwoording Kamervraag Mishandel-ing Bureau Warmoesstraat', Rapport Nr. 6.
Coornhert Liga (1975): 'Dag Diender: Het Congress dat Nooit Doorging', congres map, Amsterdam.

God, Nederland, en Oranje, no. 4, 1 Feb 1967; no. 5, 10 Mar 1967; no. 7, 7 July 1967; no. 8, 10 Sep 1967.
De Groene Amsterdammer, 18 June, 9 July 1966.

'Heldhaftig, Vastberaden, Barmhartig' (1977): Centrum Anton de Kom, Amsterdam.

Leger des Heils (1973): '25 Jaar in de Binnenstad' (Amsterdam).

'Politie en Openbare Orde' (1967): Dr. Wiardi Beckman Stichting, Ams-terdam.
Politie in Verandering (1977) (Den Haag: Staatsdrukkerij).
'Portret van een Diender' (1974): *Periodiek*, Nr. 58, Gemeentepolitie Ams-terdam.
Propria Cures, 5 Mar, 2 July 1966.
Provo, no. 2, 17 Aug 1965; no. 7, 25 Feb 1966; no. 10, 30 June 1966; no. 11, 15 Aug 1966.

Ratio, Juni/Juli 1964; Maart/April 1965; Aug 1965.

Statische Mededelingen No. 156 (1967): 'Vreemdelingenverkeer te Amster-dam' (Bureau van het Statistiek der Gemeente Amsterdam).
Statistische Mededelingen No. 175 (1971): 'Jongeren op de Dam, August 1970' (Bureau van het Statistiek der Gemeente Amsterdam).
Stichting Rechtswinkel Amsterdam (1974a): Jaarverslag, Amsterdam.
Stichting Rechtswinkel Amsterdam (1974b): 'Rechtshulp: Een Bewijs van Onvermogen', Amsterdam.

'Verslag Dam-Detachement' (1973): Gemeentepolitie Amsterdam.
'Verslag Jeudzaken' (1974): Z.J.A., Gemeente Amsterdam.
'Verzameling Rapporten in Verband met Onrust en Slaapverbod Ronde de
  Dam' (1970): Gemeentepolitie Amsterdam.

Index

225

work *and* Warmoesstraat police station
Police Journal, 181
Policemen
detectives, 2, 9, 57, 62, 78, 150, 157, 187–8, 193–4
officers, 1, 2, 9, 34, 42, 52, 57, 62, 70–2, 91–3, 122, 168, 184, 193–4
patrolmen/constables, 9, 14, 48, 58, 62–4, 70–3, 76–8, 86–8, 90–3, 96, 100–2, 104, 108–9, 117, 125–6, 129, 153, 156, 161, 165, 168, 170–2, 179, 187, 190, 193–4
patrolmen's ideology, 9, 45, 49–3, 94–5, 123, 175–6
sergeant, 2, 10, 52, 54, 56–8, 62–4, 71–2, 87, 91–3, 101, 108–9, 111, 115, 122, 164, 167, 170, 178, 185, 193–4
Police review, 76
Police work, 6, 9, 18–23, 25–7, 45, 133–4, 183–91
'backstage behaviour', 5, 18, 26, 58
car-chases, 12, 45, 112–13, 154
checking papers, 10, 118
decision-making behaviour, 4, 18, 23, 36, 45, 134, 138–9, 150, 152, 158, 176, 185
decline of police craft, 19, 38, 49–54, 93, 184–6, 191
'front-line position', 45, 182, 184–5, 188
grading of cases, 45–8, 135, 188
gratuities, 6
misconduct, 12–13, 38, 78–85, 100, 159, 162–3, 171, 178
night-duty, 1, 8–9, 57, 62–3, 108, 127, 129
non-criminal matters, 6, 41, 46–7, 60–1, 88–90, 117, 125, 133–48, 190
patrolling, 1–2, 4–5, 8–19, 25, 38, 51–2, 54, 62–4, 68–73, 76, 88, 93, 107–15, 117–48, 151, 154, 166, 172–3, 175–6, 185

plain-clothes duty, 8, 11, 13, 62–3, 75, 78, 80, 154, 168
occupational culture, 4, 13, 19, 23, 25, 37–8, 40, 44–6, 49, 51, 57, 62, 72, 77–8, 84–6, 88, 94, 98, 100, 106–16, 122–3, 125–7, 151, 179, 184, 186, 189
restriction of output, 35, 117–18, 140–3, 150, 152–3, 188
search/arrest, 11, 26, 45–7, 50, 62, 73, 75, 95, 97, 100, 103, 105, 117, 122, 130–1, 133, 140–4, 151–4, 157–8, 163, 166–8, 173, 175, 177, 188–9, 195
stop and frisk, 8, 58, 73–5, 103, 107, 115, 121, 123
use of force, 26, 94–5, 97, 99–107, 115, 121, 123, 141–2, 167, 170
Politie in Verandering, 181
Polsky, N., 14
Porn shops, 5, 65–6, 130
Preiss, J. J., 23
President's Crime Commission, 45, 180
Press, the, 34, 73, 75, 78, 81, 83, 102, 105, 115, 149, 156, 183, 185, 189–90
Prinsenhof, 43, 66, 153
Prostitutes, 17, 56, 59, 65–7, 83, 85, 109, 123–4, 127–30, 144–7, 166
Provos, 33–4
Public Prosecutor, 35, 66, 170, 193
Punch, M., 3, 6–7, 11, 13, 21, 45, 93, 134, 150, 182, 184

Quinney, R., 4

Red light district, 5, 7, 10, 19, 64–7, 117–18, 121, 123, 126, 129–30, 133, 135, 144, 158, 186–7, 191
Reenen, P. van, 32
Reiss, A. J., 2, 14, 24–5, 85, 117–18, 134–5, 147
'René', 70